Partisanship, Union Centralization and Mobility

Qiang ZHOU

Partisanship, Union Centralization and Mobility

The Political Roots of Interindustry Labor Mobility

L'Harmattan

5-7, rue de l'Ecole-Polytechnique, 75005 Paris

http://www.harmattan.fr
diffusion.harmattan@wanadoo.fr

ISBN : 978-2-343-09222-5
EAN : 9782343092225

Acknowledgements

It is my greatest pleasure to be able to thank the persons who have extended their intellectual support and friendship to me during the research, writing, and publication of this book. I began to get interested in this subject while taking a graduate seminar on Political Economy taught by Professor Helen Milner, who has been my adviser and chaired my dissertation committee until her departure for Princeton University. I have great gratitude to Helen; not only does she read, comment, and guide me through numerous drafts of the chapters, but also because she remains committed to her old student even after she left Columbia University. I am very grateful to Helen's offer of a research fellowship at the Niehaus Center for Globalization and Governance in Princeton University and a significant part of this research was written under the support of the fellowship.

I was also fortunate enough to have Professor Pablo Pinto, who came to Columbia University in 2004, to chair my dissertation committee after Helen left. Pablo has been passionate about my research project and his thoughtful and incisive comments throughout the years decisively shaped my dissertation, which constitutes the basis for this book. I am extremely grateful to Lucy Goodhart, the other adviser of mine at Columbia University, who always provided me with constructive, thorough, and insightful comments as well as greatly helped me improve the empirical analysis. I would also like to thank the Department of Political Science at Columbia University for providing me the supportive learning environment.

And this book would not materialize were it not for the urging of my research collaborator, Michel Prum, Professeur de classe exceptionnelle, at Paris Diderot University Paris 7.

This book project is also supported by National Social Science Foundation of China (No.15BZZ027).

Contents

Figures and Tables

Figures:

Tables:

Chapter 1
Introduction and Literature Review

1.1. Empirical discrepancy and the importance of interindustry factor mobility

In the primary season of the 2008 US presidential campaigns, we heard some candidates repeatedly talked about their promises to invest in job retraining programs to combat unemployment and future economic downturns, one example is the Republican candidate John McCain who said before the Michigan primary that "There are some jobs that aren't coming back to Michigan," "But it is government's job to help workers get the education and training they need for the new jobs that will be created by new businesses in this new century." (Zuckman 2007) [1]. The apparent assumption among the candidates was that such programs would facilitate workers to relocate from a declining industry into another booming industry.

In other parts of the world, for instance, Danish workers have accommodated, even welcomed globalization and its consequences such as outsourcing and job displacement, this phenomenon puzzled many critics of globalization; and a recent Time magazine article conducts a case study of Denmark that explains why (Fox 2007). From the 1990s, successive Danish governments have been engaged in some transformation of their welfare-state, and especially they greatly increase the investment in the job retraining programs. These programs, in combination with other aspects of the Danish welfare system such as generous unemployment benefits, health care and

---

[1] In Michigan the state economy hasn't been doing very well the past few years before 2008 and its unemployment was the highest among states in the US. The Democratic Party's candidates did not campaign in Michigan during the primary since the Democratic National Committee stripped the Michigan of all its delegates to the Democratic National Convention because the state scheduled its primary at an earlier date than sanctioned by the party.

portable pensions, etc., have enabled Danish workers to better adjust to employment changes induced by globalization.

Both these cases involve the ability of workers to move across industries. It is immediately clear that the degree of such ability matters a great deal for the performance of macroeconomy. In fact, workers' ability to move across industries, or technically the *interindustry labor mobility*, is a subset of the concept of *interindustry factor mobility*, which is formally defined as "the elasticity of substitution along the transformation curve that maps the conversion of a factor located in one industry for use in another industry at increasing opportunity costs" (Hiscox 2002b), where factor consists of broadly construed labor and capital. It has been acknowledged that factor mobility has important implications in political economy models. For example, highly mobile factors are the necessary conditions for Stolper-Samuelson model to work. Political economists have shown that international trade will have important distributional consequences under Stolper-Samuelson framework where locally abundant factors benefit and locally scarce factors lose, and as a result preferences toward global economic integration will usually take a class divide depending on whether capital or labor is the locally abundant factor. If interindustry factor mobility is low, however, productive assets tend to be specific to the industries that employ them and political struggles concerning trade and trade policies are likely to be dominated by industry-specific groups and idiosyncratic capital-labor coalitions. For instance, the standard Grossman-Helpman model and the specific factors, a. k. a., the Ricardo-Viner model, all assume factors are specific to the industries, and they have been used widely in the political economy literature.

Besides the study of international trade, interindustry factor mobility and especially interindustry labor mobility plays an important role in the literature on welfare state and varieties of capitalism (VoC). For example, according to Hall and Soskice (Hall and Soskice 2001), coordinated market economies (CMEs) and the liberal market economies (LMEs) differ in that the institutional complementarities established within CMEs favor the construction of long term relationship and formation of specific skills, and in LMEs the opposite tends to be true. It then follows that skills and human capital are more industry specific in CMEs than in LMEs, so the inference is that interindustry labor mobility tends to be lower in CMEs than in LMEs.

Interindustry factor mobility may also affect the trajectory of economic growth of a country. Barriers to intersectoral factor movement may take many forms, such as the coercive attachment to land (slavery, debt bondage, and seasonal compulsory labor, etc), guilds that limit the talents in and out of an industry, aristocracy that reserve the access to public service to those of noble birth, and barriers to credit where lending depends on the identity of the lender and the borrower, not on the merits of a project (Przeworski 2007). Przeworski argues that barriers to factor mobility may result in mismatching skills and opportunities and the overall productivity may be lower as a result (Przeworski 2007).

Most existing studies share the assumption that interindustry factor mobility of a country is exogenous to the domestic political economy in question; see for example (Frieden 1991; Grossman and Helpman 1994; Hiscox 2002a; Hiscox 2002b; Mukherjee, Smith, and Li 2007; Rickard 2005; Rogowski 1989). Some contemporary events, however, seem to indicate that politics and government policy interventions can be significant determinants of the levels of intersectoral factor mobility. The two cases at the inception of this section both call for active roles for governments. As another example, Swedish governments have long been engaged in interventions of the economy, arguably at the behest of the Swedish Confederation of Trade Unions, or LO[2]. LO has investigated on the topics of wage policy and full employment through its research department. Its report in 1951 called for wage restraint for the sake of wage solidarity, and advocate coordination of economic and wages policy among LO members in order to attain full employment. The LO report in 1963 made increasing labor's adaptability a center piece in their strategy to counter the volatility in labor market due to Sweden's increasing involvement in international market. The proposals for wage constraint and increased adaptivity were implemented by the governments through institutions such as National Labor

---

[2] Not coincidentally, most of the Swedish governments since the WWII are Social Democratic. I will discuss more on Sweden in the case study chapter.

Market Board (Hiscox 2002b; Katzenstein 1985; LO 1953; LO 1963).

Questions naturally follow: if only a casual look at the historical evidence indicates it is very likely that there are government interventions on levels of interindustry factor mobility, to what extent should we continue to assume that factor mobility is exogenous? Given that interindustry factor mobility is consequential as has been acknowledged in the literature, have governments ever attempted to "manage" the levels of interindustry factor mobility; and if they do, why and how?

This study will address the apparent discrepancies between theories and real-life practices. And my central argument is that interindustry factor mobility, and in specific interindustry labor mobility, can be shaped by domestic political processes.

1.2. Current literature on interindustry factor mobility

Modern production process involves three fundamental productive factors: land, capital, and labor. Because land in domestic economy is often fixed and its supply cannot easily respond to demands in ways labor and capital can, I will leave it out of the analysis here. Other scholars have looked at land factor and produced interesting hypotheses, such as in (Rogowski 1989). It is also a common feature of modern economy that we observe the flows of production factors crisscrossing industry lines. In economic terms, the flows of production factors release the factors from the firms or sectors where they are redundant and less profitable, and relocate the factors to new firms or sectors where they are in short supply and more profitable. The end-result is that the economy becomes more efficient in production.

Importantly, the ease of production factors (labor or capital) to move across industry lines, known formally as interindustry factor mobility (IFM), can have far-reaching economic and political implications as a critical structural variable underlying the domestic political economy. In international trade literature, Stolper Samuelson theorem is built on the assumption that production factors are mobile across industry lines (Stolper and Samuelson 1941), it argues that when factors of production are mobile across industries, i.e., IFM is high, and when another set of assumptions are met (full employment of factors, competitive markets, all factor owners and the economy where they reside are price takers), then trade liberalization will ensue magnification effects and the abundantly endowed factors of production domestically will benefit from open trade and the scarcely endowed factors of production domestically will lose from open trade. From this theorem, we can derive that in capital-rich countries, the support for the trade liberalization will mostly come from capital owners and the opposition against trade liberalization will come from labor owners; and in labor-rich countries, pro-liberalization forces will mostly be the labor owners and pro-protectionism will mostly come from capital owners (Wood 1995).

Specific factors or the Ricardo-Viner model is built on the contrary assumption that production factors are specific to the industries that employ them (Jones 1971; Samuelson 1971). In the specific-factor model framework, there are three factors of production; two types of factors, say two types of capital are specific to their sectors while the third factor, say labor, can be mobile across sectors. When trade liberalization happens, the industries strong enough to export will see the returns to the factors they employ increases, and industries that must compete with imports will experience decreases in the returns to the factors they employ. So the capital specific to the export industries will unambiguously gain from trade liberalization, and the capital specific to the import-competing industries will unambiguously lose from open trade, furthermore the gains for the mobile factor here (labor) will be ambiguous since the absolute gains or loss for the factor will depend on labor's consumption patterns. From this theorem, we can predict domestic coalitions will form according to the exporting or import-competing industries. Export industries will favor open trade while import-competing industries will favor protectionism.

There have also been many scholarly endeavors to test which model has more empirical traction. In researches that focus primarily on the U.S., Magee found that Ricardo-Viner model better predicted trade policy lobbying in US Congress than Stolper-Samuelson theorem (Magee 1980), since such lobbying mostly takes the form of industry-based testimonies rather than class-based ones. Beaulieu found that neither

Stolper-Samuelson nor Ricardo-Viner model can be rejected using congressional roll-call votes on trade policy, suggesting there would be bias if the district level factor composition is ignored in studies on congressional voting patterns, as well as that the real levels of interindustry factor mobility may well be in between either Ricardo-Viner or Stolper-Samuelson types (Beaulieu 2002). Using roll call vote data for the US Congress from 1963 to 1992, Ladewig managed to show that at the district level the general trend of levels of interindustry factor mobility is low (or close to what specific factors model assumes) through the later 1970s and high (or close to Stolper-Samuelson ideal) from the early 1980s to 1992 (Ladewig 2006). Using individual-level survey data, Scheve and Slaughter found evidence that the factor type dominates industry of employment in explaining support for trade barriers (Scheve and Slaughter 2001). Taking a longer view into history, Hiscox found that the interindustry factor mobility in the US is gradually shifting overtime, so that Ricardo-Viner model may better explains US politics in 1930s but Stolper-Samuelson is a better fit from 1960s on (Hiscox 1999). Rickard argued that levels of asset specificity affect the trade-related compensatory policies, high levels of asset specificity ensue higher demand for industry-specific trade compensation (Rickard 2004). In the area of American trade policy, high levels of interindustry factor mobility have been found to increase the likelihood of the members of the Congress to vote in line with their dominant constituency base: labor or working-class for the Democrats, and capital owners or big businesses for the Republicans; and low levels of interindustry factor mobility made the voting patterns less predicable based on dominant constituency types (Beaulieu 2002; Hiscox 1999; Ladewig 2006; Magee 1980).

Aside from the above-mentioned tests on which model better describes the U.S. trade policy formation, scholars have also worked on exploring other aspects of the political implications of interindustry factor mobility. For example, Rogowski assumed high levels of international factor mobility (IFM) and argued that domestic political cleavages will be formed along factoral lines and according to four types of factor endowments when the society was subject to the exposure to international trade (Rogowski 1987; Rogowski 1989). There could be advanced or backward economies roughly corresponding to high or low capital-labor ratio, combined with high or low land-labor ratio. Class conflicts would be expected when there are advanced economies combined with high land-labor ratio or when there are backward economies combined with low land-labor ratio. When there are the other two combinations, i.e., advanced economies with low land-labor ratio or backward economies with high land-labor ratio, urban-rural conflicts should arise.

Assuming low levels of interindustry factor mobility, Frieden for example argued that domestic trade coalitions will be formed around specific industries, especially, exporting industries will have distinctive pro-free trade political preferences while the import competing industries will have pro-protectionism stances (Frieden 1991). Still others won't commit to the assumptions of extreme levels of factor mobility but instead allow factor mobility levels to vary (Hiscox 2001; Hiscox 2002a; Hiscox 2002b; Rickard 2005), they found that varying levels of factor mobility will correspond to varying patterns of political coalitions on trade, with high factor mobility corresponding to class-based coalitions and low factor mobility to industry-based coalitions.

We can come to appreciate the far-reaching consequences of different levels of interindustry factor mobility through the findings of these studies. When interindustry factor mobility is rather high, class-cleavages are more likely to emerge as the fault-line of domestic political battles where issues like taxation, redistribution, and welfare state programs are contested; on the other hand, when interindustry factor mobility is rather low, various interest groups would tend to dominate the domestic political debates, these groups tend to be composed of members from both factors/classes, advocate political preferences for some specific government programs rather than comprehensive class-wide platforms, and usually come from the background of a particular industry or cluster of similar industries. Many scholars have attempted to extend the Stolper-Samuelson vs. Ricardo-Viner models so that factor mobility would be a continuum rather than the extremes (Grossman 1983; Hill and Mendez 1983).

Interindustry factor mobility can affect politics through its interaction with political institutions. Alt and Gilligan linked levels of factor mobility with types of political institutions and costs of collective action (Alt and Gilligan 1994). They argued that the type of political coalitions as Rogowski has described is only possible when the factors are mobile, when there are majoritarian political institutions and when collective action costs are low; on the other hand, the type of political coalitions described in standard trade policy models where there is intense lobbying for protection from the producer groups while the consumer groups are inactive will be possible when the factors are specific, when there are non-majoritarian institutions, and when collective action costs are high. The latter type is the classical trade coalitions described by Schattschneider (Schattschneider 1935) and other special interest groups arguments as we usually see in the study of American politics.

The literature on welfare state and the Varieties of Capitalism (VoC) also hinges closely on the role of interindustry factor mobility. Hall and Soskice argued that there are distinct types of institutional complementarities within categories of countries (Hall and Soskice 2001). They categorize the existing advanced industrial countries into the coordinated market economies (CMEs) and the liberal market economies (LMEs). In CMEs, many institutions are intertwined and any one institution is in the symbiosis relationship with other institutions. The workers in CMEs are "guaranteed" by their employers to keep their jobs and maintain their real wage levels, this "guarantee" made the workers willing to make the necessary investment into industry-specific skills that cannot be readily transferred to another industry without losses. The workers are backed by the employee's associations that negotiate with employers and when necessary support the workers through hardship. The employers and their associations make the implicit or explicit bargains with employee's associations so that in return for their guarantee for worker's wages and jobs, they get highly trained work forces that enable them to specialize and get competitive edges in international markets. The relationship is also sustained by long term finance provided by banking sectors that are not bound by short term profit goals as their counterparts do in LMEs. The breakdown of any one of these symbiotic relationships may topple the whole CME model within the country. The opposite can be said for LMEs, where market is the ultimate source of income and risks. Workers will derive their income primarily from the market alone, no guarantee or effective support from employee's associations can be expected. As a result, workers tend not to make industry-specific investment in human capital, and they invest in general skills instead. The employers in LMEs cannot expect highly skilled work forces and their best market strategy is to invest in technologies that use mostly general education and can be fit for mass production. They, and the banking sector that finance them, are subject to short term profitability constraint from the market so they expect quick results and liquidity of assets.

It follows that according to this VoC argument, one of the foundational parameters is the different level of interindustry labor mobility in CMEs or LMEs. Workers who invest in industry-specific skills in CMEs tend to have the kinds of human capital that are not readily transferable across industries, so the levels of interindustry labor mobility (ILM) tend to be low in CMEs. Conversely, workers who invest in general skills in LMEs would possess kinds of human capital that are mostly transferable across industries, so the ILM would be high in LMEs.

In the spirit of VoC literature, Estevez-Abe, Iversen, and Soskice focused on the institutional complementarities about skill formation (Estevez-Abe, Iversen, and Soskice 2001). They divided the skill types into three categories: firm-specific, industry-specific, and general skills. Employers will develop different product market strategies according to the availability of work forces in different skill categories. Workers will only make the investment into different types of skills when their future return can be guaranteed. Such guarantee can be obtained via different paths in countries with different dominant product market strategies. In a country where product market strategies require intensive use of firm-specific skills, workers will need the guarantee that investment into building such skills will be properly rewarded, which is mostly done through employment protection; if the product market strategy requires lots of industry-specific skills, then unemployment protection may play a larger role in guaranteeing proper compensation to the workers with such skills. In both cases the employers will have to be closely involved in training and certifying the quality of employees, the education and training systems in these countries act as nexus to attain the specific skill equilibrium.

But if the dominant product market strategies center around general skills, then workers' utility maximizing strategy is to invest in general skills that can be portable from employment to employment, and the employers will have little incentives to provide additional training to employees, so that the complementary institutions that work so well in the first set of countries will never develop in the second set of countries.

Mares argued that not only employees, but also employers have distinct preferences toward welfare state policies (Mares 2001). Firms' utilities for different social policies will differ along the two axes of risk redistribution and control. Firms that are affected by high incidence of risks prefer high risk redistribution policies, and those firms affected by low incidence of risks prefer low risk redistribution policies. The size and skill intensity of firms determine how firms want control of social insurance policies. Large firms or firms employing skilled workers like more control, while small firms or firms that do not employ high-skilled workers prefer less control.

The influential study by Esping-Andersen on the three worlds of welfare capitalism also closely hinges on to the underlying parameter of interindustry labor mobility (Esping-Andersen 1990). Esping-Andersen argued that in terms of the relationship between social services provision and individual well-being, there are three types of welfare states: the liberal (or Anglo-Saxon), the corporatist (or continental European), and the social democratic (or Nordic). The liberal welfare state is the residual type, where the market will dominate individual welfare, meaning there will be little social protection from the state that can be expected. The corporatist welfare state stresses privileges for sectors in certain social positions, the "natural" hierarchy among occupations, and the authority of the state, so the social welfare provision is stratified, but to a lesser degree than liberalism because of the corporatist guarantee of welfare and the safety net espoused by the coincident Catholicism movement in these countries. The social democratic welfare state provides a universal safety net to all citizens, which is non-stigmatizing, decent, and provides for a middle-class living standard. And as he emphasized, for any country there is in fact a mix of these prototypical welfare programs.

The liberal welfare state seems strikingly similar to liberal market economies as described in Hall and Soskice and the VoC literature. Workers in the liberal welfare states may just as well behave as in LMEs, where they derive their income from the market, and if the market cannot provide them with guaranteed income, they will take the matter into their own hands and reducing investing in specific skills and more on general skills. So the accompanying level of ILM may as well be relatively high in liberal welfare states. In the corporatist welfare states, ILM may be severely suppressed due to the necessity to maintain the hierarchy among occupations, and the pay structure that follows. The workers here will be most interested in getting a perk within this hierarchy, and investing in industry-specific human capital seems the best investment a worker can make. This may be the closest fit to the institutional complementarities summed up in the coordinated market economies (CMEs). According to the arguments of both Esping-Andersen and Hall and Soskice, ILM levels in CMEs or corporatist welfare states should be low. And in social democratic welfare states, governments intervene extensively to provide the safety net, and those market risks for workers whose investment on specific skills may be lost to technological updates or international market fluctuations are offset by active labor market interventions in the labor markets (Burgoon and Hiscox 2000; Hiscox and Rickard 2002). ILM therefore should be quite high among social democratic welfare states.

Therefore, we can have a tentative ranking of levels of ILM among three groups of welfare capitalism. Social democratic welfare states will have the highest ILM levels, followed by liberal welfare states, and corporatist welfare states will have the lowest levels of ILM.

From the reviews of VoC and welfare state literature it becomes clear that, beyond the realm of international trade policies, interindustry factor or labor mobility levels may be strongly correlated with the types of governments that form within the countries, for example, according to VoC argument, market-orthodox parties will be fundamentally at odds with the complex web of institutions within CMEs, but will thrive in LMEs; and according to welfare state literature, parties committed to universal safety nets could run into trouble if they try to gain footholds in liberal welfare states where market has traditionally dominated the individual welfare, and that political parties' fundamental political ideas would have to be framed to fit the domestic political contours dictated by the levels of interindustry factor or labor mobility within the countries. The mismatches between the two will make it hard for political parties to operate.

Few scholars, however, have looked at the possibility where a proactive government may take great interest in influencing the levels of interindustry factor mobility. As a peripheral argument, Alt and Gilligan argued that factor owners can invest more (less) in the industries where assets are highly specific to commit themselves to certain political course of protectionism (liberalization) and sway the government's political decisions (Alt and Gilligan 1994).

Verdier argued that factors owners in particularistic policy networks will have different levels of interindustry factor mobility than outside of those policy networks. There will be ample opportunities for politicians to influence levels of IFM by constructing the policy networks to enlarge their support base and reward the loyal supporters, or destructing policy networks among the opposition (Verdier 1995).

A recent study by Brawley argues that the dominant cleavage within the economy can be shifted by calculated government interventions (Brawley 2006). Stolper-Samuelson or specific factors models usually treat a country as a homogenous economic unit, but in reality different regions within a country will have different mix and concentration of productive factors. Brawley argues that for factor owners there is considerable ambiguity arising from the different combinations of their factor endowment and their attachment to the exporting or import-competing sectors. Governments can target the swing groups that have ambiguous attitudes on trade policies, and nudge these groups towards their favored coalitions. In doing so, the dominant cleavage within the country changes accordingly.

These researches, however, have not explained in detail the causal mechanisms through which governments may affect factor mobility, and they have not produced any systematic and reproducible evidence that levels of interindustry factor mobility are influenced in the predictable manner, beyond some interesting yet underdeveloped hypotheses. This study seeks to redress the shortcomings.

1.3. Overview of my argument

In this dissertation, I analyze the relationship between the partisanship of governments and the corresponding levels of interindustry labor mobility. From a general equilibrium model, I show that high levels of ILM lead to greater class solidarity/cohesiveness among labor owners while weakening the solidarity among capital owners. The reverse holds for low levels of ILM. Left governments would benefit from having a more cohesive working-class base and would therefore prefer high levels of ILM. For equivalent reasons, Right governments would prefer low levels of ILM for the sake of a more cohesive business class. Such partisan divergences in preferred levels of ILM, however, could be moderated by centralized labor unions, which both bring about more cohesive labor forces by themselves and possess their own preferences for high levels of ILM. I develop and test a set of conditional hypotheses concerning the interaction between partisan governments and centralized unions on ILM levels. I further argue and test the claim that one mechanism through which partisan governments can cause the changes of interindustry labor mobility levels is the manipulation of certain labor market policies.

In the process of quantitative analyses, I construct innovative new measures of interindustry labor mobility based on the formal definition of ILM, i.e., "the elasticity of substitution along the transformation curve that maps the conversion of a factor located in one industry for use in another industry at increasing opportunity costs" (Hiscox 2002a), or in other words, the elasticity of labor supply across industries upon the interindustry wage differentials. The measures are at country-year level, but they also can be disaggregated into country-year-industry level. The relationship between partisan politics and interindustry labor mobility will be corroborated and further explored by qualitative case studies of Sweden and the US.

Chapter 2
A Theory of Partisan Preferences of Interindustry Labor Mobility

This chapter presents a theory that argues for partisanship-based preferences of interindustry labor mobility by the governments and explains the possible causal mechanisms through which this preference can be attained. It consists of two main parts. Part one constructs a theory of partisan preferences of ILM, which is developed in four sections. Part two discusses the government policy intervention as a possible causal mechanism through which partisan governments may affect levels of interindustry labor mobility.

2.1. Partisan preferences on interindustry labor mobility

In this part, I seek to describe the basic relationship between partisan governments and their preferred levels of interindustry labor mobility (ILM); this is done in four steps. The first section explains the root causes of partisan governments' distinct preferences in the cohesiveness of their constituency bases. I show that Left-Right parties have distinct constituencies that correspond roughly to their factor ownership[3]. Section two presents a general equilibrium model that reveals that the solidarity or cohesiveness among labor and capitalist groups can be shaped by levels of interindustry labor mobility. Section three discusses the effect of centralized labor unions, which were not considered in the general equilibrium model, and analyzes the preferences of centralized labor unions on the levels of interindustry labor mobility. Section four combines the previous discussions together and argues that Left-Right governments tend to pursue different levels of ILM to facilitate

[3] Here I define factors in a rather general sense in line with the Heckscher-Ohlin models, that is, factors comprise at least labor and capital. More nuanced division of factors, such as in Leamer's work where he identified 11 different factors (Leamer 1984), will not add to the insight of the theory here but will unnecessarily complicate the derivation.

their implementation of partisan policies. It draws three testable conditional hypotheses regarding partisan preferences of ILM and centralized unions' preferences depending on partisanship of the governments.

2.1.1. Partisan governments and their constituencies

Modern political parties take positions in the overall policy space that reflect their general ideological preferences and the interests of their constituents. Studies on partisan politics and macroeconomic policies have found that there is a prominent Left-Right differentiation among parties, especially in advanced industrial countries. The left parties tend to be labor-oriented, working-class-based, and their main constituency would mostly include lower income individuals. The left parties and their constituents will generally favor the macroeconomic performances of low unemployment, high economic growth, and are more sympathetic to redistributive government policies. On the other hand, right parties tend to be business-oriented, upper-middle-class-based, and their core constituency composes mostly of wealthier individuals who usually hold financial capital. The macroeconomy favored by the right parties and their supporters will most likely be characterized by low inflation, moderate growth, and they are much more averse to redistributive policies than their counterparts on the left. For discussions of partisan politics and the Left/Right correspondence with roughly the labor/business classes, see for example (Alesina and Rosenthal 1995; Alesina et al. 1997; Dutt and Mitra 2002, 2005; Hibbs 1977, 1987, 1994; Iversen 2006; Przeworski and Sprague 1986). Dutt and Mitra wrote that "it is fairly standard in the political economy literature to use left-wing (right-wing) and pro-labor (pro-capital) interchangeably when describing political parties" (Dutt and Mitra, 2002: 2-3). For the partisan differentiation of macroeconomic performances and different preferences in policy space, see for example (Alesina and Rosenthal 1989, 1995; Alvarez et al. 1991; Boix 1997; Franzese 2006; Garrett 1998; Milner and Judkins 2004). Hibbs wrote that

> "...[T]he interests and preferences of core party constituencies predispose Left governments to pursue relatively expansive policies intended to raise growth and lower unemployment and Right governments to pursue relatively restrictive policies designed to contain inflation" (Hibbs 2006).

The preceding argument demonstrates that there is a close relationship between parties and different factor owning groups. The following general equilibrium model shows that interindustry labor mobility (ILM) levels can lead to changes of solidarity/cohesiveness among owners of different types of factors but in opposite directions[4]. When ILM levels are higher, labor owners will become more identified with the fact that they are members of the labor class and that their incomes are predominantly determined by their own productivity, which has been shaped by their training, education, experience and the general labor market skills they possess; rather than by their affiliation with industries of employment. That is, rising ILM levels solidify the relative economic positions of workers employed in different industries. At the same time, rising ILM levels can disequilibrate the relative economic positions of capital owners in different industries by increasing the capital return differentials to otherwise homogenous capital assets that happen to be used in different industries. Given the ability of capital owners to move their productive assets across industries upon the price incentives, i.e., given interindustry **capital** mobility levels, increasing capital return differentials tend to increase the internal tension among capital owners across industries, which will disturb the cohesiveness among capital owners. Symmetrically, the opposite effects apply when ILM levels are declining: labor owners will become more identified with the industries that employ them and capital holders more unified with each other. It follows that different levels of interindustry labor mobility will have important implications to parties that rely on the support of different factor owning groups.

Muller and Strom argued that political parties and their leaders in particular are most frequently engaged in hard struggles to find the proper balance among three distinct goals: office, policy, or votes (Muller and Strom 1999). Once in

[4] Class solidarity is indicated by the absolute differences between relative changes of returns for the same factor employed in different industries. Shrinking absolute differences indicate higher solidarity, which means that returns to different owners of the same factor across industries are more likely to be stable and the relative positions of each factor owner within the economic structure tend to be fixed; less solidarity means such structure is less stable and more prone to change. See more explanations on this point below.

government, however, parties will likely be preoccupied with whether they could implement their preferred policies or whether they can garner enough votes in the next election to remain in government. Since votes can only plausibly be instrumental goals, for parties in government, seeking to implement their ideal policies will most likely be the most important concern of the parties. Another support for emphasizing parties' policy concern comes from the literature on partisan models of party competition. According to the partisan models, parties as well as voters care about policy outcomes in addition to winning elections per se (Calvert 1985; Wittman 1977, 1983), and rather than in a Downsian model where parties choose policies in order to win elections, "parties want to be elected in order to choose policies" (Alesina and Rosenthal, 1995, p17).

The job of implementing a party's preferred policies will be made easier if the party has a unified or cohesive constituency than if the constituency is internally divided. Any rudimentary game theory textbook will tell us that an increasing number of players involved in decision-making will render the decisions harder to make, and if a compromise can be achieved, it will be farther away from the ideal positions of many players than if there were fewer numbers of involved players. We can also regard the general constituency for the governing party or party coalition as consisting of multiple segments of supporters, and each segment may be a veto player to the implementation of the party's preferred policies. Tsebelis has shown that as the number of veto players increases, the probability of making policy changes decreases (Tsebelis 2002). Higher cohesiveness among the constituency tends to decrease the number of the potential "veto players" as many segments now possess increasingly similar economic interests while internal strife tends to increase the number of veto players. To the extent that parties care about policy outcomes, they would have an interest to have a more cohesive constituency so as to decrease the number of the potential veto players. The left-leaning party or coalition of parties would favor high levels of interindustry labor mobility and right-leaning parties or party coalitions would prefer low levels of labor mobility in order to generate the more cohesive constituencies that may facilitate the implementation of their preferred policies. The following model shows explicitly how interindustry labor mobility is linked with the fundamental economic interests of factor owners of different kinds and what is the nature of the relationship between ILM and solidarity/cohesiveness among different kinds of factor owners.

2.1.2. How ILM levels can shape class solidarity?

Ronald Jones proposed a general equilibrium model of production that analyzes an economy consisting of two factors (Labor and Capital), two sectors, and two commodities; and this model has been further developed by others (Jones 1965, 1971; Hill and Mendez 1983; Parai and Yu 1989; Hiscox 2002). The model reveals a clear linkage between levels of interindustry labor mobility and the relative income of labor and capital owners; since the utility to owners of any type of factors would depend on the income derived from their assets, the model will be able to shed important insight on how the fundamental economic interests of labor and business groups are affected by different levels of interindustry labor mobility. Furthermore, the model can indicate what implications different levels of ILM will have for the cohesiveness among different types of factor owners and their political support for partisan governments[5]. The detailed derivation of the model and its conclusions can be found in the appendix. For the purpose of discussion here, we can derive the following equations from the model about the relative change of factor returns as induced by a relative change of commodity price:

---

[5] The Jones model assumes market efficiency and no unemployment, just as in the Stolper-Samuel model. (Shapiro and Stiglitz 1984) proposed that involuntary unemployment can be the equilibrium outcome in modern labor markets, when the wages are set at efficiency-levels and unemployment used as a worker discipline device. Using the efficiency-wage model framework, (Hoon 1991) and (Bretcher 1992) argued that in an open economy efficiency-wages can lead to involuntary unemployment as the jobless workers cannot bid down the wages to the full-employment level. Besides efficiency-wage argument, (Davidson et al. 1988, 1991, 1999) argued that unemployment could be the consequence of costly search processes. (Walde and Weiss 2006) combined matching process with a Jonesian specific model in the context of a small open economy. The bottom line is that unemployment can be incorporated into the above model without altering the main conclusions. In future research I will consider models with unemployment.

$$\hat{w}_1 = \left[\frac{-\theta_{K1}\sigma_2(\lambda_{K2}\eta_K - \lambda_{L2}\eta_L) - \theta_{K1} \cdot |\lambda|\eta_L\eta_K}{D} \right] \cdot \hat{p}$$

$$\hat{w}_2 = \left[\frac{-\theta_{K1}\sigma_2(\lambda_{K2}\eta_K - \lambda_{L2}\eta_L) + \eta_K(\sigma_1\lambda_{K1} + \sigma_2\lambda_{K2}) + \sigma_1\sigma_2 - \theta_{K1} \cdot |\lambda|\eta_L\eta_K}{D} \right] \cdot \hat{p}$$

$$\hat{r}_1 = \left[\frac{\theta_{L1}\sigma_2(\lambda_{K2}\eta_K - \lambda_{L2}\eta_L) + \theta_{L1} \cdot |\lambda|\eta_L\eta_K}{D} \right] \cdot \hat{p}$$

$$\hat{r}_2 = \left[\frac{\theta_{L1}\sigma_2(\lambda_{K2}\eta_K - \lambda_{L2}\eta_L) + \eta_L(\sigma_1\lambda_{L1} + \sigma_2\lambda_{L2}) + \sigma_1\sigma_2 + \theta_{L1} \cdot |\lambda|\eta_L\eta_K}{D} \right] \cdot \hat{p}$$

Where $\hat{w}_1$, $\hat{w}_2$, $\hat{r}_1$, and $\hat{r}_2$ are the relative change of wages and rates of return to capital in sectors 1 and 2, for example, $\hat{w}_1 = dw_1 / w_1$; $\hat{p}$ is the relative change of commodity prices; η_L is the interindustry labor mobility while η_K is the interindustry capital mobility [6]. Definitions of other parameters can be found in the appendix.

Given the set up of the model, we can formally derive the following two inequalities, which reveal the interesting relationship between class solidarity (among either labor or capital owners) and interindustry labor mobility levels:

$$\frac{\partial(|\hat{w}_1 - \hat{w}_2|)}{\partial \eta_L} < 0$$

$$\frac{\partial(|\hat{r}_1 - \hat{r}_2|)}{\partial \eta_L} > 0$$

In the same fashion as used by Hiscox (2002), the "class solidarity" is indicated by the absolute differences between relative changes of returns for the same factor used in different industries. In the above two inequalities, the absolute difference between $\hat{w}_1$ and $\hat{w}_2$, i.e., $|\hat{w}_1 - \hat{w}_2|$; and the absolute difference

[6] p is the price of commodity 2; since the price of commodity 1 is assumed to be unity, p can also be regarded as the commodity price ratio.

between $\hat{r}_1$ and $\hat{r}_2$, i.e., $|\hat{r}_1 - \hat{r}_2|$, indicate the degree of class solidarity among labor and capital owners respectively. The first inequality shows that for a unit increase of interindustry labor mobility level the absolute difference of relative changes of wages will shrink, which means higher level of labor class solidarity[7]. In other words, from the first inequality we can tell that with a unit increase of labor mobility, changes of wage in sector 1 tend to be more in sync with changes of wage in sector 2, thus workers employed in either sector 1 or sector 2 will be in more stable economic positions relative to one another, that is to say no groups of workers can improve their incomes relative to the other groups by simply being employed in some specific industry. This will by definition increases the class solidarity among labor owners. Hence the labor class cohesiveness monotonically improves with increases of interindustry labor mobility levels. The second inequality shows that for a unit increase of labor mobility level the absolute difference of relative changes of capital returns will also increase, which translates into lower level of capital class solidarity. Parallel to the explanation above, with a unit increase of labor mobility, changes of returns to capital in sector 1 will be more out of sync with changes of returns to capital in sector 2, thus capital owners in one industry can improve their economic positions relative to capital owners in the other industry by simply using their capital assets in the specific industry. By definition the increasing absolute difference of relative changes of capital returns will decrease the solidarity among capital owners. Hence the cohesiveness among capital owners monotonically deteriorates with increases of interindustry labor mobility levels.

Symmetrically we can infer that with a unit decrease of ILM level, the solidarity for labor class will deteriorate and the solidarity for capitalist class will improve.

---

[7] This is the partial derivative of the absolute differences with respect to interindustry labor mobility, assuming other things being equal and given the changes in commodity price ratios (or in general, given exogenous product price disturbances).

It is telling to compare, for example, the consequence of different levels of interindustry labor mobility to the economic positions of labor owners in different industries, by looking at the extreme values of labor mobility. Consider the labor class solidarity and assume interindustry capital mobility to be a positive but finite value, when labor owners do not have the ability to move across industries upon price signals, i.e., labor will be completely specific so that $\eta_L = 0$. After substituting the detailed expressions of $\hat{w}_1$ and $\hat{w}_2$, the indicator of relative income gaps among labor class $|\hat{w}_1 - \hat{w}_2|$ will be positive and its value will be determined by other factors such as the level of production technology (σ), existing economic structure (θ), composition of labor and capital in the overall economy (λ), as well as the level of interindustry capital mobility (η_K). However, when we move the economy in question ceteris paribus from having completely specific labor to having completely mobile labor so that $\eta_L = +\infty$, the indicator of labor class solidarity $|\hat{w}_1 - \hat{w}_2|$ will asymptotically be approaching zero, meaning $\hat{w}_1$ will approximate $\hat{w}_2$, and labor owners across industries will have similar economic positions in the economy according to their labor market skills and nothing else. Labor class solidarity/cohesiveness will be complete.

To further clarify the meaning of class solidarity, note that all that matter for the economic positions of factor owners are their incomes relative to each other rather than the absolute amounts of their incomes. For a simple numerical example, suppose the two sectors initially paid the annual wages of $50,000 and $10,000 to their workers, and for exogenous reasons such as a direct government decree in the second period, both sectors increase their wages by 10% (thus for both a relative upward change of 10%); then the wages in the two sectors will be $55,000 and $11,000 respectively. The absolute difference between relative changes of wages in the two sectors will be zero, which means the relative economic positions among labor owners will remain unchanged and so does the labor class solidarity; however, the interindustry wage differential actually increases, from $40,000 to $44,000.

In the context of the discussion of interindustry labor mobility, higher labor mobility can contribute to smaller absolute differences between relative changes of wages (thus higher labor class solidarity). This implies that with higher ILM, changes of wages across industries will become more concerted or coordinated, so that any specific labor owner will not be able to advance her economic position relative to others simply by virtue of being employed in a specific industry; rather, her economic payoff will generally be commensurate with her overall productivity (denoted in the general equilibrium model as a_{Lj}). It follows that with higher ILM levels, labor owners tend to derive their income more from their general labor market skills and less from their attachment with any specific industry. This basic intuition has also been used elsewhere such as in Hiscox's argument where he argues that the political coalition around trade issues tends to be broad-based or aligned along the class division when interindustry factor mobility is rather high, and the coalition tends to be industry-specific when the interindustry factor mobility is rather low (Hiscox 2002). This study focuses specifically on interindustry labor mobility and analyzes its differentiating effects for labor or capital friendly political parties.

Under higher levels of ILM, the income for any labor owner will be less associated with the industry that happens to employ her, but more with how productive the labor owner intrinsically is. Through the mechanism of labor mobility, labor owners will acquire a stake in the success of any labor-benefiting policies since they can reap gains from such policies by exercising their ability to move to more productive and thus remunerative industries[8]. Therefore with higher labor mobility, support for labor-benefiting policies from labor owners will increase.

---

[8] Theoretically, when levels of ILM are high, all policies are either labor-benefiting or non-labor-benefiting. If there are policies purported to benefit only parts of the labor force, the labor mobility mechanism will however spread the benefit to the whole labor force since, 1) high ILM ensures that high productivity workers can move into those policy-favored industries; 2) the general equilibrium model ensures that the absolute differences between

In similar logic, higher ILM levels will lead to larger absolute differences between relative changes of returns to capital assets been employed in different industries, which translates to deteriorating solidarity/cohesiveness among capital owners. As some capital owners can make economic gains relative to other capital owners by simply investing their assets in certain specific industries, the general level of support among capital owners for the capital-benefiting policies will decline.

2.1.3. The preference of centralized labor unions on ILM levels

The above general equilibrium model assumes the individual level rationality and the primacy of individual actors in deriving the relationship between interindustry labor mobility and class solidarity. And critically in terms of labor class solidarity, the model shows that levels of labor mobility are positively associated with labor class solidarity. However, studies of politics and economics have found that workers, their employers, and the governments are often not the only players in determining the labor market equilibria in capitalist democracies; among others, labor unions at various levels can play important roles in aggregating and representing the economic demands and political preferences of labor owners as well as having their independent impact on labor markets and government policies. By not dealing with labor unions, the above general equilibrium model describes what we should expect about the cohesiveness of different types of factor owners independent of the development of unionization, thus the predictions based on the model can be generally applied to situations of any level of union development.

Meanwhile, labor unions and labor market institutions that centered on unions feature prominently in many studies, for example, Alvarez, Garrett and Lange argued that when there are left governments coupled with centralized labor movement, or when there are right governments with weak labor movement, the macroeconomic performances will be better than in other combinations (Alvarez et al. 1991). Garrett further developed the idea of encompassness of labor movement and argued that

---

relative wage changes will be small with high levels of ILM, so that wages of those industries that are not policy-favored will also rise in sync with those that are policy-favored.

macroeconomic performance will be good when the political economies are coherent, that is, either where politically powerful left-wing parties are allied with encompassing labor market institutions or where right-wing dominance is combined with weak institutions in the labor market, and macroeconomic performance will be worse when the political economies are incoherent (Garrett 1998). Hall and Franzese suggested that the institutional variable of the degree of wage-bargaining coordination can have substantial effects on economic performance; that the desirable consequences of central bank independence hold only for countries with coordinated wage-bargaining systems; and in countries where the wage-bargaining is less coordinated, increasing central bank independence lowers inflation only at the cost of significant increase in unemployment (Hall and Franzese 1998). Furthermore, in the voluminous literature on comparative political economy and welfare state, labor unions and labor institutions that centered on unionism have been shown to be integral parts of modern capitalist economies, see for example (Golden and Pontusson 1992; Hall and Soskice 2001b; Huber and Stephens 2001; Pontusson 2005; Pontusson et al. 2002; Wallerstein 1990, 1999).

The development of centralized domestic labor unions, as the literature has suggested, is clearly a key variable in any study that concerns labor market, due at the very least to the fact that union movement constitutes an essential part of the labor markets in many industrial democracies. Hence it is important to examine if and how the degree of the development of domestic union movement may interfere with or moderate the hypothesized impact on ILM levels from governments' partisanship [9].

To gauge the development on domestic labor union movement, and especially the relationship between periphery organizations and the central peak associations, I adopt the operational definition by Miriam Golden, such that labor union

---

[9] It is entirely possible that a parallel process works for the organization of capital such as the employers' association but in the opposite direction, but insofar as interindustry labor mobility is concerned, labor organizations may have a first-order and more immediate interest in it than do capital's organizations. The discussion here hence considers only the organizations of labor.

centralization refers to the degree of internal authority exercised by union confederations over lower organizational bodies. Where confederations mean labor's central peak associations; they comprise individual national unions, and they are multi-sectoral, economy-wide bodies engaged to varying degrees in collective bargaining with government, etc. (Golden 1993; Golden et al. 2006). Under low union centralization, unions at industry or firm levels may be empowered to call strikes and sign agreements at their own discretion. When union centralization is high, the central confederation alone officially calls strikes and may have the authority to negotiate wage agreements, which extend to entire industries or even the whole economy (Golden 1993; Golden et al. 2006).

Labor unions therefore can be understood as organizations that represent the interests of labor owners. Poorly centralized unions lean heavily toward extending the interests of their own respective members, even if this may be at the expense of other unions and their members. These unions usually lack some institutionalized coordination among themselves, and the nominal central confederations, if they exist at all, do not possess any real sanction power against the actions by their member unions. Centralized unions, however, are distinguished by their effective coordination capacity and their possession of sanction power against stray member unions. They tend to be the hubs where decisions concerning to the welfare of workers would be collected, compromised, and implemented as well as be the focal points where the expectations of ordinary labor owners about their future economic interests converge. In this scenario, the fact that unions are centralized means that they, and in specific the central confederations, would strive to advance the interest of labor owners in general rather than some subset of labor owners, and they tend to have high capacity for collective political actions.

Based on this discussion, I make the following claims for ease of developing the argument later: centralized unions strive to improve the welfare for all labor owners; decentralized unions want to improve the welfare only for some specific groups of labor owners that belong to each union. Such claims echo the assumptions common in the literature that each union tries to maximize its members' long term utility and that centralized union movement is analytically equivalent to an enlarged union that encompasses the whole labor force (Pontusson 2005; Wallerstein 1990).

The organizational structure of labor unions allows them to mobilize their members. When levels of domestic union centralization increase, coordination among labor groups strengthens and the peak associations tend to possess more sanction power; it follows that labor groups will then be able to organize more effective collective political actions. When unions are centralized, the general interests of labor will be more salient in the overall orientation of the union movement, and centralized unions are more likely to lend their political supports to those policies that benefit labor in general. As the representative body of the general interests of labor, centralized unions tend to be more vocal and effective when different labor groups share similar economic interests than when they are at odds with each other. Since centralized organizational structure among labor groups facilitates the task of coordinating and enforcing peak-level decisions, well-coordinated unions aided by peak-level enforcement are highly likely to achieve economic outcomes that are collectively beneficial and in manners that contribute to cohesiveness among labor class. Hence centralized unions inherently entail labor class solidarity/cohesiveness. The general equilibrium model reveals that high or low ILM levels are conducive to high or low labor class solidarity. From the viewpoint of centralized unions, in order to maintain a highly cohesive labor class, they would always prefer the levels of labor mobility to be high, regardless of the partisanship of the governments.

2.1.4. Partisan preference and union moderation of ILM

Partisan governments need the political support of their constituencies to facilitate the implementation of their preferred policies. It has been shown that Left and Right parties display distinct patterns of preferred policies (Dutt and Mitra 2005; Hibbs 1977, 1987). Left-wing parties are generally pro-labor, and their constituency bases predispose them to adopt policies that generally favor labor once they control the governments. Similarly, because Right-wing parties are in general pro-capital, their constituency bases predispose them to adopt policies favoring capital once they are in power.

We have discussed that the cohesiveness of the constituency bases can have direct impact on the ease to implement different types of partisan policies. As a general observation, Left governments prefer to have cohesive labor class and Right governments prefer to have cohesive business class. We have seen that levels of interindustry labor mobility are closely linked to the solidarity/cohesiveness of different types of factor owners. Independent from the effects of labor unions, higher levels of ILM will lead to a more cohesive labor class and less cohesive capital class, and vice versa.

Centralized labor union movement enables effective coordination among various unions and helps overcome the barriers to collective actions, thus to a large degree it embodies a cohesive labor class. At the same time, due to the incentive for self-preservation centralized unions themselves have an unambiguous preference for cohesive labor force and consequently high levels of labor mobility; hence the presence or absence of centralized unions will significantly condition the pursuit of labor mobility by either Left or Right governments.

When the union centralization is low (or equivalently when the labor unions are decentralized, or when there is an absence of centralized union), Left governments prefer to have **HIGH** levels of ILM in order to facilitate the implementation of their preferred policies that tend to benefit labor. High levels of ILM ensure that the economic interests of labor owners will be determined by their characteristics as members of labor forces such as their general labor market skills and not by their affiliation with specific industries. Through the mechanism of labor mobility, economic implications of policies will spread to all labor owners; labor owners thus acquire a stake in the implementation of labor-benefiting policies, which positively affect their incomes, and with ever higher ILM levels, such stake grows larger. Since union centralization is rather low, labor cohesiveness cannot be provided through the centralized labor organizations and Left governments will have strong incentives and preferences to attain labor cohesiveness by other means. For Left governments whose predisposition was to implement labor-benefiting policies, it is rational to prefer high levels of ILM and furthermore to achieve this by engineering increases of ILM levels when needed to ensure sufficiently high levels of political support from labor owners, who are their core constituency base.

Under the same situation, that is, when the union centralization is low, Right governments prefer to have **LOW** levels of ILM to facilitate implementation of their preferred capital-benefiting policies. The finding from the general equilibrium model shows that with lower ILM levels, the absolute difference between relative changes of returns to capital across industries becomes smaller, meaning capital class solidarity will be higher[10]. Capital-benefiting policies will benefit capital owners in general, and the political support on capital-benefiting policies by capital owners tend to increase with the decrease of ILM levels (and consequently the increase of capital class solidarity). The absence of centralized unions means that there would be no effective collective actions among labor owners and coordination among their unions to constrain the policy choices of Right governments. For Right governments whose predisposition was to implement capital-benefiting policies, it becomes rational to prefer low ILM levels and to manage to decrease ILM levels when necessary in order to have higher degrees of support for their policies by capital owners, who are their core constituency base.

When the union centralization is high, coordination among labor groups will be common and effective, and labor's concerted political support for Left government's labor-benefiting policies is very likely. As the labor cohesiveness concomitant with centralized unions is high, Left governments

[10] Within the general equilibrium framework, the reason why this happens may be that low ILM levels prevent high productivity workers to respond to intersectoral wage differentials and move across industries, so that some high productivity workers are stuck within industries that would otherwise lose them. Despite being paid lower than their productivity, these workers continue to have high output so that their employers will have higher than normal rates of return to capital. Parallel to this development, there are workers with low productivity stuck in other industries that pay high wages such that those industries will have lower than normal rates of return to capital. And at equilibrium, lower or higher than normal rates of return to capital tend to cancel each other out such that capital used in different industries will earn similar rates of return when ILM levels are low. It follows that when ILM levels are low, it matters less for capital owners as to which industry they have invested their assets but more about their identity as capital owners, which tends to ensure them a certain rate of return everywhere in the economy.

can secure much of the needed political support from centralized unions, hence their direct incentives and derived preferences for high levels of interindustry labor mobility in order to achieve cohesive labor constituency tend to subside. However, the lack of incentive on the part of Left governments to aggressively pursue high levels of labor mobility may not lead to a decline of labor mobility levels, due to the moderating effects of centralized unions. Centralized union movement and its peak associations have strong interests in maintaining cohesive labor forces and for this purpose prefer high levels of ILM. As a key part of the political support base of the Left governments, centralized unions' preferences for high levels of ILM tend to be reflected in the policy choices of the Left governments. This will compensate for the original lack of Left governments' incentive to pursue high ILM levels; as a result, we can expect the ILM levels under Left governments and centralized unions to remain as high as the levels under Left governments and decentralized unions.

When the union centralization is high, coordination among labor unions is strong and the peak associations tend to possess sanction power over their member unions, labor groups will be able to organize effective collective political actions. The high capacity for collective action implies that centralized labor unions can apply considerable constraints on Right governments' policies. In terms of the policies that can have labor mobility-changing implications, had there been no centralized unions, the Right governments would likely manipulate the policies to keep labor mobility at low levels. But in the presence of centralized unions, the attempts by the Right governments to reduce labor mobility levels will likely meet strong resistance from centralized unions. The general equilibrium model reveals that low ILM levels are conducive to low levels of labor class solidarity or cohesiveness, which directly threaten the very existence of centralized union movement. We should then expect that centralized unions will exert heavy pressure on the policy choices of the Right governments, to such an extent that the outcome variable of the level of labor mobility will be significantly different than when there are no centralized unions. It may be that centralized unions can moderate the Right governments' partisan pursuit so much so that, despite their incentives for low ILM levels, the

ILM levels under Right governments and centralized unions will be significantly higher than those under Right governments and decentralized unions.

It is not unlikely that centralized union movement may constrain governments; political economists have shown that partisan governments may behave differently depending on the degree of domestic union development. For example, Garrett showed that Right governments tend to move toward the macroeconomic regime of social democratic corporatism when they face encompassing labor movement if they prefer not to have a paralyzed macroeconomic governance; similarly, Left governments tend to shift towards market liberalism if there does not exist a cooperative and encompassing labor movement (Garrett 1998). Alvarez, Garrett and Lange argued that the macroeconomic performances will be better either when there are Left governments with centralized labor movement or when there are Right governments with weak labor movement, than in any other configurations (Alvarez et al. 1991). In other words, the literature has shown that centralized labor movement tends to constrain the policy space available to governments, more so on the Right-wing governments than on Left-wing governments. The reason that centralized labor movement may differentiate the types of constraints on the Left from those on Right governments may be that centralized labor movement tends to share a set of fundamental political economic goals with the Left governments, such as lower unemployment, higher economic growth, and more redistributive welfare policies benefiting the poor; while the goals cherished by the Right governments, such as low inflation, moderate growth, and minimal governments, etc., may not echo with the labor movement (Alesina and Rosenthal 1989, 1995; Alvarez et al. 1991; Boix 1997; Garrett 1998; Huber and Stephens 2001; Pontusson et al. 2002; Przeworski and Sprague 1986; Wallerstein 1990).

To summarize, the discussions yield the following expectations about the levels of interindustry labor mobility under different partisan governments and when the moderation effect of centralized unions is considered. Other things being equal, where there are low levels of union centralization, labor mobility levels tend to be higher under Left governments than under the Right governments. When there are higher levels of union centralization, the concomitant labor cohesiveness and labor's capacity for collective action are both higher, Left governments will have less incentive to continue pursuing high ILM levels. But the lack of incentive on the part of Left governments is compensated by the strong interests for high ILM on the part of centralized unions, who can heavily influence Left governments' policies, so that the resultant ILM under the Left governments tend to stay at relatively high levels with the increases of the degree of the union centralization. Under the same situation of higher union centralization, Right governments become more constrained by the centralized unions in their choices of labor mobility changing policies, so that the resultant ILM levels under the Right governments tend to increase with the increases of the degree of the union centralization. Furthermore, as a result of the moderation by centralized unions, we will not have a clear prediction about the relativity of ILM levels under Left or Right governments when there are high levels of union centralization.

The following conditional hypotheses recapitulate the predictions:

Hypothesis 1: When the level of domestic union centralization is low, levels of ILM will be higher under Left governments than under Right governments.

Hypothesis 2: When there are Left governments, levels of ILM will not significantly change with higher levels of union centralization.

Hypothesis 3: When there are Right governments, levels of ILM will be higher with higher levels of union centralization.

Tables 2.1 and 2.2 present the predictions of conditional hypotheses schematically:

Table 2.1. Predictions of relative levels of interindustry labor mobility that will be associated with different government partisanship with the moderation of domestic union centralization

	Left governments		Right governments
High union centralization	ILM levels	?	ILM levels
Low union centralization	ILM levels	>	ILM levels

Note: "?" means there is no clear prediction

Table 2.2. Predictions of relative levels of interindustry labor mobility that will be associated with different levels of domestic union centralization when under different types of government partisanship

	Left governments		Right governments
High union centralization	ILM levels		ILM levels
Low union centralization	ILM levels		ILM levels

2.2. Can government policies affect interindustry labor mobility?

Previous studies that concern the subject of interindustry factor mobility tend to treat levels of interindustry factor mobility as exogenous. So when it comes to the relationship between politics and interindustry factor mobility, the arguments generally would be that levels of interindustry factor mobility determine the types of prevailing political coalitions (either broad class-based or industry-specific), such as in (Frieden 1991; Hiscox 2002; Rogowski 1989), but not vice versa. That is, the conventional wisdom usually assumes that political manipulations cannot change the levels of interindustry factor mobility within the economy.

Though to the author's knowledge there have been no systematic theories on the subject of endogenous interindustry factor mobility in the political economy literature, there are many studies that hinted in this direction. For example, Bhagwati and Srinivasan discussed a variety of policy instruments that concern trade, some of which, such as "factor tax cum subsidy" could fundamentally change the production frontier by changing real factor returns (Bhagwati and Srinivasan 1983). Since real factor returns are the basic motivation of intersectoral factor movement, such policy interventions would surely have factor mobility implications. The Variety of Capitalism (VoC) literature maintains that distinct types of institutional complementarities exist within different bundles of countries; one of the key areas where these country groupings differ is the skill specificity, which may determine the ability of workers to move across different sectors within the economy. VoC literature argues that workers in coordinated market economy countries are less inclined to move across sectors than their counterparts in liberal market economy countries for reasons that coordinated market economies usually have the configuration of institutional complementarities such that they allow and encourage workers to develop skill sets that tend to be specific to certain sectors and not readily transferable to other sectors within the economy, while liberal market economies have another configuration of institutional complementarities that tend to encourage general skills that are portable across sectors (Hall and Soskice 2001a; Estevez-Abe et al. 2001). As these authors suggested, such different patterns of institutional complementarities would both foster and be fostered by the intricate web of government policies and institutions, hence VoC literature can be taken to imply that interindustry labor mobility, a key component of interindustry factor mobility, may be influenced by – thus endogenous to – government manipulations. Mark Brawley suggested that for those governments whose electoral fortunes depend heavily on the dominant trade cleavages, they may engage in interventions aimed at shifting the dominant cleavage, targeting especially the swing groups (Brawley 2006). In so doing, he no longer treated societal cleavages (which can be regarded as the direct consequences of levels of interindustry factor mobility) as exogenously given, but rather argued that they are susceptible to political manipulations.

Once we allow the possibility that levels of interindustry labor mobility may be responsive to political manipulations, we can then regard the question on the relationship between labor mobility and government policies as largely empirical; that is, can we or can we not discern some persistent causal patterns that link certain government policies to subsequent levels of interindustry labor mobility? Recalling that interindustry labor mobility is defined as the elasticity of interindustry labor supply in the economy in response to interindustry wage/earning differentials, we can therefore attempt to describe the general conditions under which government policies may make an impact on the levels of ILM. First, such government policies should relate to labor market institutions in general; for instance, government programs to fund job centers where workers can either search for new employment opportunities or receive job-training would have implications for cross-industry labor movement. As a case in point, a recent article in the Time magazine showed an interesting case study of Denmark (Fox 2007). From the 1990s, successive Danish governments have been engaged in some transformation of their welfare-state, by especially investing in the job retraining programs in a big way. These programs, in combination with other aspects of the Danish welfare system such as generous unemployment benefits, health care and portable pensions, etc., have enabled Danish workers to better adjust to employment changes, and may have contributed in no small part to the impressive macroeconomic performance of Denmark ever since. Second, such government policies may aim at influencing the equilibrium prices of labor factor; for example, unemployment compensation scheme is usually available for all eligible unemployed workers, while other government programs such as Trade Adjustment Assistance, subsidized employment, trade protection, and industrial subsidies may only target some subgroups of labor (for discussion on broad vs. narrow forms of redistributive policies, see (Rickard 2005)). The government policies that cover a large swath of the labor forces may be more likely to have appreciable impact on labor mobility levels. Last but not least, government policies may directly stipulate the movement of workers across industries, thus manipulating the regulatory barriers for interindustry labor movement. Though not the same as interindustry labor mobility, it (interindustry labor movement) may have close relationship to labor mobility. An example of the attempt by a government to stipulate domestic labor movement (much of it would be cross-sectoral) is the 2006 turmoil in France over the French government's effort to pass a new law that would allow employers to fire young workers without justification during a two-year trial period.

Based on these rather crude criteria, one would expect the potential policies that can causally affect labor mobility levels should contribute to the general improvement of the labor market in that the given wage levels of workers must be justified by the given levels of their labor market skills. I therefore expect to find that many, if not all, of the following public social expenditure programs may have significant impact on levels of interindustry labor mobility. These public social spending programs are: public expenditure on health, public expenditure on active labor market programs (which contain five subcategories)[11], and public expenditure on unemployment benefits. I choose to look closely at public social expenditure programs because despite the rising levels of government spending during the post-war era (Cameron 1978; Pierson 1996; Rodrik 1997), the different combinations of various programs within the overall spending packages could still reflect the differing priorities for different governments (Huber et al. 1993; Rickard 2004, 2005), and the literature has acknowledged that governments can use public social spending programs as important policy instruments to selectively intervene into the economy (Burgoon and Hiscox 2000; Martin and Swank 2004). There also exist systematic data of these public expenditure programs over the years that enable cross-country comparison among the OECD countries. Furthermore, the definitions of these government programs indicate that they focus on certain important aspects of labor market I just mentioned, such as subsidies, training, employment services, and alternative income; hence these programs are more likely to affect the elasticity of labor supply across industries within the economy. In the ensuing chapters, I will empirically analyze the hypothesized causal relationship from these government policies to the subsequent levels of ILM.

2.3. Conclusion

Combining the predictions summarized in tables 2.1 and 2.2 as well as the discussion in part 2.2; it is straight forward to conclude that the incentive to implement their preferred policies would drive partisan governments to pursue separate strategies on levels of interindustry labor mobility. The patterns of the partisan preference and association with ILM levels as well as the centralized unions' moderating effects are developed in part 2.1 and summarized in the conditional hypotheses. Part 2.2 discusses the possible impact of government policies and

[11] These five categories are: employment services and administration, labor market training, special programs for youth, subsidized employment, and special programs for the disabled.

reveals that partisan governments can engage in a repertoire of policy instruments in order to pursue their desirable levels of ILM.

Appendix to Chapter 2:

Following Jones (1965, 1971), I construct a general equilibrium model of production. Assume an economy that has two sectors that produce two commodities, x_1 and x_2; production of any commodity requires input of two factors, labor L and capital K. Following Hill and Mendez (1983), I assume the aggregate supplies of both factors are fixed and exogenous, but the degree of factor mobility between sectors is left open, that is, intersectoral factor movements are allowed to take place in response to changes in earnings differentials, no assumption is made concerning the degree of responsiveness in factor supplies to those differentials. There are essentially four factor markets: two labor markets with wages w_1 and w_2, and two capital markets with rentals r_1 and r_2.

To set up the model, I have the following relationships.

$$L = L_1 + L_2 \qquad (1)$$

$$K = K_1 + K_2 \qquad (2)$$

Let a_{ij} represents the quantity of factor i required per unit output of x_j, the equations (1) through (8) show the endowment of each factor.

$$x_1 = \frac{L_1}{a_{L1}} \qquad (3)$$

$$x_1 = \frac{K_1}{a_{K1}} \qquad (4)$$

$$x_2 = \frac{L_2}{a_{L2}} \qquad (5)$$

$$x_2 = \frac{K_2}{a_{K2}} \qquad (6)$$

$$a_{L1} \cdot x_1 + a_{L2} \cdot x_2 = L \qquad (7)$$

$$a_{K1} \cdot x_1 + a_{K2} \cdot x_2 = K \qquad (8)$$

The equations (9) and (10) show the competitive profit relationships, here to simplify notations I assume the first commodity x_1 to be the numeraire, thus it has the price of unity, and the price of x_2 is p; w_1, r_1, w_2, and r_2 denote the returns to labor and capital in industry 1 and 2 in terms of the numeraire.

$$a_{L1} \cdot w_1 + a_{K1} \cdot r_1 = 1 \qquad (9)$$

$$a_{L2} \cdot w_2 + a_{K2} \cdot r_2 = p \qquad (10)$$

With competition, unit costs are minimized and each a_{ij} will depend on the ratio of factor prices in industry j, so I have the following equation.

$$a_{ij} = a_{ij}\left(\frac{w_j}{r_j}\right), \text{ where } i = L, K \quad j = 1, 2 \qquad (11)$$

Totally differentiate (11) gives me the following useful relationships.

$$da_{L1} = a'_{L1} \frac{dw_1 \cdot r_1 - dr_1 \cdot w_1}{r_1^2}$$

$$da_{L2} = a'_{L2} \frac{dw_2 \cdot r_2 - dr_2 \cdot w_2}{r_2^2}$$

$$da_{K1} = a'_{K1} \frac{dw_1 \cdot r_1 - dr_1 \cdot w_1}{r_1^2}$$

$$da_{K2} = a'_{K2} \frac{dw_2 \cdot r_2 - dr_2 \cdot w_2}{r_2^2}$$

Throughout the model, a caret " ∧ " over a variable denotes the percentage change in that variable, (e.g., $\hat{x}_1 = dx_1 / x_1$).

Denote η_{ij} as the elasticity of supply of factor i to industry j with respect to earnings differentials, so that,

$$\eta_{L1} = d\ln(L_1) / d\ln(w_1 / w_2)$$

$$\eta_{K1} = d\ln(K_1) / d\ln(r_1 / r_2)$$

$\eta_{L2} = d\ln(L_2)/d\ln(w_1/w_2)$

$\eta_{K2} = d\ln(K_2)/d\ln(r_1/r_2)$

The elasticity of supply of factor i everywhere in the economy with respect to earnings differentials are:

$\eta_L = d\ln(L_1/L_2)/d\ln(w_1/w_2)$

$\eta_K = d\ln(K_1/K_2)/d\ln(r_1/r_2)$

Where $\eta_L \geq 0$ and $\eta_K \geq 0$

Denote $\lambda_{L1} = \frac{L_1}{L}$, $\lambda_{L2} = \frac{L_2}{L}$, $\lambda_{K1} = \frac{K_1}{K}$ and $\lambda_{K2} = \frac{K_2}{K}$, we can have:

$$\lambda_{L2} \cdot \eta_L = (L_2/L) \cdot d\ln(L_1/L_2)/d\ln(w_1/w_2) = (dL_1/L_1)/d\ln(w_1/w_2) = \eta_{L1}$$

This is because from $L = L_1 + L_2$ and L being fixed and exogenous, we have $dL = dL_1 + dL_2 = 0$, therefore,

$$(L_2/L) \cdot d\ln(L_1/L_2) = (L_2/L) \cdot (d\ln L_1 - d\ln L_2) = (L_2/L) \cdot \left(\frac{dL_1}{L_1} - \frac{dL_2}{L_2}\right)$$

$$= (L_2/L) \cdot \left(\frac{dL_1}{L_1} + \frac{dL_1}{L_2}\right) = (L_2/L) \cdot dL_1 \cdot \frac{L_1 + L_2}{L_1 L_2} = dL_1/L_1$$

And similarly,

$\lambda_{L1} \cdot \eta_L = \eta_{L2}$

$\lambda_{K2} \cdot \eta_K = \eta_{K1}$

$\lambda_{K1} \cdot \eta_K = \eta_{K2}$

It follows that,

$\eta_{L1} + \eta_{L2} = \eta_L$

$\eta_{K1} + \eta_{K2} = \eta_K$

Furthermore, we have,

$$\eta_{L1}\eta_{K2} - \eta_{K1}\eta_{L2} = -(\lambda_{L1}\lambda_{K2} - \lambda_{L2}\lambda_{K1}) \cdot \eta_L \eta_K = -|\lambda| \cdot \eta_L \eta_K$$

Where $|\lambda| = \lambda_{L1}\lambda_{K2} - \lambda_{L2}\lambda_{K1}$

Define θ_{ij} as the distributive share of factor i in the value of output in industry j, or in other words, the fraction of unit costs in industry j attributable to factor i, so for equations (9) and (10), divide both sides by the prices of respective commodities, we have:

$$a_{L1} \cdot w_1 + a_{K1} \cdot r_1 = \theta_{L1} + \theta_{K1} = 1$$

$$\frac{a_{L2} \cdot w_2}{p} + \frac{a_{K2} \cdot r_2}{p} = \theta_{L2} + \theta_{K2} = 1$$

From the cost minimizing condition, we have [12],

$$\theta_{Lj}\hat{a}_{Lj} + \theta_{Kj}\hat{a}_{Kj} = 0 \qquad j = 1,2 \qquad (12)$$

The derivation of this equation goes as the following: the typical competitive entrepreneur will try to minimize costs for any given level of output, that is, he will minimize the unit costs, the entrepreneur will treat factor prices as fixed and vary a's so as to set the derivative of costs equal to zero. For the first industry we have from (9) $a_{L1} \cdot w_1 + a_{K1} \cdot r_1 = 1 \rightarrow da_{L1} \cdot w_1 + da_{K1} \cdot r_1 = 0 \rightarrow \hat{a}_{L1} \cdot \theta_{L1} + \hat{a}_{K1} \cdot \theta_{K1} = 0$

From (10),

$$a_{L2} \cdot w_2 + a_{K2} \cdot r_2 = p \quad \rightarrow \quad \frac{a_{L2} \cdot w_2}{p} + \frac{a_{K2} \cdot r_2}{p} = 1 \quad \rightarrow$$

$$\frac{da_{L2} \cdot w_2}{p} + \frac{da_{K2} \cdot r_2}{p} = 0 \rightarrow$$

$$\hat{a}_{L2}\theta_{L2} + \hat{a}_{K2}\theta_{K2} = 0$$

The elasticity of factor substitution within each industry can be defined as,

$$\sigma_j = \left(\hat{K}_j - \hat{L}_j\right)/\left(\hat{w}_j - \hat{r}_j\right) \qquad j = 1,2$$

Or equivalent to,

$$\sigma_j = \left(\hat{a}_{Kj} - \hat{a}_{Lj}\right)/\left(\hat{w}_j - \hat{r}_j\right) \qquad j = 1,2 \quad (13)$$

Solving (12) and (13), I can get

$$\hat{L}_j = \hat{x}_j - \theta_{Kj}\sigma_j \cdot \left(\hat{w}_j - \hat{r}_j\right) \qquad j = 1,2 \quad (14)$$

$$\hat{K}_j = \hat{x}_j + \theta_{Lj}\sigma_j \cdot \left(\hat{w}_j - \hat{r}_j\right) \qquad j = 1,2 \quad (15)$$

From the full employment of labor in (1) we can get,

[12] For more detail on this, see Jones (1971) footnote 4 and Jones (1965), esp. pp.558-560.

$$\hat{L} = \lambda_{L1}\hat{L}_1 + \lambda_{L2}\hat{L}_2 \qquad (16)$$

The elasticity definition of interindustry factor mobility gives that for labor,

$$\hat{L}_1 - \hat{L}_2 = \eta_L \cdot (\hat{w}_1 - \hat{w}_2) \qquad (17)$$

Solving (16) and (17) yields,

$$\hat{L}_1 = \hat{L} + \eta_{L1} \cdot (\hat{w}_1 - \hat{w}_2) \qquad (18)$$

$$\hat{L}_2 = \hat{L} + \eta_{L2} \cdot (\hat{w}_2 - \hat{w}_1) \qquad (19)$$

Repeat these steps for K:

From the full employment of capital in (2) we can get,

$$\hat{K} = \lambda_{K1}\hat{K}_1 + \lambda_{K2}\hat{K}_2$$

The elasticity definition of interindustry factor mobility gives that for capital,

$$\hat{K}_1 - \hat{K}_2 = \eta_K \cdot (\hat{r}_1 - \hat{r}_2)$$

Solving the above two gives,

$$\hat{K}_1 = \hat{K} + \eta_{K1} \cdot (\hat{r}_1 - \hat{r}_2) \qquad (20)$$

$$\hat{K}_2 = \hat{K} + \eta_{K2} \cdot (\hat{r}_2 - \hat{r}_1) \qquad (21)$$

From (14), (15), (18), (19), (20), and (21) I have,

$$\hat{L} + \eta_{L1} \cdot (\hat{w}_1 - \hat{w}_2) = \hat{x}_1 - \theta_{K1}\sigma_1 \cdot (\hat{w}_1 - \hat{r}_1) \qquad (22)$$

$$\hat{L} + \eta_{L2} \cdot (\hat{w}_2 - \hat{w}_1) = \hat{x}_2 - \theta_{K2}\sigma_2 \cdot (\hat{w}_2 - \hat{r}_2) \qquad (23)$$

$$\hat{K} + \eta_{K1} \cdot (\hat{r}_1 - \hat{r}_2) = \hat{x}_1 + \theta_{L1}\sigma_1 \cdot (\hat{w}_1 - \hat{r}_1) \qquad (24)$$

$$\hat{K} + \eta_{K2} \cdot (\hat{r}_2 - \hat{r}_1) = \hat{x}_2 + \theta_{L2}\sigma_2 \cdot (\hat{w}_2 - \hat{r}_2) \qquad (25)$$

From $a_{L1} \cdot w_1 = \theta_{L1}$, $a_{K1} \cdot r_1 = \theta_{K1}$, $a_{L1} \cdot w_1 + a_{K1} \cdot r_1 = 1$ and $\hat{a}_{L2}\theta_{L2} + \hat{a}_{K2}\theta_{K2} = 0$, we can verify that,

$$\hat{w}_1\theta_{L1} + \hat{r}_1\theta_{K1} = 0 \qquad (26)$$

From $\frac{a_{L2} \cdot w_2}{p} = \theta_{L2}$, $\frac{a_{K2} \cdot r_2}{p} = \theta_{K2}$, $a_{L2} \cdot w_2 + a_{K2} \cdot r_2 = p$ and $\hat{a}_{L2}\theta_{L2} + \hat{a}_{K2}\theta_{K2} = 0$, we can verify that,

$$\hat{w}_2\theta_{L2} + \hat{r}_2\theta_{K2} = \hat{p} \qquad (27)$$

Equation (24) - (22) gets,

$$(\sigma_1 + \eta_{L1})\hat{w}_1 - \eta_{L1}\hat{w}_2 - (\sigma_1 + \eta_{K1})\cdot \hat{r}_1 + \eta_{K1}\hat{r}_2 = \hat{K} - \hat{L} \quad (28)$$

Equation (25) - (23) gets,

$$-\eta_{L2}\hat{w}_1 + (\sigma_2 + \eta_{L2})\hat{w}_2 + \eta_{K2}\hat{r}_1 - (\sigma_2 + \eta_{K2})\cdot \hat{r}_2 = \hat{K} - \hat{L} \quad (29)$$

From the assumption of fixed and exogenously given factors K and L, $\hat{K} = \hat{L} = 0$. So we can have the following matrix:

$$\begin{pmatrix} \theta_{L1} & 0 & \theta_{K1} & 0 \\ 0 & \theta_{L2} & 0 & \theta_{K2} \\ \sigma_1 + \eta_{L1} & -\eta_{L1} & -(\sigma_1 + \eta_{K1}) & \eta_{K1} \\ -\eta_{L2} & (\sigma_2 + \eta_{L2}) & \eta_{K2} & -(\sigma_2 + \eta_{K2}) \end{pmatrix} * \begin{pmatrix} \hat{w}_1 \\ \hat{w}_2 \\ \hat{r}_1 \\ \hat{r}_2 \end{pmatrix} = \begin{pmatrix} 0 \\ \hat{p} \\ 0 \\ 0 \end{pmatrix} \quad (30)$$

Let D be the determinant of the coefficient matrix, and D is given by

$$D = \sigma_1\sigma_2 + \sigma_1(\eta_{L2}\theta_{K2} + \eta_{K2}\theta_{L2}) + \sigma_2(\eta_{L1}\theta_{K1} + \eta_{K1}\theta_{L1}) + |\theta|\cdot|\lambda|\cdot\eta_L\eta_K$$

Or

$$D = \sigma_1\sigma_2 + \eta_L(\theta_{K2}\sigma_1\lambda_{L1} + \theta_{K1}\sigma_2\lambda_{L2}) + \eta_K(\theta_{L2}\sigma_1\lambda_{K1} + \theta_{L1}\sigma_2\lambda_{K2}) + |\theta|\cdot|\lambda|\cdot\eta_L\eta_K$$

Where $|\lambda| = \lambda_{L1}\lambda_{K2} - \lambda_{L2}\lambda_{K1}$ and $|\theta| = \theta_{L1}\theta_{K2} - \theta_{L2}\theta_{K1}$. From Hill and Mendez, there is no factor intensity reversal in the value sense and hence D is positive. The sign of $|\lambda|$ describes the physical factor intensity: $|\lambda| > 0$ when sector 1 is labor intensive, $|\lambda| < 0$ when sector 1 is capital intensive.

Solve for the relative change of factor prices as induced by a relative change of commodity price, we have:

$$\hat{w}_1 = \left[\frac{-\theta_{K1}\sigma_2(\lambda_{K2}\eta_K - \lambda_{L2}\eta_L) - \theta_{K1}\cdot|\lambda|\eta_L\eta_K}{D}\right]\cdot\hat{p}$$

31)

$$\hat{w}_2 = \left[\frac{-\theta_{K1}\sigma_2(\lambda_{K2}\eta_K - \lambda_{L2}\eta_L) + \eta_K(\sigma_1\lambda_{K1} + \sigma_2\lambda_{K2}) + \sigma_1\sigma_2 - \theta_{K1}\cdot|\lambda|\eta_L\eta_K}{D}\right]\cdot\hat{p}$$

(32)

$$\hat{r}_1 = \left[\frac{\theta_{L1}\sigma_2(\lambda_{K2}\eta_K - \lambda_{L2}\eta_L) + \theta_{L1}\cdot|\lambda|\eta_L\eta_K}{D}\right]\cdot\hat{p}$$

(33)

$$\hat{r}_2 = \left[\frac{\theta_{L1}\sigma_2(\lambda_{K2}\eta_K - \lambda_{L2}\eta_L) + \eta_L(\sigma_1\lambda_{L1} + \sigma_2\lambda_{L2}) + \sigma_1\sigma_2 + \theta_{L1}\cdot|\lambda|\eta_L\eta_K}{D}\right]\cdot\hat{p}$$

(34)

As discussed in Hiscox (2002), equations (31) to (34) show the relationships between commodity price (or price ratio indeed) p and factor prices depending on levels of interindustry capital and labor mobility. The Specific Factors and Stolper-Samuelson models appear as special cases here. When we let $\eta_K = 0$, the specific factors model results will follow; and if we let $\eta_L = \eta_K = \infty$, we will have the Stolper-Samuelson results.

The "class solidarity" is indicated by the absolute differences between relative changes of returns for the same factor in different industries. The extent as to how levels of factor mobility will affect class solidarity under a certain change of commodity price can be seen through the partial derivative of the absolute difference with respect to factor mobility. From (31) to (34) we can have:

$$\frac{\partial(|\hat{w}_1 - \hat{w}_2|)}{\partial\eta_L} < 0 \qquad (35)$$

$$\frac{\partial(|\hat{r}_1 - \hat{r}_2|)}{\partial\eta_K} < 0 \qquad (36)$$

$$\frac{\partial\left(\left|\hat{w}_1 - \hat{w}_2\right|\right)}{\partial \eta_K} > 0 \tag{37}$$

$$\frac{\partial\left(\left|\hat{r}_1 - \hat{r}_2\right|\right)}{\partial \eta_L} > 0 \tag{38}$$

In proving these inequalities, I have used the assumption that $|\theta| \cdot |\lambda|$ is positive. Hill and Mendez (1983) and Jones (1971) have argued that this term is positive if there are no factor-price differentials in the initial equilibrium. The technical note to this appendix shows step by step how the four inequalities can be derived within the model's framework, and it can be acquired from the author by request.

From (35) (36), we can see that for any change in commodity prices, the income effects for workers (capitalists) will be more similar when labor (capital) mobility is higher. But from (37) (38), we can see that the income effects for workers (capitalists) will be more dissimilar when capital (labor) mobility is higher.

Chapter 3
Measurement of Interindustry Labor Mobility

The full spectrum of interindustry factor mobility will include both interindustry labor and interindustry capital mobility. Since the focus here is that of labor, I deal with interindustry labor mobility (ILM) and its measurement in this chapter.

Much has been said about the intersectoral factor mobility in general and ILM in particular, however there is no consensus on what ILM means in the economic literature, let alone how to measure it properly. There are broadly three meanings in economic literature when interindustry labor mobility is the focus of the study. First, ILM could generally mean interindustry labor movement (Lilien 1982; Wacziarg and Wallack 2004). The general focus for the authors in this category is usually the intersectoral labor shifts, and the various measures of the intersectoral labor shifts are used either as independent variables to analyze cyclical unemployment (as in Lilien) or dependent variables to gauge the impact of trade liberalization episodes (as in Wacziarg and Wallack). Some political scientists have picked up these measures of intersectoral labor shifts as their measures of ILM, which in turn have been used as either independent variables (Hiscox and Rickard 2002; Rickard 2004, 2005), or dependent variables (Hiscox and Rickard 2002).

Second, ILM may mean the degrees of interindustry wage differentials or the interindustry wage dispersions. Most economists may associate themselves with this way of defining ILM (Edin and Zetterberg 1992; Krueger and Summers 1988). The underlying rationale for this way of defining ILM is the law of one price, where it is assumed that the differences of wages across industries will be arbitraged away when differences of job attributes and worker skills are controlled for. In many of his works, Hiscox also adopted this version of ILM definition when he used coefficient of variation (COV) of wages across industries to approximate the levels of ILM prevailing in the economy (Hiscox 2001, 2002a, 2002b).

Third, economic literature also defines ILM in a rather formal fashion, for example as Hiscox suggested that interindustry factor mobility "is best represented formally as the elasticity of substitution along the transformation curve that maps the conversion of a factor located in one industry for use in another industry at increasing opportunity costs" (Hiscox 2002b). Similarly, ILM should be the elasticity of substitution of productive labor constrained by opportunity costs for the use of the same labor factor in different industries. The elasticity of substitution definition of ILM is most common in trade literature (Stolper and Samuelson 1941; Jones 1971; Hill and Mendez 1983), but it can also be found in studies of taxation (McLure 1970) or cyclical upgrading of labor (McLaughlin and Bils 2001). The advantage of elasticity measure over either the real labor movement or the variation of interindustry wage differentials is that it takes into account of both employment shifts in the labor market and the factor price (i.e., wages) changes that purport to incentivize the employment shifts. In other words, it looks at the sensitivity of rational labor owners to the observable wage differentials across industries[13]. Ideally, higher degrees of the sensitivity of labor to factor price differentials would mean higher levels of ILM, and vice versa for lower degrees of sensitivity. Therefore, empirically we should be able to distinguish economies that have higher labor mobility from economies that have lower labor mobility by finding higher degrees of labor-price sensitivity in the former and lower degrees of labor-price sensitivity in the latter set of economies.

The rest of this chapter proceeds as follows. In the next section I discuss various extant measures of ILM, and in the process I argue that these existing measures suffer from either the problem I just mentioned or other empirical problems. I then propose the elasticity measure of ILM in section 3.2. Despite common acknowledgement in the literature that labor mobility should capture the essence of conversion of labor to different

[13] Obviously the rationality assumption of workers implies that workers are utility maximizing and for this purpose they maximize their lifetime wage incomes.

uses at changing opportunity costs, existing ILM measures in the literature try to arrive at the goal through rather detour approaches. In the dissertation I construct a direct measure of ILM using the elasticity of substitution instead of the first two meanings of ILM in the literature. I will measure ILM both by calculation and by estimation. In section 3.3 I compare the performance of both calculated and estimated elasticity measures of ILM as well as with other ILM measures. I have applied the measurements discussed in this chapter to test specific theories; to maintain the coherence of the text I put the applications in appendix. In appendix 3.A I compare the performance of various measures with what the literature has argued in the case of the U.S., and I further compare the ILM levels in the US with those in Europe. In appendix 3.B I use these measures of interindustry labor mobility to cross-examine the claims made in welfare state and variety of capitalism literature.

3.1. Current measures of ILM in the literature

3.1.1. Measuring ILM as observed interindustry labor movement

As discussed above, there are about three ways to directly measure ILM. The first way is to measure the observed interindustry labor movement. In his study of cyclical unemployment, David Lilien proposed a proxy measure of the dispersion of employment demand conditions throughout the labor market as the variance of net hiring among industries. For a sample of 21 two-digit manufacturing industries from 1958-77, he gave the following measure:

$$\hat{\sigma}_t = \left\{ \sum_{i=1}^{21} c_i \left[\Delta e_{it} + q_{it} - \left(\Delta E_t + Q_t \right) \right]^2 \right\}^{\frac{1}{2}}$$

Where $\hat{\sigma}_t$ is the proxy for employment dispersion, c_i is the i th industry's median year in the sample share of total manufacturing employment, Δe_{it} is the rate of change of employment in industry i and q_{it} is the quit rate for the industry. Capitalized e and q are for the whole sample (Lilien 1982).

Wacziarg and Wallack collected three measures of intersectoral labor movement in their study of how episodes of trade liberalization affect movement of labor across sectors (Wacziarg and Wallack 2004). Their first measure of intersectoral labor movement is structural change of employment at the sector level:

$$CH_{st}(\tau) = \left| S_s^{\,t} - S_s^{\,t-\tau} \right|$$

Where $S_s^{\,t}$ is the share of sector s in total employment for each country in any given year t, τ is the interval of years from t that we want to measure changes. This measure gives structural change for every country-sector-year. It also contains two components: movement of labor across sectors, and sectorally differentiated changes in aggregate employment such as those resulting from population growth and uneven entry into the labor market.

Hiscox and Rickard modified this measure to get economy-wide structural adjustment for every country-year pair (Hiscox and Rickard 2002). Their measure of structural adjustment is:

$$SA_{t-z} = 0.5\sum_{i=1}^{N} \left| S_i^{\,t} - S_i^{\,t-z} \right|$$

Where $S_i^{\,t}$ is the share of i th industry in total employment at time t. The summation is over all industries (in their case, 26 manufacturing industries). This index measures net changes in the distribution of workers over the period from $t-z$ to t.

The second measure of sectoral shifts in Wacziarg and Wallack is the excess job reallocation, or compensated changes in the structure of employment[14]. This is the same measure used by Davis et al. for plant level data (Davis et al. 1996).

$$SH_t(\tau) = \frac{\sum_{s=1}^{S} \left| E_s^{\,t} - E_s^{\,t-\tau} \right| - \left| \sum_{s=1}^{S} E_s^{\,t} - \sum_{s=1}^{S} E_s^{\,t-\tau} \right|}{0.5\sum_{s=1}^{S} (E_s^{\,t-\tau} + E_s^{\,t})}$$

[14] Which is the employment changes resulting from pure shifts of jobs across sectors.

Where E_s^t is the employment in sector s at time t, τ is again the interval of years from t that we want to measure reallocation. This measure controls the sectorally differentiated changes in aggregate employment and only measures "compensated" movement of labor across sectors.

This same measure was adopted by Hiscox and Rickard and Rickard in their studies (Hiscox and Rickard 2002; Rickard 2004, 2005), and used as their main measure of ILM. Their industry reallocation is:

$$IR_{t-z} = \frac{\sum_{i=1}^{N}\left|E_i^t - E_i^{t-z}\right| - \left|\sum_{i=1}^{N} E_i^t - \sum_{i=1}^{N} E_i^{t-z}\right|}{0.5\sum_{i=1}^{N}(E_i^{t-z} + E_i^t)}$$

Where E_i^t and E_i^{t-z} are employment in the ith industry at times t and t-z. In the numerator, the term on the left represents the total number of employment changes (jobs lost and gained) between t and t-z. The summation of absolute values counts each job gained or lost as a change in the structure of employment. The term on the right is the total number of jobs lost or gained and not offset by a gain or loss in other industries; these are the total numbers of uncompensated changes in employment. Subtracting the uncompensated from the total changes in employment provides a measure of total job reallocations between industries, or the compensated changes in the structure of employment, meaning employment changes resulting from pure shifts of jobs across sectors. The value is divided by total employment (the average across t and t-z) to obtain a measure expressed as a rate.

Wacziarg and Wallack noted that SH_t will be zero whenever all sectors experience employment changes in the same direction.

This measure is naturally meant for the real volume of labor movement, not the sensitivity of workers' employment choices in response to price signals, and we can make erroneous conclusions about labor mobility levels if they are based on this measure only. For example, if a country in fact has only moderate to low levels of ILM, and an external shock such as a major trade liberalization happens, then either from Stolper-Samuelson perspective or Specific factor model we should expect to see the comparatively advantaged industries (those use abundant factor intensively or export) expand and the comparatively disadvantaged industries (those use scarce factor intensively or compete with imports) contract. A measure of ILM based purely on real labor movement may pick up high levels of interindustry labor movement during the transition period, which will be interpreted as high levels of ILM, when in fact the true levels of ILM should be moderate to low. Similarly, if a country truly has high levels of ILM, and trade liberalization has already happened, which means that the comparatively advantaged or disadvantaged industries have either expanded or contracted already, then a measure of real interindustry labor movement may be rather small, despite the high levels of true ILM. From this discussion, I agree that measures of ILM using only real labor movement can be good "first-cut", but we should exert caution on conclusions that are based on these measures.

The third measure of sectoral labor shifts according to Wacziarg and Wallack is one based on aggregate employment, which basically measures the growth in employment:

$$EM_t(\tau) = \frac{\sum_{s=1}^{S} E_s^{\,t} - \sum_{s=1}^{S} E_s^{\,t-\tau}}{0.5\sum_{s=1}^{S}(E_s^{\,t-\tau} + E_s^{\,t})}$$

Where similarly $E_s^{\,t}$ is the employment in sector s at time t, τ is the interval of years from t that we want to measure reallocation.

3.1.2. Measuring ILM as interindustry wage differentials

The second way to measure ILM is by measuring industry wage differentials. Krueger and Summers studied wage differentials empirically, and they found strong support for efficiency wage theories that there are important variations in wages which cannot be explained by standard competitive theories (Krueger and Summers 1988). In testing the merits of competitive theories, they estimated for each industry the standard cross-section wage equation on how industry dummy variable affected relative wages when controlling for human capital, demographic background, and working conditions [15]. The assumption behind the wage equations is that under competitive conditions industry dummy should have no impact on relative wages, and the deviations from zero as shown by the coefficients of industry dummy variables should be measures of the degree of how true the efficiency wage theories are. The smaller the industry wage differentials, the more efficient the labor market is, and the higher are labor mobility levels. The economy-wide variability in industry wages is the adjusted standard deviation of the industry wage differentials:

$$SD(\beta) \approx \sqrt{\operatorname{var}(\hat{\beta}) - \sum_{i=1}^{K} \hat{\sigma}_i^{\,2} / K}$$

Where $\hat{\sigma}_i$ is the standard error of $\hat{\beta}_i$, and $\hat{\beta}_i$ is the estimated wage differential for each industry $i = (1,\ldots,K)$. The adjustment is due to the fact that the standard deviation of $\hat{\beta}$ is an upwardly biased estimate of the standard deviation of β. This bias occurs because $\hat{\beta}_i$ equals $\beta_i + \hat{\varepsilon}_i$, where $\hat{\varepsilon}_i$ is a least squares sampling error.

Edin and Zetterberg compared results for Sweden using the same procedure as Krueger and Summers with that of the US, they found that the magnitude of interindustry wage differentials in Sweden is much smaller than in the US, meaning labor mobility levels are higher in Sweden than in the US, and they attributed the cross-country difference mostly to labor-market institutions (Edin and Zetterberg 1992). Their formula for economy-wide standard deviation of wage differentials is the same as above[16].

Robert Flanagan studied economic equality and wage setting in Swedish labor markets. He found that if quit rate in industry

---

[15] They used survey data from Current Population Surveys (CPS) in the estimations.

[16] Their formula in the paper had slight difference from that in Krueger and Summers, though they claimed it to be the same. This leads me to believe the difference in formula is due to printing error, and not substantive difference.

is taken as a measure of voluntary mobility, then Sweden would have essentially the same rate as in the US, even though the wage dispersion in Sweden as measured by the Coefficient of Variation (COV) was much more compressed (mainly) as a result of solidaristic wage policy than in the US (Flanagan 1987). In a sense, Flanagan refuted the argument that wage differentials are the essential incentive device for workers so that high wage differentials are necessary to bring high volumes of interindustry labor movement.

Hiscox also used COV of wages across industries within the domestic economy "as a crude, general indicator of interindustry labor specificity" (Hiscox and Rickard 2002), as other measures of interindustry wage differentials, the COV measure of ILM is based on the assumption of "law of one price", i.e., factor price equalization. The measure for interindustry capital mobility is similarly defined as the COV of rental rates (profits) of capital across industries. Hiscox argued that under the assumption of factor price equalization, if there were return differentials for different factors such as labor and capital, the differentials would be arbitraged away through factor movements. The quickness of the adjustment process would be captured by the range of variation in returns; a high variation showed low levels of interindustry factor mobility, and a low variation showed high levels of factor mobility (Hiscox 2001, 2002b).

The formula for the Hiscox measure, to take the example of interindustry labor mobility, is:

$$Cov = \frac{\sqrt{\left(\sum_{i=1}^{N}(W_i - \overline{W})^2\right)\frac{1}{N-1}}}{\left(\sum_{i=1}^{N}W_i\right)\frac{1}{N}}$$

Where W_i is average wage per employee in the i th industry, and $\overline{W}$ the mean wage of the whole economy.

But a measure of ILM based on interindustry wage differentials may suffer many deficiencies. First, the "law of one price" assumption is restrictive. As shown above, almost none of the authors found support for a pure competitive market condition, and their empirical findings revealed that factor price equalization almost never happened. In fact, they found industry characteristics or labor-market institutions to have significant impact on the interindustry wage structure even after standard controls. This apparent empirical irregularity casts doubts on the validity of a measure that rests squarely on factor price equalization assumption. Second, wage differentials could persist if there are technological breakthroughs that happen sporadically within the economy that bring returns to some industries out of sync with returns to others, which can lead to persistent wage disparities alongside little actual labor movement. We can think of this process as if there is a certain probability in any industry that a technological break-through will happen over one period, and when taking the society as a whole, factor returns would be "constantly" out of steps with those predictions that fail to consider technological shocks. Third, as Rosenbloom noted, factor owners may possess objectives other than maximizing real income (Rosenbloom 1989). Considering that we have considerable difference between the real observed interindustry labor movement and the measure of interindustry wage differentials that is based on the ideal of factor price equalization and that is purported to describe the same concept as the observed interindustry labor movement, it is a logical development to rethink such definition of ILM and an alternative measurement strategy[17].

3.1.3. Measuring ILM as elasticity of labor supply to wage differentials

The third way to measure ILM will consider the flows of labor movement across industries and the price incentives faced by the workers simultaneously, and this is a direct measure of ILM in terms of how ILM is defined in the economic and especially trade literature. There have been other attempts to do this. For

[17] It will be unwise to jettison COV measure of factor mobility altogether. This is because although COV suffers from the apparent empirical irregularity, IN THE LONG TERM, it has been argued and shown that factor prices do tend to converge, just as Heckscher-Ohlin model holds true in the long run. So as an indicator that tells the trends of levels of factor mobility over a rather long period, such as decades or 5-year intervals, COV could be valuable. Another advantage of using COV is that it, like the interindustry labor movement measures, has minimal data requirement, since it can be calculated whenever we have data on earnings (or employment for labor movement measures) across industries during the same period.

example, Flanagan mentioned "and criticized" the way to measure the mobility of Swedish labor forces using simple correlations between relative wage and employment changes. He argued such measure missed the standard simultaneity problems when the labor markets experienced shifts in both the supply and demand schedules for labor, ignored the investment character of labor market decisions (such as young workers take low-pay jobs to accrue skills for high-pay jobs later in their career), and ignored non-pecuniary compensation on labor market choices (Flanagan 1987). But the alternatives of focusing only on relative wages or employment changes may fare no better than the one that considers these two simultaneously, as the evolvement of wages may persistently defy the law of one price, and changes of employment structure may equally be susceptible to the problems Flanagan mentioned. Furthermore, a more sophisticate way to consider labor movement and price incentives simultaneously is to look at the rational workers' responsiveness in terms of employment shifts upon a perceived wage differential, instead of simple correlations. This is the elasticity of substitution for labor factor between different uses subject to opportunity cost concern. We can even put in controls in deriving the elasticity measures, thus mitigating the concerns such as simultaneity of supply and demand shocks.

The idea of considering both labor movement and price incentives simultaneously when it comes to describe interindustry labor mobility can be traced to Stolper and Samuelson. In their path-breaking article in 1941, Stolper and Samuelson assumed each factor to have perfect complete physical mobility (Stolper and Samuelson 1941). Along with assumptions of full employment of both factors and pure competition, it is straightforward to deduce that physical labor movement must be justified by wage differentials in the Stolper-Samuelson framework.

Ronald Jones formally defined elasticity of substitution in a series of general equilibrium models (Jones 1965, 1971). In his models, elasticity of substitution measures the changes of distributive shares of mobile factor across different industries upon changes in the factor price. Gene Grossman formally model the degree of capital mobility through the percentage loss in relative efficiency when a physical unit of capital is reallocated (Grossman 1983). Hill and Mendez sought to accommodate any degree of mobility in the capital and labor factors in a two-sector general equilibrium model (Hill and Mendez 1983). They measured the mobility of factor i, denoted η_i, using the elasticity of the ratio of its supplies to the two sectors with respect to the relative earnings differential. Therefore, the ILM will be measured as:

$$\eta_L = d\ln(L_1 / L_2) / d\ln(w_1 / w_2)$$

Where L_1 and L_2 are amounts of labor factor been used in sector 1&2, w_1 and w_2 are wages in the two sectors.

Empirical measure of ILM based on this formulation should be able to capture the essence of labor mobility that is close to what most theorists have in mind. One problem in practice, however, is that this measure of ILM is based on a two-sector economy framework, and in most real economies there would have more than two sectors, which leave us the choice of how to find the two representative sectors to calculate the elasticity. I will consider this issue in the next section.

And a way to still use elasticity as measure of ILM but bypass the need to find two representative sectors is through estimation, not calculation. Similar methods have been used in economics for a long time (Tinbergen 1946; Polak 1950; Morrissett 1952). A more recent example was by Kenneth McLaughlin and Mark Bils to measure the cyclical sensitivities of industry's employment and wages (McLaughlin and Bils 2001). Using surveys of establishments data, for each industry they regressed industry-specific variables on the aggregate employment E_t, which is their measure of the business cycle, according to the following two equations:

$$\ln(E_{it} / E_t) = a_i^e + \alpha_i^e t + \beta_i^e \ln E_t + \varepsilon_{it}^e$$

$$\ln(W_{it} / W_t) = a_i^w + \alpha_i^w t + \beta_i^w \ln E_t + \varepsilon_{it}^w$$

Where variables without industry indices are aggregates, E_{it} and W_{it} are industry i's employment and wage respectively,

β_i^e and β_i^w are the industry level cyclical sensitivities of employment and wages, respectively.

By modifying this setup, we can estimate the elasticity of labor movement to wage differentials for the whole economy. I will discuss this way of estimating ILM in the next section.

3.1.4. Other measures of ILM

Besides these measures, other political scientists have proposed their disparate ways of measuring ILM. In the Varieties of Capitalism literature, the premise is that in coordinated market economies (CMEs) workers tend to acquire industry or firm specific skills and therefore have high level of factor specificity (i.e., low ILM); while in liberal market economies (LMEs) workers tend to acquire general skills and thus have low level of factor specificity (or high ILM). So logically comparative levels of ILM could be inferred from data on vocational training programs, countries with highly institutionalized vocational training systems would lean closer to CMEs and have low levels of ILM, countries with poorly institutionalized vocational training systems would lean towards LMEs and have high levels of ILM (Iversen and Soskice 2001). Or cross-national levels of labor specificity could be measured by rates of turnover among employees, such as the median length of tenure: the longer the tenure, the higher the labor specificity (or the lower the ILM), and vice versa (Estevez-Abe et al. 2001). Jeffrey Ladewig offered an indirect way of measuring interindustry factor mobility. From the assumption that either Specific Factors or the Stolper-Samuelson model describes what is really going on in the economy, Ladewig went on to use J-Test on an indirect linear combination of the two models to determine which one fits the data better. For the two coefficients denoting two models in the J-Test, the better performing model should have a significant coefficient; and in case neither coefficient was significant, the appropriate model couldn't be assessed (Ladewig 2006). Using roll call vote data for the US Congress from 1963 to 1992, Ladewig managed to describe the general trend of levels of interindustry factor mobility as low (or close to what specific factors model assumes) through the late 1970s and high (or close to Stolper-Samuelson ideal) from the early 1980s to 1992.

In another general review of existing measures of asset specificity (factor mobility), Hainmueller and Hiscox covered six measures of interindustry labor mobility: Training, Job Change, Labor Movement, Wage Differentials, Occupational Classifications, and Responses to Survey Questions (Hainmueller and Hiscox 2007). Clearly much of my review so far in this chapter overlaps theirs.

3.2. Elasticity measure of ILM

3.2.1. Calculated elasticity measure of ILM

I adopt a definition of interindustry factor mobility as the ability of the factors (i.e., their owners) to respond to the price incentives they are facing by physically moving (their assets) across industries. Therefore the measure of interindustry labor mobility should stress the **responsiveness** of workers' employment choices upon interindustry wage differentials. For this reason, I first return to the common definition of interindustry factor mobility in economic literature, that is, the elasticity of substitution between different uses of a factor, to find the measure that is theoretically sound as well as practically feasible. I will first focus on calculating the elasticity measure of ILM. My goal is to find for each country and each year a measure of economy-wide ILM level, so the unit of the measure will be at country-year level. And I include as many countries as I can find data of in order to construct a cross-national panel of interindustry labor mobility over time.

As mentioned in the previous section, the elasticity measure of ILM is inspired by Stolper and Samuelson, Jones, Grossman, and particularly Hill and Mendez. Suppose in a framework of 2x2x2 (two sector, two factor, two commodities) model, there are two sectors in the economy, which are denoted by 1 and 2. There are a total number of E^t workers in the labor market at time t, with $E_1^{\ t}$ and $E_2^{\ t}$ in sectors 1 and 2 respectively ($E_1^{\ t} + E_2^{\ t} = E^t$). The average wages at time t for sectors 1 and 2 are $w_1^{\ t}$ and $w_2^{\ t}$. Following Krueger and Summers I assume equally skilled workers (Krueger and Summers 1988)[18].

[18] This may be a grossly simplified assumption, but it is useful to make comparison with the benchmark of competitive labor market consisting of

Compare with the formula mentioned earlier in Hill and Mendez on labor factor mobility that is also based on a 2x2x2 framework, reproduced here, $\eta_L = d\ln(L_1/L_2)/d\ln(w_1/w_2)$, it's clear that I need to define L_1, L_2, w_1 and w_2.

It is obvious that E_1^t and E_2^t can replace L_1 and L_2. And to ensure that labor factor owners move their productive assets only after they perceived the factor price differentials, I lagged the wages by one period in my calculations. Therefore, the baseline formula to calculate the elasticity measure of interindustry labor mobility is the following[19]:

$$\eta_L^t = d\ln(E_1^t/E_2^t)/d\ln(w_1^{t-1}/w_2^{t-1})$$

The operationalization of elasticity measure of ILM is:

$$\eta_L^t = d\ln(E_1^t/E_2^t)/d\ln(w_1^{t-1}/w_2^{t-1}) \Rightarrow$$

$$\eta_L^t = d\ln(E_1^t/E_2^t)/d\ln(w_1^{t-1}/w_2^{t-1}) = \frac{d\frac{E_1^t}{E_2^t}\Big/\frac{E_1^t}{E_2^t}}{d\frac{w_1^{t-1}}{w_2^{t-1}}\Big/\frac{w_1^{t-1}}{w_2^{t-1}}}$$

Rearrange and divide both nominator and denominator by dt will yield

$$\eta_L^t = \frac{d\frac{E_1^t}{E_2^t}\Big/dt}{d\frac{w_1^{t-1}}{w_2^{t-1}}\Big/dt} * \frac{\frac{w_1^{t-1}}{w_2^{t-1}}}{\frac{E_1^t}{E_2^t}}$$

As a practical step to estimate the first order derivative with respect to time when only annual data are available, let $dt = 1$

---

homogenous work forces. Unimpeded labor movement upon price incentives in such markets would naturally lead to higher measure of elasticity (or ILM) than hampered labor movement upon the same incentives.

[19] Besides this, I also experiment a version where I assume the labor factor owners would respond to the past ten year average wage differential instead of just the past year wage differential. The detailed derivation of that version is in the appendix 3.1. The results are not reported and can be available upon request.

so that $d\frac{E_1^t}{E_2^t}\Big/dt = \frac{E_1^t}{E_2^t} - \frac{E_1^{t-1}}{E_2^{t-1}}$

and $d\frac{w_1^{t-1}}{w_2^{t-1}}\Big/dt = \frac{w_1^{t-1}}{w_2^{t-1}} - \frac{w_1^{t-2}}{w_2^{t-2}}$. From these relations I can operationalize the measurement of interindustry labor elasticity at time t.

$$\eta_L^t = \frac{\frac{E_1^t}{E_2^t} - \frac{E_1^{t-1}}{E_2^{t-1}}}{\frac{w_1^{t-1}}{w_2^{t-1}} - \frac{w_1^{t-2}}{w_2^{t-2}}} * \frac{\frac{w_1^{t-1}}{w_2^{t-1}}}{\frac{E_1^t}{E_2^t}}$$

Since the way on how to divide the economy into two sectors seems to significantly change the results, I experiment three variations. The first variation is to take any industry as the first sector, and use the whole economy (including the industry taken as the first sector) as the second sector. The rationale here is that the whole economy will be much bigger than any single industry, so using either the whole economy or the whole economy less this single industry will make virtually no difference. Operationally, setup like this can allow me to treat E_1 / E_2 as a probability, which will be easier to explain. In the end, because the basic unit in the available data is at country-year-industry level, I will have for every country-year-industry a value denoting the level of ILM under this variation. Thus for any country-year I will have multiple values of ILM. In order to get the most representative value for that country-year, I take the median of the multiple values belonging to any country-year pair[20].

[20] Wacziarg and Wallack also used UNIDO data in their study (Wacziarg and Wallack 2004). As they discovered, there could be numerous measurement errors in the data such as many abnormally large employment jumps for some industries over a short period of time. I also found huge changes of elasticity measure in many cases, so much so that even if I took means or weighted means by employment shares within every country-year, the year by year changes of ILM levels still seemed suspiciously large. And I found median value could be least affected by industry-specific abnormality as the

The second variation is to take any industry as the first sector, and use the whole economy less the first sector/industry as the second sector. This setup is more pertinent to the original elasticity definition of interindustry labor mobility in economic literature. The potential difficulty is that E_1 / E_2 will be treated as the odds of being employed in sector 1, and odds will be a bit tricky to explain. Like the first variation, I will end up having a value denoting level of ILM corresponding to each observation (i.e., country-year-industry); hence I will have multiple values of interindustry labor mobility for any country-year pair. I take the median among the multiple values belonging to any country-year pair as the most representative value for that country-year.

The third variation in calculating elasticity measure of interindustry labor mobility is to make the two sectors in the model to be of roughly equal size. For each country-year, I identify all industries that pay more than the median wage (in that country-year) as sector 1, and all industries that pay less than or equal to the median wage as sector 2. Sector 1 and 2 will now have roughly equal sizes in terms of people employed. This setup ameliorates the problem embedded in the previous two variations that the two sectors are of hugely different sizes. Again, E_1 / E_2 will be the odds of being employed in sector 1, which is the sector that pays more than the median wage. Under this variation, I will have a unique measure of ILM for each country-year pair.

A common problem for calculating the elasticity measure is the two-sector restriction. First of all, we know in reality people consider employment choices among far more than just two sectors. Second, in any of the above three variations, one can argue that enormous amount of variations in terms of interindustry labor movement in response to wage differentials could have happened within one of the rather bulky hypothetical "sectors" (sector 2 in variations 1 and 2, and both sectors in variation 3), therefore, calculating the elasticity measurement under a two-sector framework may miss a

abnormality would only affect the ranking, not the value of representative ILM.

considerable portion of responsiveness by the labor factor owners to interindustry wage differentials that I hope a good measurement of interindustry labor mobility should capture. Therefore, an alternative method to measure labor mobility is called for.

3.2.2. Estimated elasticity measure of ILM

The second strategy is to estimate, rather than calculate, the elasticity measure of ILM. Following the example of (McLaughlin and Bils 2001) and continuing to assume equally skilled workers, suppose a rational individual worker makes decision of employment choice at the start of every period, the probability that this individual chooses industry i at time t can be denoted as the proportion of industry i's employment within the total employment at the same period. I express the probability to be employed in industry i in the probability's natural log form[21]. In competitive labor markets where there are no industry-specific barriers, wage differentials between the wage of industry i and the average wage of the whole economy should be the primary motivators of interindustry labor movement for workers within industry i. Specifically, changes of wage differentials in the past period should explain the changes of employment proportions in industry i at time t. For every country-year, I estimate the following equation:

$$\ln(E_{it} / E_t) = \alpha_t + \beta_t * \ln(w_{it-1} / w_{t-1}) + \varepsilon_{it}$$

Where E_{it} is the employment in industry i at time t, E_t is total employment of the economy at time t, w_{it-1} is the average wage in industry i at time $t-1$, w_{t-1} is the economy-wide average wage at time $t-1$, ε_{it} is the error term that is assumed to be independent and normally distributed, α_t is the constant term, and β_t is the estimated elasticity measure of ILM in this country-year.

[21] All other variables in the regression are also expressed in their natural log forms. This makes clear the mathematical meaning of the estimated coefficients as relative (or percentage) changes, which is how elasticity is defined.

The mathematical meaning of β_t becomes straightforward if we take the first order derivative of the dependent variable $\ln(E_{it} / E_t)$ in the above equation with respective to the independent variable $\ln(w_{it-1} / w_{t-1})$, so that:

$$\beta_t = \frac{d\ln(E_{it} / E_t)}{d\ln(w_{it-1} / w_{t-1})}$$

Note this mathematical expression is the same as the one we discussed above, and the same derivation will follow. So the coefficient β_t would be the estimated elasticity measure of ILM for this particular country-year.

3.2.2.1. Caveats

At the same time, there may be the concern that the observed wage levels may have ***already*** anticipated changes in the industrial employment structure, so that relative changes of wage differentials last period are not independent from relative changes of employment proportions in this period, which have been anticipated, and this may lead to potential endogeneity problem in the above measure of ILM[22]. In order to control for these anticipation effects, I use a two stage least square procedure. The key here is to find good instruments that can predict the changes of interindustry wage differentials but are unrelated to the changes of interindustry employment proportions, i.e., unrelated with the disturbance term of the dependent variable in the above measure. Once I derive the *unbiased* predicted relative wages from the first stage, I can estimate the labor elasticity just as before in the second stage.

In the first stage, I regress the changes of sectoral wages differentials (which is the ratio of current wage in industry i over current economy-wide average wage) on several exogenous variables that are purported to be unrelated to changes of employment structure; these are: aggregate employment less industry i, aggregate output less industry i,

[22] Clearly, the materialization of this endogeneity concern depends on the assumption that the anticipated changes of employment proportions closely track real changes of employment proportions.

and the ratio of male to female workers (M/F) in industry i.[23] Aggregate employment less industry i roughly indicates business cycle and the overall health of the economy, changes of this variable may indicate fluctuations of the overall labor supply, thus affect relative changes of wages, but it may have little to do with relative change of employment in a specific industry. Aggregate output values less industry i show the size of the economy and its changes may be the basis for relative wage changes; and it is not obvious how changes of aggregate output can affect the changes of specific industrial employment. Lastly changes of male to female ratios may also be important to predict changes of sectoral wage differentials, but it is not clear how the gender ratio will affect changes of industrial employment. The first stage estimation will be according to the following equation:

$$\ln(w_{it} / w_t) = \alpha_t + \beta_{1t} \cdot \ln E_t^{\bar{i}} + \beta_{2t} \cdot \ln V_t^{\bar{i}} + \beta_{3t} \cdot \ln(M / F)_t^{i} + \varepsilon_{it}$$

Where $E_t^{\bar{i}}$ is the aggregate employment at time t less the employment in industry i, $V_t^{\bar{i}}$ is the aggregate output values at time t less the output in industry i, and $(M / F)_t^{i}$ is male to female ratio in industry i at time t. The residual ε_{it} is the error term[24].

In the second stage, I estimate elasticity according to equation in section 3.2.2, but instead of using actual observed sectoral wage differentials $\ln(w_{it} / w_t)$, I use predicted sectoral

[23] I choose the aggregates less industry i for the following reason. Operationally, since the basic unit of my data is country-year-industry, and the aggregate employment and output variables are country-year aggregates, hence they will not vary. To enable industry-level variability, for each of these variables I calculate their country-year-industry values by calculating the country-year values without the value of the corresponding industry. All these variables are expressed in their natural log forms.

[24] When applying this equation to the data, there are too few data on gender ratio at the industry level, so the variable on male to female ratio has to be dropped in order not to lose too many observations.

wage differentials $\hat{y}_{i,t} = \ln(w_{it} / w_t)^{predicted}$ from the first step, and as usual I lag it one period, so the estimation equation becomes:

$$\ln(E_{it} / E_t) = \alpha_t + \beta_t * \hat{y}_{i,t-1} + \varepsilon_{it}$$

The coefficient β_t here is the elasticity measure of ILM for this particular country-year, after controlling for possible endogeneity.

The second caveat I call attention to is that, when the elasticity measures are finally generated, there are quite a lot of negative values. The models on which these measures are based on however assume the elasticity measure to be positive. How to square the obvious discrepancy? A deeper look at the construction of my measures will reveal that I didn't impose the assumption that all employment movement must be rational, that is, moving from lower paid industries in time T-1 to higher paid industries in time T. Yet the data would show that such neat correspondences are not always what happened. Various reasons such as an expectation that the currently low paying industries will encounter a boom in the near future may explain some of the odd employment behavior. However, a far more likely culprit for the negative elasticity values may be the existence of barriers to interindustry labor movement, such that workers employed in lower paid industries do not have the ability to move across industry lines to take advantage of higher wages elsewhere that commensurate with their human capital; instead, workers with high human capital cannot enter the higher paid industries and resort to lower paid industries. In this sense, negative elasticity values reveal the extent of the existence of interindustry labor movement barriers and indicate the lack of interindustry labor mobility.

3.2.3. Summary

Above I discussed my proposed measures of interindustry labor mobility, which directly use the elasticity of labor supply upon interindustry wage differentials. From the design of these measures, we can infer that in "normal" situations where one percentage increase (decrease) of interindustry wage differentials induces one percentage increase (decrease) of interindustry labor reallocation, the elasticity measure of ILM will take the value of one. Any values larger than one will mean that one percentage increase (decrease) of wage differentials will bring more than one percentage increase (decrease) of labor reallocation; vice versa for values less than one. It is interesting to note that there are considerable numbers of values less than zero. They represent the cases where the increase (decrease) of interindustry wage differentials actually induces the decrease (increase) of interindustry labor reallocation, in other words, higher wages in one industry induce workers in that industry to leave and lower wages in one industry induce workers from other industries to enter. Conventional wisdom may attribute such behavior to reasons such as worker irrationality, workers harboring motives other than utility maximizing, workers anticipating the structural change of the economy, or technological innovations (Hiscox 2002a; Rosenbloom 1989; Rothenberg 1988); in addition I argue that these negative values of elasticity measure simply reveal the severity of barriers to interindustry labor movement upon wage signals. The lesser or even the more negative these values are, the harder it is for the workers to realize their economically rational responses to wage differentials, and the lower are the labor mobility levels.

3.3. Comparative performance of different measures of ILM

3.3.1. Summaries, correlations, and histograms for global sample

I apply the different elasticity measures discussed above to empirical data, and compare them with the other measures in the literature, i.e., either of interindustry labor movement (a la Rickard) or of interindustry wage differentials (a la Hiscox). All these methods require that we have data on the number of employees and their average wages at the industry-level and preferably the data are recurring; the data should also allow for international comparison across time. United Nations Industrial Development Organization (UNIDO) provides a systemic Industrial Statistics Database at the 3-digit level of ISIC code (rev.2) for 217 countries over the period from 1961 to 2003; the data only cover the manufacturing sectors, which comprises 29 categories. Because the data primarily speak about manufacturing sectors, the various measures derived here would be best understood as indicating levels of interindustry labor mobility among manufacturing sectors. However, in my study I will extrapolate the economy-wide ILM levels from the manufacturing sectors, and treat values derived from manufacturing sectors as if they represent the economy-wide ILM[25].

In a global setting where all countries and all years available are used, the summary statistics of all measures of ILM discussed above are the following[26] :

Table 3.1. Summary statistics of various measures of ILM for global sample (annual data)

Variable	Obs	Mean	Std.Dev	Min	Max	Skewness	Kurtosis
Calculated Elasticity v1	2947	.076	1.138	-16.720	20.084	3.041	123.071
Calculated Elasticity v2	2919	.072	1.194	-18.368	20.440	1.586	122.991
Calculated Elasticity v3	2919	-3.736	340.808	-14722.2	7690.026	-24.460	1291.579
Estimated elasticity (no endogeneity control)	3157	-.340	1.158	-7.271	4.588	.316	4.978
Estimated elasticity (endogeneity control)	2780	-1.246	14.631	-293.033	291.262	1.762	144.333
Hiscox measure	3423	40.325	25.486	5.133	256.364	2.436	13.636
Rickard measure	2699	3.080	3.872	0	53.717	3.376	24.260

[25] I could corroborate the findings here using data from either ILO or STAN. But ILO data aggregate the economic activities in very broad categories, and STAN data have too many missing values.

[26] A symmetric distribution should have a skewness of 0, and a score larger than 2 or less than -2 shows skewness to a significant degree. A distribution that is skewed to the left, e.g., when the mean is less than the median, has a negative skewness. Kurtosis is a measure of the heaviness of the tails of a distribution. A normal distribution has a kurtosis of 3. Variables with high kurtosis (greater than 3) tend to have a distinct peak near the mean, decline rather rapidly, and have heavy tails. Variable with low kurtosis (less than 3) tend to have a flat top near the mean rather than a sharp peak.

As discussed above, from the theoretical arguments behind the measuring of interindustry labor mobility as the elasticity of labor supply upon given interindustry wage differentials, we can roughly expect that in an ideal situation, one percentage rise (or fall) of interindustry wage differentials would bring one percentage increase (or decrease) of cross-industry employment reallocation. So the "normal" level of elasticity measure of ILM should be one. Levels above one indicate one percentage rise (or fall) of wage differentials brings more than one percentage increase (or decrease) of employment reallocation, thus higher levels of ILM; while levels below one indicate lower levels of ILM.

A good elasticity measure of ILM, therefore, should display desirable validity and reliability and should consistently center on the value of one, as well as being rather symmetric in its distribution. From this criterion, the third version of calculated elasticity clearly fares the worst, since it has mean of almost –4, a wide dispersion, and heavy skewness. The other four elasticity measures have reasonably good qualities. The two calculated elasticity measures both have positive means and symmetric distributions, with the version 2 slightly preferred over version 1 because it has smaller degree of skewness. Among the two estimated elasticity measures, the one with no endogeneity control tends to display better qualities such as mean closer to one and concentrated and symmetric distribution. There are no expected ranges as to where the values of Hiscox and Rickard's measures of ILM levels should be in.

The pairwise correlation coefficients between these measures are the following:

Table 3.2. Matrix of pairwise correlation and significance level of different measures of ILM for global sample (annual data)

	Calculated Elasticity v1	Calculated Elasticity v2	Calculated Elasticity v3	Estimated elasticity (no endogeneity control)	Estimated elasticity (endogeneity control)	Hiscox measure
Calculated Elasticity v1	1.0000					
Calculated Elasticity v2	0.9416 0.0000					
Calculated Elasticity v3	0.0059 0.7490	0.0059 0.7507				
Estimated elasticity (no endogeneity control)	0.0130 0.4796	0.0156 0.3996	0.0073 0.6929			
Estimated elasticity (endogeneity control)	-0.0048 0.7990	-0.0014 0.9406	-0.0583 0.0021	0.3292 0.0000		
Hiscox measure	0.0154 0.4030	0.0171 0.3567	0.0161 0.3844	-0.0616 0.0005	-0.0414 0.0291	
Rickard measure	0.0676 0.0007	0.0837 0.0000	0.0063 0.7539	0.0529 0.0060	-0.0490 0.0166	0.2057 0.0000

The pairwise correlations confirm that the third version of calculated elasticity is not a solid measure of ILM as it has almost nothing to do with all other ILM measures. The remaining two calculated elasticity measures have high correlation between them, but they tend to have very little correlations with either the two estimated elasticity measures or the Hiscox and Rickard measures. The two estimated measures have modest correlation between them (0.33); they are negatively (and significantly) correlated with the Hiscox measure but correlated with the Rickard measure in mixed directions. Finally, Hiscox and Rickard measures are positively correlated. However, such correlation is more worrisome than encouraging. Recall that Hiscox measure is the coefficient of variation of cross-industry wages, so higher values mean higher wage dispersion across industries and should indicate lower levels of ILM. The Rickard measure is the compensated intersectoral labor movement, so higher values show higher labor movement and should indicate higher levels of ILM.

Economic theories would predict that arbitraging acts such as increasing interindustry labor movement will lead to shrinking of intersectoral wage differentials (often quickly) so we should see negative correlations. Therefore, by design of these two measures, if they measure the same thing, we should expect negative correlation between these two, and in fact negative correlations between the Hiscox measure and elasticity measure as well (higher values of calculated or estimated elasticity should mean higher sensitivity of labor owners upon price signals, thus better ability to move across industries and higher levels of ILM). The correlation table here confirms the negative correlations between two versions of estimated elasticity and the Hiscox measure, but not between calculated elasticity and the Hiscox measure. The table also provides only mixed confirmation to the predicted positive correlation between elasticity measures and Rickard measure. These results could be interpreted as that more caution should be exerted when picking the right proxies for interindustry labor mobility.

Figure 3.1 shows the histograms of all these ILM measures except version 3 of the calculated elasticity.

[Figure 3.1 about here]

3.3.2. Summaries, correlations, and histograms for OECD sample

One may argue that given that measurement errors are prevalent in datasets that allow international comparison across time, the problem is probably more serious in developing countries than in developed countries, due either to the inferior information gathering infrastructure or to the weaker institutions that are susceptible to various pressures in developing countries. For this reason, I reproduce the above descriptive statistics for a sub-sample composed solely of OECD countries, which are commonly thought to have higher quality data.

Table 3.3. Summary statistics of various measures of ILM for OECD sample (annual data)							
Variable	Obs	Mean	Std.Dev	Min	Max	Skewness	Kurtosis
Calculated Elasticity v1	773	.075	1.335	-16.720	19.861	2.120	102.243
Calculated Elasticity v2	747	.068	1.345	-16.609	19.221	1.832	94.643
Calculated Elasticity v3	747	-7.900	640.549	-14722.2	7690.026	-14.114	403.309
Estimated elasticity (no endogeneity control)	800	-.114	1.241	-3.123	4.588	.772	3.622
Estimated elasticity (endogeneity control)	736	.585	11.105	-44.468	88.508	2.867	20.497
Hiscox measure	827	26.634	15.098	11.377	212.877	6.606	71.565
Rickard measure	733	1.549	1.569	0	12.564	2.605	14.049

The same basic conclusion would emerge here, that the third version of calculated elasticity measure performs badly; among the two other calculated elasticity measures, both have positive means and clustered and symmetric distributions, with version 2 slightly less skewed than version 1. Of the two estimated elasticity measures, the one without endogeneity controls performs very similar as in the global sample but with narrower distribution, the one with endogeneity controls also has narrower distribution but now has mean closer to the ideal value of one. The Hiscox and Rickard measures have narrower distributions and smaller standard deviations in OECD sample.

From the pairwise correlation table, we can tell that calculated elasticity versions 1 and 2 have even higher correlation in OECD sample, the same is true for the two estimated elasticity measures. The two relevant calculated measures now have higher correlations with the estimated elasticity with no controls and the correlations are significant, though the two calculated measures and estimated elasticity with controls still have no correlation. All relevant elasticity measures of ILM have negative correlations with the Hiscox measure of ILM, which is how we should expect from the design of the measurements; but all relevant elasticity measures also have negative correlations with Rickard measure of ILM, which is contrary to the expectations based on measurement designs. Finally, Hiscox and Rickard measures of ILM continue to have positive correlation, albeit smaller than in the global sample, suggesting at least one of the two measures is not a valid measurement of interindustry labor mobility[27].

Table 3.4. Matrix of pairwise correlation and significance level of different measures of ILM for global sample (annual data)

	Calculated Elasticity v1	Calculated Elasticity v2	Calculated Elasticity v3	Estimated elasticity (no endogeneity control)	Estimated elasticity (endogeneity control)	Hiscox measure
Calculated Elasticity v1	1.0000					
Calculated Elasticity v2	0.9931 0.0000					
Calculated Elasticity v3	0.0157 0.6678	0.0151 0.6805				
Estimated elasticity (no endogeneity control)	0.1115 0.0019	0.1147 0.0017	0.0083 0.8204			
Estimated elasticity (endogeneity control)	-0.0056 0.8789	-0.0081 0.8266	-0.1630 0.0000	0.4531 0.0000		
Hiscox measure	-0.0102 0.7762	-0.0067 0.8560	0.0489 0.1823	-0.0893 0.0115	-0.1507 0.0000	
Rickard measure	-0.1112 0.0031	-0.1066 0.0053	-0.0056 0.8834	-0.0321 0.3853	-0.0411 0.2864	0.0707 0.0557

The histograms describing these ILM measures as they are applied to OECD sample are shown in figure 3.2.

[Figure 3.2 about here]

27 And from the discussions I would suggest that interindustry wage differential measure of ILM is preferred over the intersectoral labor movement measure.

To briefly recap, among the elasticity measures, calculated elasticity version 2 is the preferred measure. And the estimated elasticity measure without endogeneity control is slightly preferred over the instrumented version. In chapter 4, I will show that instrumented version improved little (if any) over the un-instrumented estimated elasticity measure of ILM.

Appendix 3.1:

To further guarantee that labor factor owners adjust their employment choices according to not only the wage differential of the last period, but that of the last several periods, I use the weighted average wage for sectors 1 and 2 for the last 10 periods prior to the period of measurement. Thus, for observations where data for the preceding 10 years are available, I have

$$ww_1^t = (1/2)*w_1^t + (1/2)*0.5*w_1^{t-1} + (1/2)*(0.5)^2*w_1^{t-2} + (1/2)*(0.5)^3*w_1^{t-3} + (1/2)*(0.5)^4*w_1^{t-4} + (1/2)*0.5)^5*w_1^{t-5} + (1/2)*(0.5)^6*w_1^{t-6} + (1/2)*(0.5)^7*w_1^{t-7} + (1/2)*(0.5)^8*w_1^{t-8} + (1/2)*(0.5)^9*w_1^{t-9} + (1/2)*(0.5)^{10}*w_1^{t-10}$$

And

$$ww_2^t = (1/2)*w_2^t + (1/2)*0.5*w_2^{t-1} + (1/2)*(0.5)^2*w_2^{t-2} + (1/2)*(0.5)^3*w_2^{t-3} + (1/2)*(0.5)^4*w_2^{t-4} + (1/2)*(0.5)^5*w_2^{t-5} + (1/2)*(0.5)^6*w_2^{t-6} + (1/2)*(0.5)^7*w_2^{t-7} + (1/2)*(0.5)^8*w_2^{t-8} + (1/2)*(0.5)^9*w_2^{t-9} + (1/2)*(0.5)^{10}*w_2^{t-10}$$

Where ww_1^t and ww_2^t are the weighed average wages for sectors 1 and 2.

I choose the multiplier 0.5 because the minimization of $y = (1/2)*(1+\sum_{t=1}^{10} x^t) - 1$ yields x=0.5 as the best value.

For observations where previous data run short of the past 10 years, I choose the weights attached to each year according to solution to the following equation:

$$x + \sum_{t=2}^{n} x^t = 1$$

Therefore, if an observation only has data for three preceding years, I will solve this equation: $x + x^2 + x^3 + x^4 = 1$, which gives me $x \approx 0.51879054$. And the weights I assigned to this year's wage w^t, last year's wage w^{t-1}, and wages for the last two and three years w^{t-2} and w^{t-3} are:

$0.51879054, (0.51879054)^2, (0.51879054)^3$ and $(0.51879054)^4$, respectively.

In light of discussions above, the operationalization of elasticity measure of ILM is:

$$\eta_L = d\ln(E_1^t / E_2^t) / d\ln(ww_1^{t-1} / ww_2^{t-1})$$

This can be rewritten as

$$\eta_L = d\ln(E_1^t / E_2^t) / d\ln(ww_1^{t-1} / ww_2^{t-1}) = \frac{d\frac{E_1^t}{E_2^t} \Big/ \frac{E_1^t}{E_2^t}}{d\frac{ww_1^{t-1}}{ww_2^{t-1}} \Big/ \frac{ww_1^{t-1}}{ww_2^{t-1}}}$$

Rearrange and divide both nominator and denominator by dt will yield

$$\eta_L = \frac{d\frac{E_1^t}{E_2^t} \Big/ dt}{d\frac{ww_1^{t-1}}{ww_2^{t-1}} \Big/ dt} * \frac{\frac{ww_1^{t-1}}{ww_2^{t-1}}}{\frac{E_1^t}{E_2^t}}$$

As a practical step to estimate the first order derivative with respect to time when only annual data are available, let $dt = 1$ so that $d\frac{E_1^t}{E_2^t} \Big/ dt = \frac{E_1^t}{E_2^t} - \frac{E_1^{t-1}}{E_2^{t-1}}$ and $d\frac{ww_1^{t-1}}{ww_2^{t-1}} \Big/ dt = \frac{ww_1^{t-1}}{ww_2^{t-1}} - \frac{ww_1^{t-2}}{ww_2^{t-2}}$. From these relations I can operationalize the measurement of interindustry labor elasticity at time t.

$$\eta_L^t = \frac{\frac{E_1^t}{E_2^t} - \frac{E_1^{t-1}}{E_2^{t-1}}}{\frac{ww_1^{t-1}}{ww_2^{t-1}} - \frac{ww_1^{t-2}}{ww_2^{t-2}}} * \frac{\frac{ww_1^{t-1}}{ww_2^{t-1}}}{\frac{E_1^t}{E_2^t}}$$

When estimating the elasticity measure of ILM, I also try the weighted average wage over the past ten years as similarly defined above, to ensure comparability with the calculated elasticity measure of ILM and to allow rational labor factor owners to respond to wage differentials over a long enough time, so the equation I would be estimating is:

$$\ln(E_{it} / E_t) = \alpha_t + \beta_t * \ln(ww_{it-1} / ww_{t-1}) + \varepsilon_{it}$$

On estimated elasticity controlling for endogeneity, again, to ensure comparability with the calculated elasticity measure of ILM and to allow rational labor factor owners to respond to wage differentials over a long enough time, I adopt the weighted average wage over the past ten years as similarly defined before.

Appendix 3.A: What the data tell us about ILM in the U.S. and a US-Europe comparison

3.A.1. Measuring the U.S. Interindustry labor mobility levels

A good way to corroborate whether these measures of ILM have the desired validity is to compare their performance to those in the literature. The political economy literature has produced extensive studies on the U.S, which I can use to cross-check various measures of ILM here.

Hiscox argued that coefficients of variation (COV) across wages of different industries should measure the levels of interindustry labor mobility, with higher COVs denoting lower levels of ILM and lower COVs denoting higher levels of ILM. Using data on manufacturing industries, he found that the COV levels have been increasing from 1960s to 1990s, which means that ILM levels have been declining during the same period (Hiscox 2002b, 2002a).

Magee found that industrial affiliations determined the lobbying activities of various groups more than the factoral attachment, and in the Trade Reform Act of 1973 labor and business groups were on the same side of the debate. So we can infer from Magee that at least around mid-1970s, industry-specific model dominated and ILM levels were relatively low (Magee 1980).

Beaulieu also tested the validity of Stolper-Samuelson model in the US but looking at Congressional votes on three key trade legislations: CUSTA (Canada-US Free Trade Agreement) in 1988, NAFTA in 1993, and GATT in 1994. He found more support of industry-specific model than the factor-industry detachment corollary. Thus we can infer from Beaulieu that from late 1980s to mid 1990s, ILM levels in the US were relatively low (Beaulieu 2002).

However, Ladewig showed an opposite pattern of US factor mobility. From analyzing Congressional roll call votes on a series of trade legislations, he showed that US factor mobility levels were relatively low but rising during the 1960s and 1970s, reaching a pivot point in the late 1970s and subsequently remaining relatively high during the 1980s and 1990s (Ladewig 2006). Using a 1993 survey on the preferences of individual Americans regarding international trade policy, Scheve and Slaughter argued that factoral attachment is more salient in their political preferences (Scheve and Slaughter 2001). We can infer here that US interindustry factor mobility levels were relatively high during the mid 1990s.

In figure 3.A.1 I plot the levels of US ILM levels using the six available measures discussed here. Roughly we can see that all four elasticity measures indicate declining ILM levels in the US, with the trend more prominent in the two estimated measures than in the calculated elasticity. The COV or the Hiscox measure is rising steadily from 1960s to 2000, indicating a steady decline of ILM, which confirms the findings from the elasticity measures. The plot of Rickard measure looks bi-modal and may be increasing over time.

[Figure 3.A.1 about here]

From figure 3.A.1, the elasticity measures corroborate with the Hiscox measure well in the US setting. ILM levels as indicated by elasticity measures were moderate during the 1970s, lower than in the 1960s, but higher than in the 1980s and afterwards. This roughly conforms to the argument in Magee that ILM levels in the 1970s were low. The elasticity measures, as well as the Hiscox measure, conform to the Beaulieu argument well, that US ILM levels in the late 1980s and afterwards were relatively low. All these measures, however, are contrary to the arguments in Ladewig and Scheve and Slaughter, that labor mobility levels in the 1990s were rather high. Maybe such can be attributed to the fact that Ladewig and Scheve and Slaughter were discussing interindustry factor mobility, while here I focus on interindustry labor mobility, which is part of, but not equivalent to, factor mobility.

3.A.2. A perceived Atlantic divide: is U.S. labor mobility higher than the Europe?

I have argued that Right-leaning governments more often would prefer lower levels of interindustry labor mobility than the Left-leaning governments, hence we may observe that countries consistently having more conservative governments would have lower labor mobility levels than countries consistently having more labor-friendly governments. We do not need to look far for such examples. It has been generally accepted that the U.S. tends to be more market oriented and its economic and political orthodoxy tend to be more conservative than the countries in continental Europe, which frequently form social democratic governments. According to the theory proposed here we would expect that the levels of labor mobility in the U.S. be lower than those in continental European countries. This runs counter to the popular belief that the U.S. economy has far more flexibility and dynamism, especially in its labor market, than the Europe, that U.S. interindustry labor mobility levels must be higher than those in Europe.

Schmitt and Zipperer show that the alleged superiority of U.S. labor market over the European ones may not stand up to scrutiny. In many indices such as the unemployment rate, unemployment among the youth (15-24 years old) or those with less-than-high-school education, employment-to-population rates, incorporation of women into paid labor force, and employment rates for the youth, the U.S. labor market performs better than some, but not other European countries. Yet in terms of economic mobility, measured either by the share of low-income families (those earn less than half of the national median income) that managed to escape from low-income status over a three-year period in the mid-1990s, or by the degree of correlation between fathers' and sons' income at different points in time, the U.S. has decidedly lower economic mobility than continental European countries (Schmitt and Zipperer 2006).

In figure 3.A.2, I plot the ILM levels measured in six different ways for the US and the average of European countries[28]. The results show that when using the calculated elasticity, ILM levels in the US and Europe are indistinguishable from each other. When using the estimated elasticity, the data show that prior to the 1980s, US tended to have higher ILM levels than an average European country but after the 1980s, the reverse tends to be true. Using the Hiscox measure confirms this rather general observation, when the

[28] These European countries include Austria, Belgium, Czech Republic, Denmark, Finland, France, Germany, Greece, Hungary, Iceland, Ireland, Italy, Luxemburg, Netherlands, Norway, Poland, Portugal, Slovak Republic, Spain, Sweden, Switzerland, and United Kingdom.

switch of positions happened around the 1975 and after 1975 COV of wages tended to be lower in Europe than in the US. The Rickard measure tends to produce indistinguishable result. This figure also corroborates the conclusion in Schmitt and Zipperer's study since their conclusion was largely based on empirical data of 1990s and 2000s and in this period US had lower labor mobility levels than in Europe.

[Figure 3.A.2 about here]

Appendix 3.B: Testing existing theories using different measures of ILM

I engage in some comparisons of different measures of ILM to different sets of countries. The Varieties of Capitalism (VoC) literature distinguishes countries into Coordinated Market Economies (CMEs) and Liberal Market Economies (LMEs), and argues that CMEs have highly structured labor market and should have highly specific-skilled labor forces and consequently lower ILM. On the contrary, LMEs have flexible labor market and general-skilled labor forces and thus should have higher levels of ILM (Hall and Soskice 2001; Estevez-Abe et al. 2001; Iversen and Soskice 2001). The CMEs would include Austria, Belgium, Denmark, Finland, Iceland, Germany, Japan, Netherlands, Norway, Sweden and Switzerland; the LMEs would include Australia, Canada, Ireland, New Zealand, UK and United States. Hiscox and Rickard however, found such distinction to have only limited empirical support (Hiscox and Rickard 2002). In the next table, I report the summary statistics for LME and CME countries respectively, and to be more economical in using space, I will not use versions 1 and 3 of calculated elasticity, because version 2 consistently outperforms version 1, and version 3 has been shown to be a bad measure.

Table 3.B.1. Summary statistics of various measures of ILM, according to VoC categorization

Liberal Market Economies							
Variable	Obs	Mean	Std.Dev	Min	Max	Skewness	Kurtosis
Calculated Elasticity v2	208	.227	1.532	-4.986	19.221	9.072	115.483
Estimated elasticity (no endogeneity control)	215	-.493	.850	-2.290	2.312	-.013	2.629
Estimated elasticity (endogeneity control)	206	-2.696	2.916	-10.393	3.965	-.147	2.481
Hiscox measure	223	26.702	22.012	13.536	212.877	7.098	56.856
Rickard measure	200	1.451	1.774	0	13.099	3.613	21.150
Coordinated Market Economies							
Variable	Obs	Mean	Std.Dev	Min	Max	Skewness	Kurtosis
Calculated Elasticity v2	315	.058	1.154	-5.330	9.516	2.780	28.075
Estimated elasticity (no endogeneity control)	354	.235	1.335	-3.123	4.588	.456	3.210
Estimated	308	3.416	16.377	-44.468	88.508	1.604	9.120

I perform mean comparison “ttest” of these measures using the VoC categorization, and report the results below:

Table 3.B.2. Mean comparison "ttest" of various measures of ILM, using VoC categorization			
Group 1=LMEs, group 2=CMEs, the null hypothesis is Ho: diff= mean(1)-mean(2)=0, the three alternative hypotheses are: diff<0, diff!=0, and diff>0.			
	[Ha: diff < 0]	[Ha: diff != 0]	[Ha: diff > 0]
Variable	Pr(T<t)=	Pr(|T|>|t|)=	Pr(T>t)=
Calculated Elasticity v2	0.9125	0.1750	0.0875
Estimated elasticity (no endogeneity control)	0.0000	0.0000	1.0000
Estimated elasticity (endogeneity control)	0.0000	0.0000	1.0000
Hiscox measure	0.9839	0.0321	0.0161
Rickard measure	0.5048	0.9904	0.4952

From this table we found that for calculated elasticity measure version 2 and for the Rickard measure of intersectoral labor movement, we cannot reject the null hypothesis that mean levels of ILM in LMEs are the same as in CMEs. But for the two versions of estimated elasticity and the Hiscox measure of interindustry wage differentials, we can reject the null hypothesis in favor of the alternative hypothesis that mean levels of ILM in LMEs are different from those in CMEs. Specifically, ILM levels measured by these three methods are significantly lower in LMEs and higher in CMEs. This result casts the main contention of VoC approach in doubt, and suggests the levels of interindustry labor mobility may just be the opposite as VoC approach would argue.

Intuitively, figure 3.B.1 shows the bar charts comparing levels of ILM as measured by these five methods. I take the mean values of ILM levels for all liberal market economies and coordinated market economies. This graph thus is highly aggregated and may subject to influences from outliers.

[Figure 3.B.1 about here]

From the graph we can see that three measures of ILM: estimated elasticity with and without endogeneity controls, as well as COV of wages, all indicate that CMEs tend to have higher ILM levels than LMEs. On the other hand, calculated elasticity and the indicator of compensated employment changes indicate that generally CMEs have lower ILM levels than LMEs.

Another prominent argument concerning ILM is by Esping-Andersen (Esping-Andersen 1990). He argued that in terms of the relationship between social services provision and individual well-being, there are three types of welfare states: the liberal (or Anglo-Saxon), the corporatist (or continental European), and the social democratic (or Nordic). The liberal welfare state is the residual type, where the market will dominate individual welfare, meaning there will be little social protection from the state that can be expected. The corporatist welfare state stresses privileges for sectors in certain social positions, the "natural" hierarchy among occupations, and the authority of the state, so the social welfare provision is stratified, but to a lesser degree than liberalism because of the corporatist guarantee of welfare and the safety net espoused by the coincident Catholicism movement in these countries. The social democratic welfare state provides a universal safety net to all citizens, which is non-stigmatizing, decent, and provides for a middle-class living standard.

The liberal welfare state seems strikingly similar to liberal market economies as described in VoC approach. Workers in the liberal welfare states may just as well behave as in LMEs, where they derive their income from the market, and if the market cannot provide them with guaranteed income, they will take the matter into their own hands and reducing investing in specific skills and more on general skills. So the accompanying level of ILM may as well be relatively high in liberal welfare states. In the corporatist welfare states, ILM may be severely suppressed due to the necessity to maintain the hierarchy among occupations, and the pay structure that follows. The workers here will be most interested in getting a perk within this hierarchy, and investing in industry-specific human capital seems the best investment a worker can make. This may be the closest fit to the institutional complementarities summed up in the coordinated market economies (CMEs). According to the arguments of both Esping-Andersen and VoC, ILM levels in CMEs or corporatist welfare states should be low. And in social democratic welfare states, governments intervene extensively to provide the safety net, and those market risks for workers whose investment on specific skills may be lost to technological updates or international market fluctuations are offset by active labor market interventions in the labor markets (Burgoon and Hiscox 2000; Hiscox and Rickard 2002). ILM therefore should be quite high among social democratic welfare states.

Therefore, we can have a tentative ranking of levels of ILM among three groups of welfare capitalism states. Social democratic welfare states will have the highest ILM levels, followed by liberal welfare states, and corporatist welfare states will have the lowest levels of ILM. According to Esping-Andersen's decommodification classification, the social democratic welfare states are: Austria, Belgium, Netherlands, Denmark, Norway and Sweden; the liberal welfare states are: Australia, United States, New Zealand, Canada, Ireland and UK; and the corporatist welfare states are: Italy, Japan, France, Germany, Finland, and Switzerland. I report summary statistics for this grouping of countries below.

Table 3.B.3. Summary statistics of various measures of ILM, according to decommodification classification

Liberal Welfare States							
Variable	Obs	Mean	Std.Dev	Min	Max	Skewness	Kurtosis
Calc elas v2	208	.227	1.532	-4.986	19.221	9.072	115.483
Esti elas (no endo control)	215	-.4933	.850	-2.290	2.312	-.013	2.629
Esti elas (endo control)	206	-2.696	2.916	-10.393	3.965	-.147	2.481
Hiscox	223	26.702	22.012	13.536	212.877	7.098	56.855
Rickard	200	1.451	1.774	0	13.099	3.613	21.150
Corporatist Welfare States							
Variable	Obs	Mean	Std.Dev	Min	Max	Skewness	Kurtosis
Calc elas v2	130	-.082	1.084	-6.211	4.647	-1.785	16.659
Esti elas (no endo control)	163	-.377	1.026	-3.025	2.664	.818	3.595
Esti elas (endo control)	128	-.702	4.899	-22.184	8.309	-1.944	9.483
Hiscox	170	23.873	8.002	15.141	56.713	1.817	6.676
Rickard	151	1.185	1.323	0	8.065	2.431	10.765489
Social Democratic Welfare States							
Variable	Obs	Mean	Std.Dev	Min	Max	Skewness	Kurtosis
Calc elas v2	207	.079	1.225	-3.501	9.516	3.774	30.042
Esti elas (no endo control)	215	.326	1.413	-3.123	4.588	.397	3.252
Esti elas (endo control)	200	5.651	19.072	-44.468	88.508	1.299	6.830
Hiscox	223	20.545	8.305	11.377	71.847	2.684	14.946

I perform mean comparison "ttest" again to the three worlds of capitalism country groupings. Since there are three groups of countries while "ttest" only compares any two groups, I explore all three possible combinations of any two out of the three groups. The three combinations are: social democracies vs. liberal, social democracies vs. corporatist, and liberal vs. corporatist.

Table 3.B.4. Mean comparison "ttest" of various measures of ILM, using three worlds of capitalism categorization

Combination one: Group 1=social democratic states, group 2=liberal states, the null hypothesis is Ho: diff= mean(1)-mean(2)=0, the three alternative hypotheses are: diff<0, diff!=0, and diff>0.

Variable	[Ha: diff < 0] Pr(T<t)=	[Ha: diff != 0] Pr(|T|>|t|)=	[Ha: diff > 0] Pr(T>t)=
Calc elas v2	0.1389	0.2779	0.8611
Esti elas (no ctrl)	1.0000	0.0000	0.0000
Esti elas (control)	1.0000	0.0000	0.0000
Hiscox	0.0001	0.0001	0.9999
Rickard	0.7644	0.4713	0.2356

Combination two: Group 1=social democratic states, group 2=corporatist states, the null hypothesis is Ho: diff= mean(1)-mean(2)=0, the three alternative hypotheses are: diff<0, diff!=0, and diff>0.

Variable	[Ha: diff < 0] Pr(T<t)=	[Ha: diff != 0] Pr(|T|>|t|)=	[Ha: diff > 0] Pr(T>t)=
Calc elas v2	0.8962	0.2075	0.1038
Esti elas (no ctrl)	1.0000	0.0000	0.0000
Esti elas (control)	1.0000	0.0000	0.0000
Hiscox	0.0000	0.0001	1.0000
Rickard	0.9918	0.0165	0.0082

Combination three: Group 1=liberal states, group 2=corporatist states, the null hypothesis is Ho: diff= mean(1)-mean(2)=0, the three alternative hypotheses are: diff<0, diff!=0, and diff>0.

Variable	[Ha: diff < 0] Pr(T<t)=	[Ha: diff != 0] Pr(|T|>|t|)=	[Ha: diff > 0] Pr(T>t)=
Calc elas v2	0.9846	0.0308	0.0154
Esti elas (no ctrl)	0.1198	0.2397	0.8802
Esti elas (control)	0.0000	0.0000	1.0000
Hiscox	0.9613	0.0775	0.0387
Rickard	0.9459	0.1082	0.0541

From combinations one and two, we can have pretty high confidence that social democracies have the highest ILM levels among all three country groupings, as both estimated elasticity measures, and Hiscox COV of wages measure all indicate social democracies have higher mean ILM vis a vis the other category in the combination. Rickard measure of compensated employment changes also lends to this confirmation in the second combination. However, the evidence is mixed for combination three, which compares liberal and corporatist states. We would infer from Esping-Andersen's work that the corporatist welfare states will have the lowest levels of ILM and thus lower ILM than liberal states. Yet only the calculated elasticity and the Rickard measure seem to back up this inference, as they tend to confirm that liberal states have higher mean ILM than corporatist states. But the estimated elasticity measures and the Hiscox measure seem to indicate otherwise, that labor sensitivity to wage difference is higher and the interindustry wage differentials are narrower in corporatist than in liberal states.

Figure 3.B.2 shows the bar charts comparison of ILM levels using these measurements. The results using the two estimated elasticity and the Hiscox measure corroborate with each other, where Social democracies have the highest ILM, corporatist welfare states tend to have the second highest ILM, and the liberal welfare states have the lowest ILM. Rickard measure confirms that Social democracies have the highest ILM, but liberal states tend to have higher ILM than corporatist states. And finally, using the calculated elasticity measure, liberal welfare states would have the highest ILM, followed by Social democracies and the corporatist states. This may hint that there is innate bias in the calculated elasticity measure, which may probably be due to the aggregation of the whole economy into only two sectors.

[Figure 3.B.2 about here]

Although the measures I discuss here generally lend support to Esping-Andersen's argument and cast doubt on the contention concerning labor mobility in the VoC approach, given the fact that the data I use here were only those on manufacturing sectors, any conclusions should only be tentative and more definite inferences should be based on more complete data that cover the whole economy and on more sophisticated analyses. Nevertheless, this exercise shows that these new measures add more options to the study of the political economy of factor mobility and could shed light on many arguments in CPE and IPE.

Figure 3.1: Histograms of different ILM measures global sample

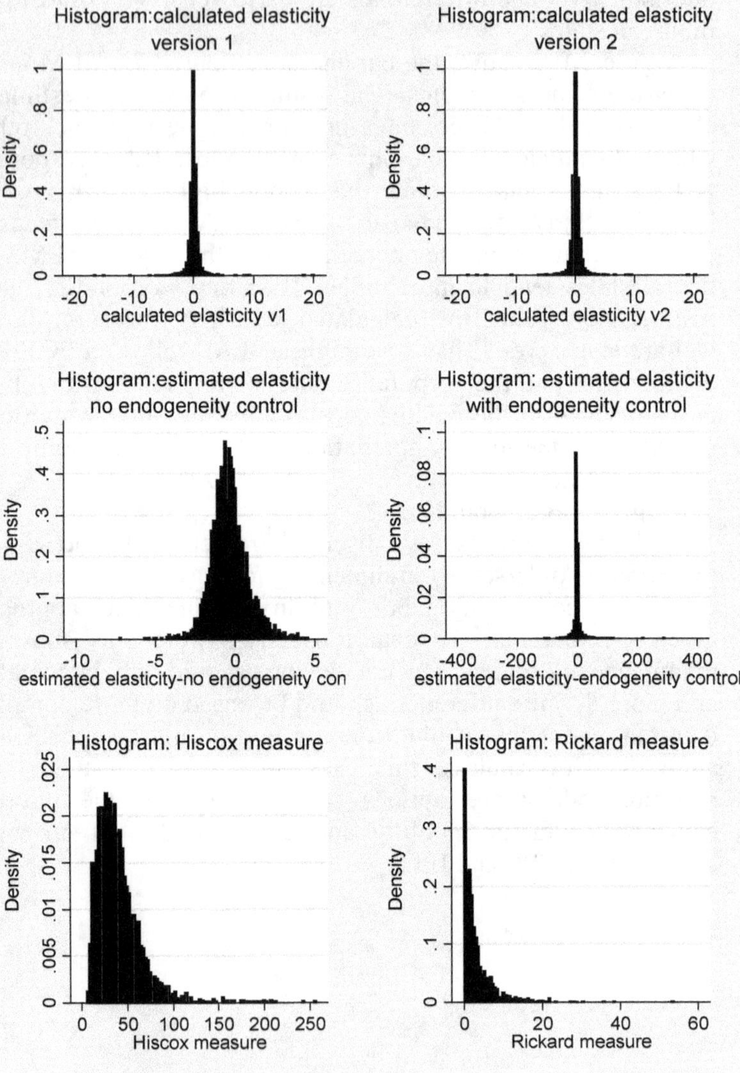

Figure 3.2: Histograms of different ILM measures OECD sample

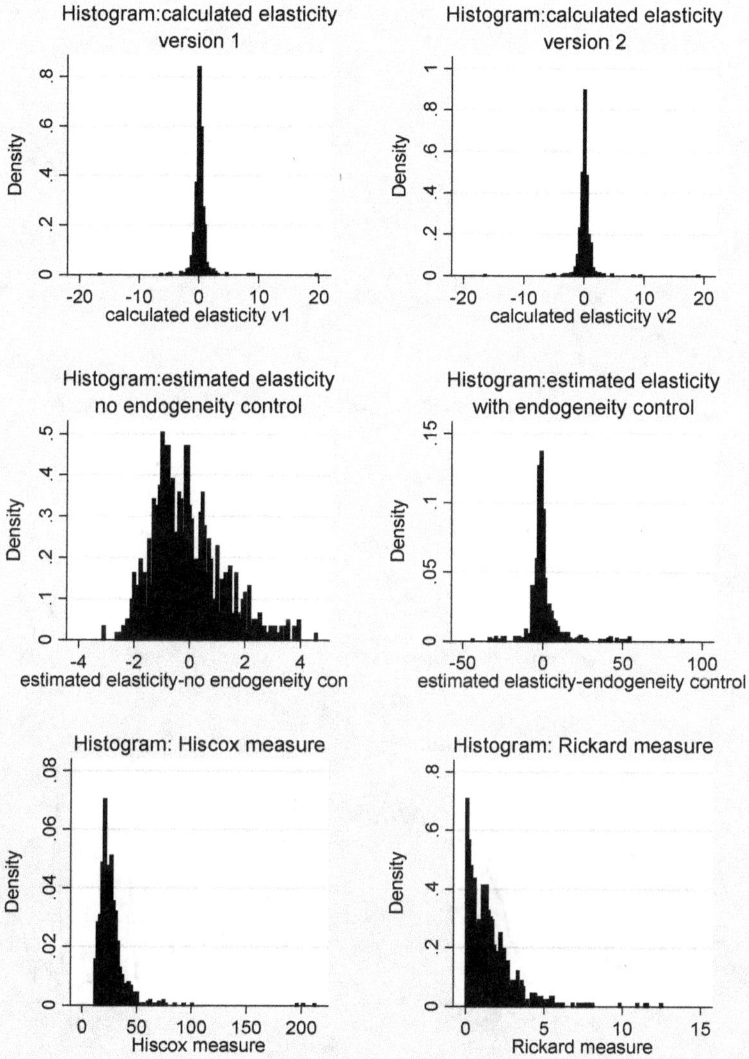

Figure 3.A.1: Interindustry labor mobility levels in the US six available measures

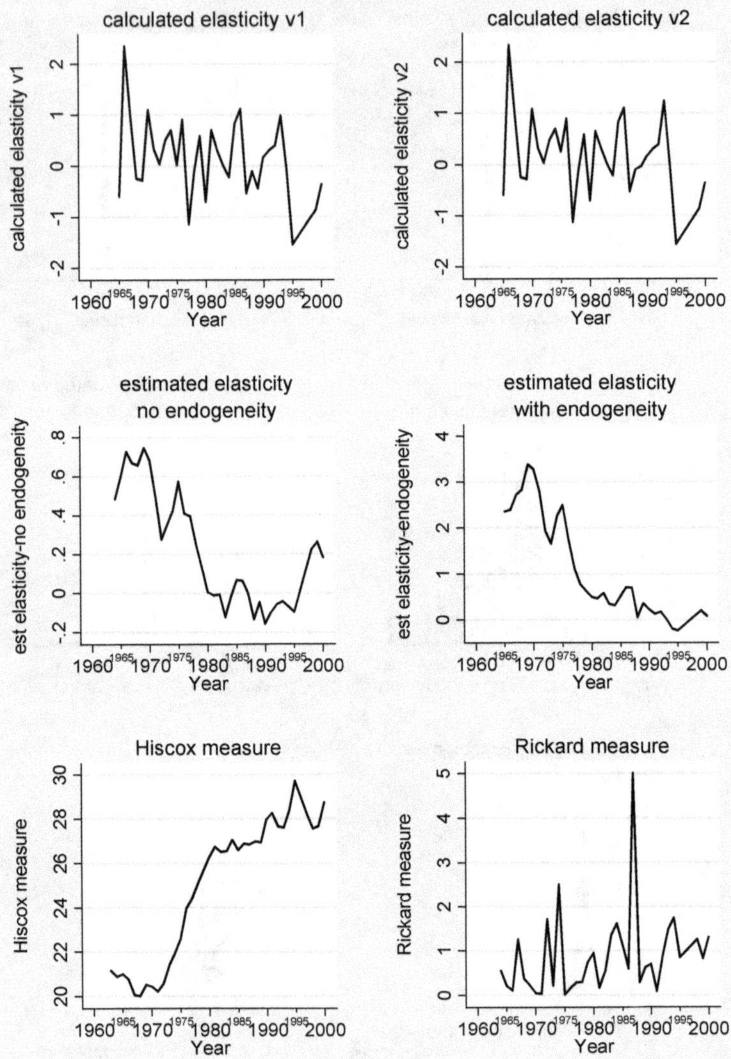

Figure 3.A.2: Comparing ILM levels in the US and Europe six available measures

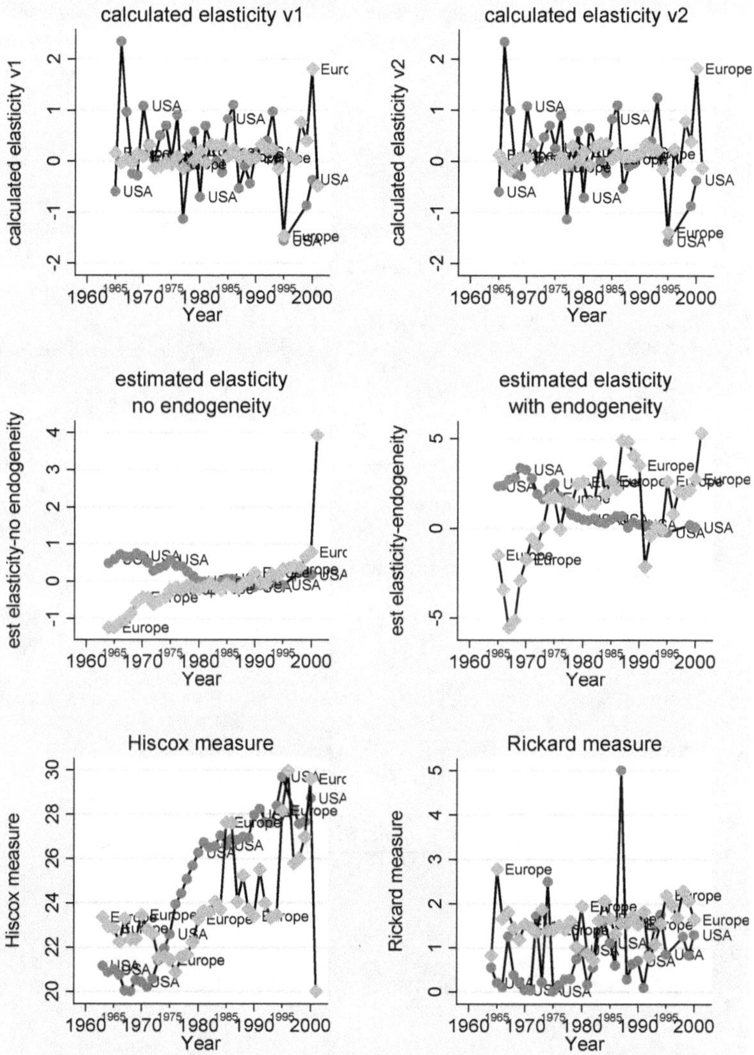

Figure 3.B.1: Bar charts comparison of ILM levels
Averages within VoC categorization

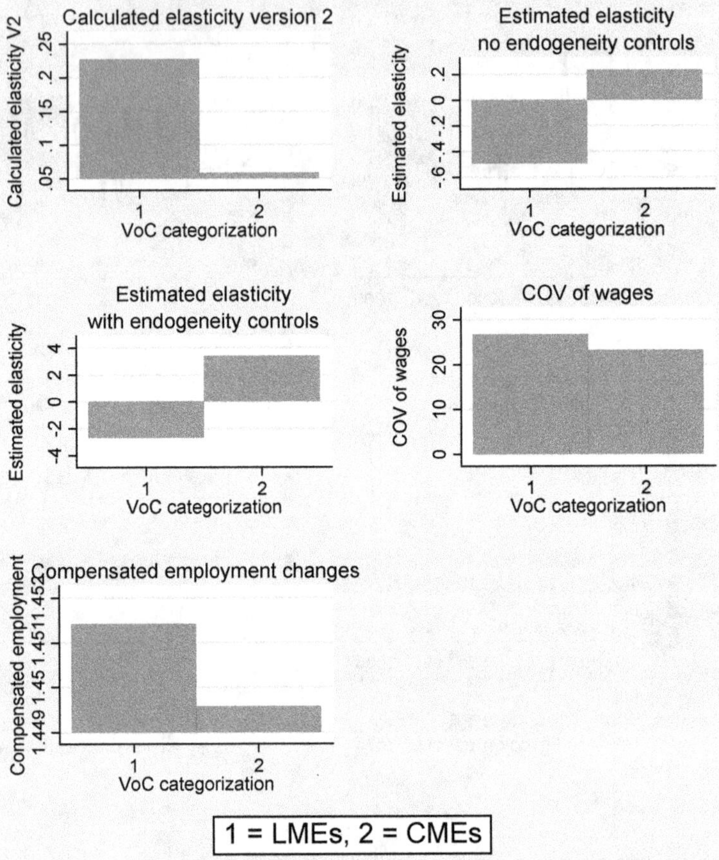

Figure 3.B.2: Bar charts comparison of ILM levels
Averages within Decommodification categorization

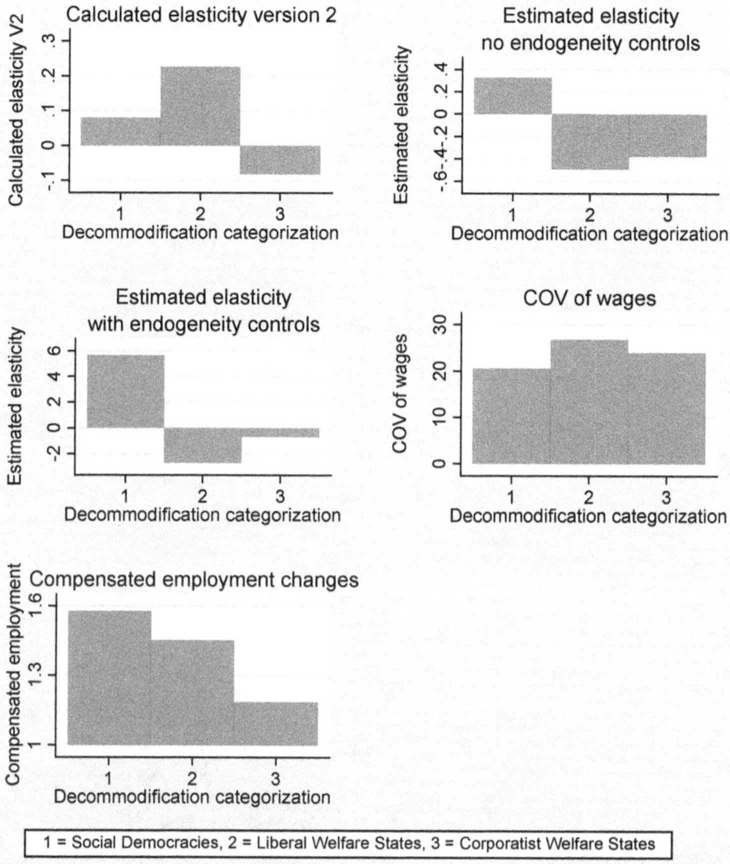

Chapter 4
Empirical Analysis of Partisan Political Influence on Interindustry Labor Mobility

This chapter will mainly consist of two parts; first I test the conditional hypotheses about the partisan political influence on levels of interindustry labor mobility, then I seek to show that government policies can bring changes to levels of ILM. If the results from these two parts are both confirmatory, then it is straightforward to conclude that partisan governments could, among other things, employ the set of policy tools that include those mentioned here for the purpose of influencing ILM levels. The following two chapters will embark on two country case studies, of Sweden and the U.S., to provide more details on the partisan preferences on labor mobility and about the policies through which governments influence the levels of intersectoral labor mobility.

The data for the empirical analysis in this chapter is only about OECD countries, for several reasons. First, in the theory a considerable degree of government accountability to societal demands and pressure is critical, and since all OECD countries are democracies such government accountability can be assured. Second, reliable data that enable cross-country comparison over time are readily available for OECD countries, making empirical analysis possible, but such data are difficult to get for other countries. Third, the hypotheses are stated in general terms so that we expect to observe the relationship between partisanship, union centralization, policies and corresponding ILM levels whenever data become available. OECD sample is used here to test the general validity of the hypotheses and I include controls like GDP per capita and indices of democracy and political rights to control the possible attributes that may be particular to the OECD country grouping.

4.1. Government partisanship and interindustry labor mobility

I begin the analysis of the relationship between government partisanship and interindustry labor mobility by showing some over-time plots that can convey the general pattern and bivariate correlation. I then use time-series-cross-sectional techniques to test the conditional hypotheses that partisan influences on levels of ILM will be moderated by degrees of domestic union centralization. In testing the conditional hypotheses, I use multiplicative terms in regressions and report statistical significance in tables as well as in graphs, as suggested by Brambor, Clark and Golder (Brambor et al. 2006; Golder 2006). Below, I describe the variables and data first.

4.1.1. Variables and sources

4.1.1.1. Measurement of dependent variable

In this part of the empirical analysis the dependent variable is levels of interindustry labor mobility (ILM). The main results will be drawn using the elasticity measure of ILM that I constructed, which is discussed in detail in chapter 3. In specific, I use the basic version, that is, the un-instrumented version of estimated elasticity in the empirical testing. I choose not to use calculated elasticity because of the concern that whichever way I divide the whole economy into two sectors, aggregation of many industries into one "sector" will eliminate much of the variance across industries and which may lead to biases in estimation using such a measure. I also choose not to use the version of elasticity measure that uses instruments to control for the endogeneity of intersectoral wage differentials. This is because once I construct the instrumented elasticity measure of ILM using the 2SLS approach, then construct the un-instrumented elasticity measure of ILM using OLS, and then use Hausman Specification Test; the results show that 2SLS is not an improvement over OLS in almost 98% of the cases using Hausman tests, which inform me that it is safe to use the un-instrumented elasticity measure of ILM.

I corroborate these results using coefficient of variation (COV) among interindustry wages as the DV, which Hiscox has used to approximate interindustry labor mobility. This measure is negatively correlated with the elasticity measure; higher values of COV of wages denote lower levels of ILM, and vice versa. I choose not to use the measure of structural employment change because it is shown to be positively correlated with COV of wages and negatively with elasticity measures, which is just the contrary to how it is purported to perform, calling question into the reliability of it as a measure of interindustry labor mobility.

I derived the elasticity measure of ILM from United Nations Industrial Development Organization (UNIDO) Industrial Statistics Database at 3-digit level of ISIC (Rev.2) (UNIDO 2005). The database covers manufacturing sector that comprises 29 categories, it contains data on all countries or equivalent political entities of the world (217 countries as of 2005) from 1961 to 2003 (43years).

4.1.1.2. Independent variables

The two main independent variables in this part of the empirical analysis are indicators of government partisanship and labor union centralization. For the former, I choose to use the variable on government partisanship created by Kim and Fording (Kim and Fording 2002). This measure of government partisanship is basically constructed in two steps. First, Kim and Fording created a measure of party ideology for each country for each election year according to comparative party manifesto data. They identified within a party manifesto the percentage of pro-Left statements and the percentage of pro-Right statements according to the 26 categories identified by (Laver and Budge 1992), and computed a standardized measure ranging from 0 to 100 with higher number denoting more Left-leaning. Second, they collect yearly data for the number of cabinet portfolios for each party in each country and then take the weighted average of party ideology scores, where the weights are the proportion of total cabinet portfolios held by each party. The series of weighted average of party ideology scores will be the final measure of government partisanship. In their words, "for countries where unified control of government occurs on a regular basis, the government partisanship score reduces to the party ideology score for the party in power. For multi-party governments, however, the measure takes advantage of the information we have about the varying ideologies of the parties and their relative shares of power."(Kim and Fording 2002, 191) Originally, this government partisanship measure has a range of 0 to 100, with higher number denoting more Left-leaning; and it only has values for election years[29].

This measure of government partisanship does not have values for the United States. To deal with this issue, I manage to find in another publication by Kim and Fording where they use similar method to calculate median voter ideology and the resultant measure contains data for the US (Kim and Fording 2001). I convert this earlier measure of median voter ideology into the same scale as the later measure of government partisanship so that they will have the same mean; then I fill in the missing values for the US using the converted earlier version of median voter ideology values. This way, I have a measure of "government" partisanship that contains US data. For ease of explanation, I recreate this series of government partisanship so that it still has a range of 0 to 100, but with higher number denoting more right-leaning[30]. Throughout the empirical analysis here, I will use this series of government partisanship that contains data for the US[31]. Since 1998 is the last year Kim and Fording measure has available data and in order that all observations are in the same time frame, I will use the year 1999 as the last year in my estimation.

This measure of government partisanship is preferred over the alternative measure of a trichotomy in the Database of Political Institutions, which denotes the chief executive's partisanship, because this measure has much more variation to generate useful statistical results.

For the indicator of labor union centralization, I use the level at which wages are determined from a dataset on Union Centralization constructed by Miriam Golden, Peter Lange, and Michael Wallerstein (Golden et al. 2006). This variable takes the value from 1 to 5, with 1 denotes plant-level wage-setting, 2 denotes industry-level wage-setting without sanctions, 3 denotes industry-level wage-setting with sanctions, 4 denotes central wage-setting without sanctions, and 5 denotes central

---

[29] Strictly speaking, this measure registers a value when a government is formed. Whenever there is an election, a government will be formed; however multiple governments may form between two elections and they will register multiple values in this measure.

[30] This is done through the following procedure: New Var = 100 – Old Var.

[31] I did, however, run the same regressions using the government partisanship series without the US data, and the results are essentially the same.

wage setting with sanctions. So the higher is this indicator, the stronger is the union centralization.

In this categorization of union centralization, however, it is not clear what the difference between two values really means. For example, it is not clear to the readers that if a country's union centralization increases from 1 to 2, the workers' collective bargaining power will increase by the same amount as when a country's union centralization increases from 4 to 5. In order to alleviate this problem and in light of the data structure of this variable, I recode union centralization to a more broadly defined categorical variable so that a value zero will mean low union centralization, which is when the original variable takes the values of 1 and 2; a value one in the new variable will mean middle level union centralization, which is when the original variable takes the value of 3; and a value two in the new variable will mean high union centralization, which is when the original variable takes the values of 4 and 5.

4.1.1.3. Control variables

I include a set of control variables that might influence levels of ILM. For demographics, I control for the old age population. Huber, Ragin and Stephens (Huber et al. 1993) suggest that demographic structure of population could be a significant determinant of welfare spending. It may be that all else being equal, older people are less likely to change occupations as younger people would do. Such a measure is also highly correlated with the size of the total population and total labor forces. So I add a measure of *total number of people over 65*. The data come from World Development Indicators.

I add five economic controls in the analysis. As a key indicator of labor market conditions, *unemployment rate as percent of the total labor force* is put into the analysis to control its social economic implications. A major limitation of this control is that systematic data for unemployment rate started only in 1980, so adding this control will essentially limit the analysis to post-1980 era. High unemployment may elicit competition among workers for the limited number of job vacancies, thus higher unemployment may be conducive to higher labor mobility. I control the economic conditions using *GDP per capita*, which measures levels of economic development of a country. As Alt and Gilligan argues, higher economic development would involve increasing differentiation and specialization, and would increase the frequency of specific factors, i.e., decrease factor mobility (Alt and Gilligan 1994). Another reason is that if workers are wealthier, small levels of wage differentials may not be able to entice them to change occupations or re-join the work force since the wage differentials represent only a small fraction of their wealth. Therefore higher GDP per capita may lower labor mobility to some extent. In my current sample, there are considerable variations of GDP per capita across time for a given country, and the most significant cross-country variation for this variable comes from Turkey.

Stephanie Rickard suggested that the degree to which a country is exposed to exogenous economic shocks will affect the observed rate of interindustry labor movement, which is her measure of labor mobility (Rickard 2005). She argues that "Exposure to international trade may generate incentives for labor to move between industries", thus more *openness* will lead to higher interindustry labor mobility. *GDP growth* also indicates the general health of an economy. The higher the GDP growth, the better the economy, and the fatter a typical worker's pay schedule usually becomes. It follows that a larger than usual wage differential would be required for a worker to consider changing industries, therefore the elasticity of labor supply, i.e., my measure of ILM, will be lower. Finally, I add the economic variable of the *inflation rate*, as measured by the percentage change on the same period of the previous year of the consumer prices of all goods and services. Inflation is a critical macroeconomic indicator that connects with labor market closely. There are strong economic arguments on the trade-off between inflation and unemployment in an economy such as in Phillips curve, and political economists have shown that there exist partisan differences with respect to inflation levels. I include this control with the expectation that it will have opposite impact on ILM as unemployment. The data of these economic controls come from World Development Indicators and OECD Main Economic Indicators (MEI) database.

In order to control for social and political conditions, I have considered two institutional variables. The first is the Freedom House measure of *political rights*. It is measured on a one to seven scale, one representing the highest degree of freedom and seven the lowest. Higher degrees of political rights (or equivalently, lower scores of the value of this control) enable improved worker participation in the political process, which may have implications on levels of ILM. However, **a priori** claim on how political participation of workers will change labor mobility may be impossible to make; after all, an extensive literature showed that some people may want high mobility while others want low mobility, depending on whether the groups are in class or sector based political coalitions (Frieden 1991; Rogowski 1989; Rickard 2004; Hiscox 2002). Furthermore, in the dataset this variable only has marginal variability, with most cases of low degrees of political rights come from Turkey only. The second institutional variable is the Polity IV measure of the *institutionalized democracy*. It is an additive eleven-point scale (0-10), 0 means the lowest level of institutionalized democracy, 10 means the highest level. No theory that I know of argues for a definitive relationship between democracy and ILM levels. More institutionalized democracy allows its citizens better access to monitor and influence their governments, but again, voters in democracies could have diverse preferences for the prevailing level of ILM, therefore there is no clear prediction on the effect of democracy. And just as the last variable, most variation of this variable comes from Turkey alone. Due to the concern that these two institutional variables do not vary much in an OECD sample, I will only include them in the robustness check.

4.1.2. Over-time scatter plots and regressions

Using the over-time scatter plots, I present a first-cut analysis of the relationship between Left-Right partisanship and their preferred levels of ILM. From the discussions in the theory chapter we have learned that Left and Right governments have distinctively different constituency bases and policy goals, and without the consideration of centralized unions, governments of any type of partisanship will prefer to have cohesive constituency to facilitate the implementation of their policies. The general equilibrium model presented in the theory chapter indicates a positive relationship between levels of interindustry labor mobility and labor cohesiveness and a negative relationship between ILM and capital cohesiveness. So in a long term perspective and without the consideration of centralized unions, we should expect that Left government partisanship should be associated with high levels of ILM and Right government partisanship should be associated with low levels of ILM. For OECD countries from 1960 to 1999 I compile a dataset that contains yearly measurements of ILM levels and measure of government partisanship, which ranges from 0 to 100 with higher values meaning more right-leaning. Figure 4.1 shows the scatter plots of average ILM levels against average values of government partisanship for each country from 1960 to 1999. In panel A I use the elasticity measure of ILM that I constructed, in panel B I corroborate the results using coefficient of variation (COV) of intersectoral wages.

[Figure 4.1 about here]

From the plots we can discern a relationship as predicted in the theory. In panel **A** as average government partisanship moves to the right (i.e., it becomes more Right-leaning in ideology), the corresponding levels of ILM decline, as can be seen through the fitted line that is downward sloping. The correlation is at –0.44 and significant at 5% threshold. In panel **B** as government partisanship moves to the right, the COV of wages rises, indicating a decline of ILM levels, which also confirms the prediction. The correlation is 0.42 and also significant at 5% level. The pattern of country clustering in the figure also confirm our knowledge from the literature, that countries with rather strong social democratic tradition and high welfare state, such as Sweden, Norway, Finland, and the Netherlands, tend to have more Left governments and higher ILM, as they cluster in the upper left quadrant in panel **A** and lower left quadrant in panel **B**. On the other hand, countries with strong liberal market tradition, such as Ireland, UK, US, and Australia, tend to have more Right governments and lower ILM, as they cluster in the lower right quadrant in panel **A** and (not so strongly) upper right quadrant in panel **B**.

A simple cross-sectional bivariate regression using the aggregate ILM levels as the dependent variable and the aggregate government partisanship as the independent variable corroborates the graphical results. Table 4.1 reports the results. Column one shows that when we use the elasticity as the ILM measure, more right-leaning governments tend to be significantly associated with lower levels of labor mobility. Column two shows that when using the COV of wages as the ILM measure, more right-leaning governments tend to be significantly associated with higher COV, hence lower levels of labor mobility.

Table 4.1. Bivariate regression of aggregate partisan influence on levels of ILM		
	DV=Elasticity (Aggregate)	DV=COV of wages (Aggregate)
Aggregate Gov Partisanship	-0.043**	0.383**
	(0.019)	(0.180)
Constant	1.805*	9.702
	(0.869)	(8.161)
Observations	23	23
R-squared	0.193	0.178
Estimated using REGRESS. Standard errors in parentheses		
* p<.10, ** p<.05, *** p<.01		

Nevertheless, this evidence is rather crude and highly aggregated, it is only intended as a first-cut evidence. In order to show the relationship in presence of a set of controls and critically the moderation effect of centralized unions, I need to employ other econometric techniques to reveal the nuances.

4.1.3. Testing the conditional hypotheses

I argue that partisan governments will have different influences on the levels of interindustry labor mobility, and such influences will be moderated by the degree of union centralization within the economy. I replicated the conditional hypotheses here.

Hypothesis 1: When the level of domestic union centralization is low, levels of ILM will be higher under Left governments than under Right governments.

Hypothesis 2: When there are Left governments, levels of ILM will not significantly change with higher levels of union centralization.

Hypothesis 3: When there are Right governments, levels of ILM will be higher with higher levels of union centralization.

4.1.3.1. Specification and estimation method

Rather than using country-year as the basic unit of analysis, I use country-administration as the basic unit of analysis in testing the conditional hypothesis. There are two rationales for doing so. First and substantively, partisan manipulation on ILM levels, were it to happen at all, may not automatically occurs at any time period but it will almost certainly happen during the course of an administration. This is because when subject to a given set of constraints, the partisan governments would likely have the best knowledge available about their prospects to pass their preferred policies and would marshal their resources accordingly to maximize such prospects as well as trading off other pressing priorities. Manipulation of ILM levels will most likely be done according to their peculiar political schedules so that even though the immediate or short-term effects of such manipulation may not be perceptible, the cumulative effects over an administration are more likely to be significant. Secondly, the measure of government partisanship I use here is reported for each country per government/administration. As a main independent variable, it is preferable that the time frame in the analysis coincide with independent variable so as to avoid the odd scenario where the dependant variable (i.e., the yearly ILM level) varies but the independent variable(s) do not, since the ILM levels are measured annually and a usual administration will last more than a year.

Therefore for government partisanship variable, its value will be the same as when the particular government was formed [32] throughout the duration of the government/ administration; in the few cases where multiple governments were formed within the same calendar year, I take the average of the multiple government partisanship scores. For all other variables in the analysis, I take the averages over every country-administration. The final dataset thus constructed for OECD countries between 1960 and 1999 will have 381 observations with 24 units (countries) and on average 16 time periods (administrations), with the maximum of 34 administrations over the 40 years in Switzerland (followed by Italy with 24 governments and Denmark and Turkey with 22).

The specification of my baseline model is as follows.

$$
\begin{aligned}
Mobility_{it} = {} & \alpha + \beta_1(gov\_partisanship_{it}) + \beta_2(union\_centralization_{it}) \\
& + \beta_3(par_{it} * cent_{it}) + \beta_4(pop\_over65_{it}) + \beta_5(unempl\_rate_{it}) \\
& + \beta_6(GDP\_pc_{it}) + \beta_7(GDP\_growth_{it}) + \beta_8(openness_{it}) \\
& + \beta_9(cpi\_index_{it}) + \beta_{10}(Time_i) + u_i + \varepsilon_{it}
\end{aligned}
$$

[32] A technical note: the start date of an administration/government is the calendar year in which this government was formed, whether it was in January or December.

In the above specification, I include the appropriate control variables along with "*Time*", which indicates the temporal order of administrations within a country. If interindustry labor mobility actually is not only driven by those variables identified here but also moves upward or downward over time, the "*Time*" variable will pick up such a trend. I control for country-specific fixed effects. According to Beck (2001), for time series cross sectional data such as in this dataset, fixed effects are usually the appropriate specification. To ensure fixed effects are warranted, I check with two methods. First, I make sure that the F-test after fixed-effects OLS estimation is significant. Second, I run models in random effects and then perform a Breusch and Pagan Lagrangian multiplier test and make sure the test rejects the null hypothesis of no country-specific variance.

Since this dataset is in a time series cross sectional (TSCS) set up, estimation of such a dataset needs to check whether the error processes in the model follow certain patterns and if they do, to model such processes (Beck 2001). I check first whether there is cross sectional heteroskedasticity, this is done the following way. For each model I run fixed-effects OLS regressions first and then apply a modified Wald test for groupwise heteroskedasticity. The test will indicate whether I should reject the null hypothesis of homoskedasticity. If the test indicates I should reject the null, then I will model heteroskedasticity in estimations. Second, for each model I also check whether there is first order serial autocorrelation. I perform a Wooldridge test for autocorrelation in panel data and the test indicates whether I could reject the null hypothesis of no first-order autocorrelation. If the test shows that I should reject the null, then I will model the first-order autocorrelation, i.e., AR1, in the estimations.

Based on the structure of the data I have here, both feasible generalized least squares (FGLS) and OLS with panel corrected standard errors (PCSEs) could be used as the estimation methods. Both of them allow estimation in the presence of AR(1) autocorrelation within panels and panel-specific heteroscedasticity. Beck et al. have pointed out that FGLS correction of contemporaneously correlated errors is only valid as long as the time period T is at least as big as the units N (Beck and Katz 1995; Beck et al. 1993), and OLS with panel corrected standard errors (PCSEs) does not require T to be larger than N (Beck and Katz 1995, 1996). However this advantage of PCSE over FGLS does not apply to the data used here, since the maximum number of time periods (34 administrations in Switzerland) is larger than the number of units (24 countries), so the T is actually larger than N. Another reason both can qualify to be the estimation methods is that I should not assume the errors are contemporaneously correlated across units because this assumes that at any given time a common shock can affect all countries. In this particular analysis the "time period" is administration, and since different countries have different political schedules, generating different number of administrations over the same span of time, so a number of, say 5, does not necessarily mean a shock is happening at the same time but at the fifth administration, which may not be the same time for all countries. I therefore do not model contemporaneous correlation, and since tests of all my subsequent models show that I should allow errors to be panel-level heteroskedastic, so I specify the models to assume unit-level heteroskedasticity only. The main inference in the text will be drawn from results using FGLS; to corroborate the findings I run as robustness check using OLS with PCSEs. Finally, ordinary least squares (OLS) may be consistent in estimating the correlation coefficients, but because it cannot control for the possible disturbances in error structure, we may have little confidence in inferences that are based only on OLS.

4.1.3.2. Empirical results

For the dataset of OECD countries from 1960 to 1999 that use country-administration as the unit of analysis, table 4.2 summarizes the variables.

Table 4.2: Summary statistics of variables used in the analysis					
Variable	Obs	Mean	Std. Dev.	Min	Max
Independent variables					
Government partisanship (0=Left, 100=Right)	376	44.73	17.01	4.83	92.09
Union centralization (0=low, 1=middle, 2=high)	291	1.25	.68	0	2
Controls					
Over 65 years old (log)	381	14.22	1.51	9.66	17.35
Unemployment (%)	193	6.96	4.29	.2	23
Per capita GDP (thousand current PPP)	260	13.63	6.72	1.65	39.19
GDP growth	369	3.26	2.33	-7.28	12.15
Openness	371	59.48	33.37	7.99	227.29
Inflation/CPI index	372	8.93	12.44	.04	89.11
Political rights	284	1.20	.56	1	5
Democracy	345	9.69	.96	2	10
Dependent variables					
Interindustry labor mobility (estimated elasticity)	314	-.17	1.12	-2.65	3.58
Interindustry labor mobility (COV of wages)	323	25.57	13.74	11.75	203.18

4.1.3.2.1. Testing hypothesis one

In this subsection I seek to test the first conditional hypothesis.

Hypothesis 1: When the level of domestic union centralization is low, levels of ILM will be higher under Left governments than under Right governments.

Table 4.3 presents the results using FGLS according to the baseline specification. Model 1 uses the un-instrumented estimated elasticity as the dependent variable, and the main independent variables are: first, the government partisanship ranging from 0 to 100, with higher values denoting more Right-leaning; second, the 3-level categorical measure of union centralization, from 0 to 2, with higher values denoting higher union centralization; and third, their interaction term. Model 2 also uses the un-instrumented estimated elasticity as the dependent variable, but for the independent variables it recodes government partisanship into a dummy variable, where those partisanship scores higher than the population mean (44.73) will be coded as 1, meaning the Right-wing government partisanship; and those partisanship score lower than population mean will be coded as 0, denoting the Left-wing partisanship. In model 2, union centralization measure will still be the 3-level categorical variable. Models 3 and 4 differ in that they use the coefficient of variation (COV) among wages as the dependent variable, and the independent variables in model 3 will be the same as in model 1, while independent variables in model 4 will be the same as in model 2. For every model, I check for first order serial autocorrelation and for cross sectional heteroskedasticity to determine whether these assumptions are warranted; and the results indicate that they are. Following Beck et al I assume the serial correlation is constant across countries (Beck et al. 1993, 946). Breusch and Pagan Lagrangian multiplier test confirms that it is proper to use fixed effects model.

[Table 4.3 about here]

First look at the coefficient of the government partisanship variable, which shows a point estimate of the impact of government partisanship on ILM levels when union centralization takes the value of zero. In model 1, the coefficient for government partisanship variable is significant and negative, meaning the labor mobility levels will decrease with an increase of partisanship scores (or when governments become more Right-leaning), the coefficient is (-0.016), and this point estimate should be read when the moderating variable takes the value of zero, meaning when there is low level of union centralization. This coefficient translates to that when there are low levels of union centralization, moving from a typical Left government (with mean partisanship score of 31) to a typical Right government (with mean partisanship score of 58) will correspond to a decline of ILM of 0.432, which is over one-third of the standard deviation of ILM as measured in elasticity. Hence this point estimate in model 1 confirms the prediction in hypothesis 1 that when the level of domestic union centralization is low, levels of ILM will be higher under Left governments than under Right governments, when a host of variables have been controlled for. In model 2, government partisanship as measured by a dummy variable has a significant and negative impact on ILM levels, the coefficient is (-0.526). Again, this point estimate should be read when the moderating variable of union centralization takes the value of zero, and it says that under such a situation when moving from a broadly defined Left government (when partisanship dummy is 0) to a broadly defined Right government (when partisanship dummy is 1), the corresponded ILM level will decline by 0.526, which is over half the standard deviation of ILM as measured in elasticity. This result also confirms the claim in hypothesis 1.

Models 3 and 4 use the Coefficient of Variation among wages as the alternative measure of ILM, where **higher** COV means **lower** labor mobility and all regression coefficients should have the **opposite** signs as those in models 1 and 2. The continuous partisanship variable has positive impacts on ILM in model 3, meaning when union centralization is low levels of labor mobility tend to be lower with more Right-leaning governments; but the coefficient is not significant at conventional level[33]. In model 4, the dummy partisanship variable has positive and significant impact on ILM, corroborating model 2. Most other variables in models 3 and 4 exhibit opposite signs as their counterparts in models 1 and 2 just as expected, such as the interaction term, GDP per capita, and time trend.

As a robustness check, in table 4.4 I use OLS with PCSEs to replicate models 1 through 4. The estimated coefficients are similarly signed and of the same magnitudes. Compared to FGLS results, however, the point estimate of the coefficient of the partisanship variable tends to lose its statistical significance; the exception is the model 1'.

[Table 4.4 about here]

The specification of interaction term in the model and consequent statistical results allow us to tell the marginal influence of one main independent variable over a range of values of the other interacting variable, thus the conditional effect. Statistical tables 4.3 and 4.4 not only help us confirm the hypothesis 1, but also reveal the relativity of ILM levels under Left or Right governments as union centralization increases. From tables 4.3 and 4.4, it is not obvious to read how the

[33] It is significant at 13.9%.

government partisanship variable will influence ILM levels over a range of values of the moderating variable of union centralization. As a number of scholars have demonstrated, a better way to report the conditional effects is to present them in graphs (Braumoeller 2004; Brambor et al. 2006). In figures 4.2, I report the marginal influence of government partisanship on ILM levels and the corresponding 95% confidence intervals based on regression results in table 4.3. In each panel of graph, the marginal influence of government partisanship on levels of ILM is represented by the solid lines, and the top and bottom dashed lines represent the 95% confidence intervals. Panels (a) through (d) correspond with models 1 through 4 respectively.

[Figure 4.2 about here]

In each panel of graph, the left-most tip of the solid line shows the marginal influence of government partisanship on ILM levels when union centralization is low, for example, in panel (a) in figure 4.2 the solid line starts from the point where union centralization is zero and marginal effect is about -0.016, which is the regression coefficient for government partisanship in model 1 in table 4.2. As we move along the solid line, for every point the corresponding value on the vertical axis denotes the marginal partisan influence on ILM levels. To read the statistical significance, for any point on the solid line, we can draw a line perpendicular to the horizontal axis, if the intersections with the two dashed lines are both on the same side of the horizontal axis, then we will have confidence at 95% level that the estimation at this particular point is statistically significant. For example in panel (a) an imaginary perpendicular line through the left-most tip of the solid line will correspond to two points on the dashed lines that are both below the horizontal axis, then the estimated coefficient of the partisan influence on labor mobility levels when union centralization takes the value of zero is statistically significant at 95% level.

Let us look at the slopes now. When union centralization increases, in panels (a) (b) the solid lines will have upward slopes and in panels (c) (d) they will have downward slopes. This shows that when union centralization increases (or as unions become more centralized), the tendency that ILM levels will be higher under Left governments than under Right governments will become less and less so; and this observation is valid whether interindustry labor mobility is measured by elasticity of labor supply or by COV of wages. Such observation is also compatible with the theory that argues that the moderation effect of centralized unions tends to modify the behavior of partisan governments in different ways so that rising union centralization levels will obscure the relatively straightforward prediction of partisan correspondence with ILM levels when there are decentralized unions.

In sum, by using two different measures of ILM, applying multiple estimation methods and presentation techniques, and varying the coding about government partisanship, the evidence reported in this subsection allows me to confirm the conditional hypothesis 1. Furthermore, among the control variables, higher unemployment rates may significantly increase the elasticity of labor supply upon intersectoral wage differentials, implying that probably higher lateral pressure induces more vigorous searching efforts on the part of workers, but unemployment has no significant impact on intersectoral wage differentials themselves. Inflation has almost no impact on either elasticity of labor supply or COV of wages. Contrary to expectation, higher GDP per capita contributes to a significant increase of labor mobility using both measures, which means more wealth enables workers to better able to respond to price incentives and relocate to a more suitable line of work.

I also perform robustness checks of all these models by excluding any one country from the sample and run the regression for the rest of countries. In the interest of space, I do not report these robustness check results here[34]. This robustness check can make sure that the results are not driven by the disproportion of the number of observations distributed among countries in the sample, for example, over the time period of 40 years, Switzerland had 34 governments and Italy had 24, while Luxemburg had 9 and U.S. had 10 governments. The estimated results using this robustness check are similar in signs, magnitudes and significance as those reported in tables 4.3 and 4.4.

---

[34] This is done using Jackknife command in STATA where I exclude one country at a time and run regression for the rest of countries. The results can be available upon request.

4.1.3.2.1.1. A discussion of some seemingly counterintuitive results

An overview of figure 4.2 shows that when union centralization is low, say, around zero, levels of ILM tend to be higher under Left-leaning governments than under the Right governments, as all panels have shown except in (c)[35]. As union centralization levels increase, it first becomes statistically indistinguishable that ILM levels will be higher under Left governments than under the Right governments when there are moderate level of union centralization (i.e., when it takes the value of one). Furthermore in panels (a) and (b), when union centralization is high, ILM levels tend to be higher under the Right-leaning governments than under those governments to their Left.

At first glance, it appears somewhat counterintuitive to have a ceteris paribus result that when the union centralization is high, under the Right governments there may have higher labor mobility levels than under the Left governments, since higher levels of labor mobility would contribute to more unified labor forces that may constrain Right governments' ability to promote their ideal policies. However, the result is compatible with the theory laid out before. First of all, from this result we cannot draw the conclusion that Left governments would decrease ILM levels under centralized unions as the result is silent on such a prediction. What the result can tell us is that under centralized unions and ceteris paribus, levels of ILM may become higher under a Right government than under a Left government. Second, the result is possible since the theory argues that the institutional variable of union centralization may interfere with the partisan influence on ILM levels. Under highly centralized unions, labor forces will already have a high level of cohesiveness among themselves, hence Left governments will have less incentives to pursue high ILM in order to attain cohesive labor; meanwhile Right governments will face strong scrutiny and constraint from centralized unions, and will likely encounter organized labor' strong opposition to their attempts to pursue low ILM level. The declining incentive to pursue high ILM on the part of Left governments will however be

---

35 Since union centralization is a 3-level categorical variable, there are 43 obs when its value is zero, 126 obs when its value is 1, and 122 obs when the value is 2.

moderated by strong preferences of the centralized unions for high ILM levels, so that the Left governments would continue to adopt policies favorable for the maintaining of high ILM levels. At the same time, there is the increasing need for compromise with organized labor on the part of Right governments, who may eschew their natural preferences for low ILM levels and tilt toward certain labor mobility enhancing policies favored by the centralized unions. The twin development thus leads to ambiguity in predicting the relativity of ILM levels under Left or Right governments when the union centralization is high, and the eventual relativity of ILM levels may well be an empirical question.

Intuitively, highly centralized unions have high capacity to organize collective actions among labor owners, and they tend to possess enormous political power. The natural predisposition of labor movement will be to support labor-friendly Left parties and mobilize to counter Right parties, so much so that in countries where labor movement has historically been more centralized, the overall political environment will be favorable to the emergence and survival of Left governments but hostile to Right governments. In order to survive the hostile political environment in countries with highly centralized unions, Right governments will become likely to adapt to the constraints and demands of centralized unions and moderate their urge to reduce labor mobility levels. Left governments, on the other hand, tend to thrive in environment with highly centralized unions and they are not highly incentivized to further increase labor mobility levels.

According to the dataset used in this analysis, the following table lists the number/incidence of governments formed in each country within different combinations of partisanship types and levels of union centralization.

Table 4.5. Incidences of governments/administrations in each country, within different combinations of partisanship types and levels of union centralization

Left Gov + High Union Centralization		Right Gov + High Union Centralization		Left Gov + Low Union Centralization		Right Gov + Low Union Centralization	
Australia	4	Australia	6	Canada	4	Canada	8
Belgium	2	Belgium	2	France	6	France	3
Denmark	12	Denmark	8	UK	2	UK	6
Finland	10	Finland	3	Spain	3	Australia	2
Italy	15	Italy	9			USA	8
Netherlands	6	Netherlands	2				
Norway	16	Norway	1				
Spain	1	Spain	3				
Sweden	11	Sweden	5				
		France	1				
		Germany	1				
		UK	1				
Total	77		42		15		27

Left or Right governments are defined the same as in the text: partisanship scores higher than the population means (44.73) will be coded as the Right-wing government partisanship; those lower than population mean will be coded as the Left-wing partisanship. High union centralization is when the categorical measure of union centralization equals 2; low union centralization is when it equals 0; the cases with medium union centralization when it equals 1 are not considered.

Note: The only UK case with high union centralization happened in 1973. It appeared that from mid 1960s to mid 1970s, UK had a period of relatively high union centralization; but the centralized union movement had since disappeared from the late 1970s. Spain displayed a long term decline of its union centralization. Up to the mid 1980s, the data showed that Spain had relatively high union centralization, but its union centralization had since declined to low levels throughout the 1990s.

From table 4.5, it is clear that over the same span of time, i.e., from 1960 to 1999, when union centralization is high, there are more Left governments than Right ones, 77 to 42; conversely, when union centralization is low, there are more Right than Left governments, 27 to 15. This shows that in general, high union centralization favors the emergence and survival of Left governments, and low union centralization favors Right governments. In any individual country with high union centralization, there are likely more Left governments than Right ones (except in Australia and Spain); similarly, in any individual country with low union centralization, there are likely more Right governments than Left ones (except in France). The relatively high hazard rate for Right governments under high union centralization could indicate that they may have a strong incentive to adapt to the demands of centralized unions in order to survive. Other things being equal and for

Right governments, the corresponding ILM levels tend to be higher when they are under high union centralization than when they are under low union centralization where there are no obvious constraints from the unions.

Another interesting observation worth pointing out from table 4.5 is that union movement tends to be more centralized in the European, especially the Nordic countries than in countries with Anglo-Saxon traditions, and presumably also due to this reason, Left governments are more likely to emerge in the former than in the latter country grouping.

4.1.3.2.1.2. Other robustness tests of hypothesis one

Aside from corroborating the empirical findings using OLS with PCSEs and the jackknife estimations where I "shave" one country each time, I also experiment other robustness checks. First, I include controls of political rights and democracy. Even in an OECD sample, there would still have limited changes of the levels of political rights and democracy, and as I acknowledged earlier, most of the variance of these two variables comes from Turkey alone. It is interesting to see if adding these two controls would alter the results.

For another robustness check, I drop all control variables in order to maximize the number of observations. As I have mentioned before, since it is known that in this dataset the unemployment rate variable only has data after 1980, the estimation results reported in tables 4.3 and 4.4 are essentially that of post-1980 era. It is worthwhile to check if these results will hold when pre-1980 data are included. Taking out unemployment rate variable will not be sufficient since the GDP per capita started only since 1975, furthermore, even leaving out both of these variables may not extend the effective time period long enough since other controls may either have occasional missing values or have poor coverage for pre-1975 years. Therefore, as a rather crude robustness check, I dispose of control variables altogether and only include "Time" to control for time trend.

I use both measures of ILM and alternate the coding of government partisanship as either continuous or dummy. Table 4.6 reports models 5-8, which use the elasticity of labor supply as the measure of ILM. Models 5-6 include the controls for political rights and democracy, with model 5 using continuous variable of government partisanship and model 6 using the dummy variable of government partisanship. Models 7-8 do not use control variables at all, with model 7 using continuous government partisanship variable and model 8 the dummy variable. Similarly, table 4.7 reports models 5'-8' that use the COV of wages as the ILM measure. Models 5'-6' include controls for political rights and democracy, with model 5' using continuous variable of government partisanship and model 6' using the dummy partisanship variable. Models 7'-8' do not use controls at all and model 7' uses continuous partisanship variable while model 8' uses dummy partisanship variable.

[Table 4.6 about here]

[Table 4.7 about here]

Models 5-6 produce results very similar to those from models 1-2. This shows that when including the two controls for political institutions, there is virtually no impact on the main independent variables. Removing all control variables almost doubles the number of available observations. The results from models 7-8 show that the regression coefficients of government partisanship and the interaction term are correctly signed, however, the main independent variable of government partisanship is no longer statistically significant[36].

Adding the two controls of political rights and democracy strengthens the estimation results using COV of wage as ILM measure. Compare models 5'-6' with models 3-4, we can see that the coefficients for key independent variables of government partisanship and the interaction term are correctly signed in all models but with increased statistical significance in models 5'-6'. And if we remove all controls to increase the number of observations, as in models 7'-8', the key independent variables continue to be correctly signed and statistically significant, despite the possibility of omitted variables.

4.1.3.2.2. Testing hypotheses two and three

Based on estimation results in tables 4.3 and 4.4, I can also test the hypotheses 2 and 3, reproduced below, which argue about

[36] Because no proper controls are in use, these two models are prone to have omitted variable problem. The regression results are also sensitive to methods used. For example, using PCSE instead of FGLS on models 7-8 would generate statistically significant coefficient of government partisanship variable, the results are not reported in this study.

the ILM levels when union centralization increases given the type of government partisanship.

Hypothesis 2: When there are Left governments, levels of ILM will not significantly change with higher levels of union centralization.

Hypothesis 3: When there are Right governments, levels of ILM will be higher with higher levels of union centralization.

To test these hypotheses, we need to find out for a given value of the government partisanship and ceteris paribus the marginal influence of union centralization on ILM levels. The test is best performed in a conditional specification by replicating the procedures for conditional hypothesis testing above. First look at the statistical results reported in tables 4.3 and 4.4. When government partisanship is measured as a dummy variable, as in models 2, 4, 2', and 4', the coefficient for the union centralization variable reveals the marginal influence of union centralization on ILM levels when the moderating partisanship dummy takes the value of zero (i.e. when there are Left governments). Aside from model 2', the coefficients for union centralization variable are all statistically insignificant, which supports the claim in hypothesis 2. Similarly, when government partisanship is a continuous variable, as in models 1, 3, 1', 3', the coefficients for union centralization variable will show the marginal influence of union centralization on ILM levels when the partisanship variable takes the imaginary value of zero. Since the continuous partisanship variable ranges from 0-100 with low values denoting Left-leaning governments, these coefficients should be generally construed as when there are Left governments. All these coefficients for union centralization variable are all statistically insignificant, confirming hypothesis 2.

To test hypothesis 3, however, we cannot directly read from the tables. Using graphs is the more intuitive way and it conveys the exact same information as the tables. The following graphs test the hypothesis 3, and they corroborate the preceding discussions on hypothesis 2 as well. To save space, the graphs are based only on FGLS results as presented in table 4.3.

[Figure 4.3 about here]

Note that in all panels of figure 4.3, when government partisanship is at the most Left-wing position, the corresponding marginal effect of union centralization variable is statistically insignificant, meaning the ILM levels will not statistically be different with higher levels of union centralization. This finding is robust whether I measure government partisanship as 0/1 dummy with 0 denoting Left governments, or as a continuous variable from 0 to 100 with lower values denoting Left-leaning governments. The graphical evidence thus confirms hypothesis 2.

On the Right ends of all panels in figure 4.3, almost all panels [37] strongly support the claim that when there are Right governments and other things being equal, levels of ILM will be higher with higher levels of union centralization, hence confirming hypothesis 3.

In addition to using the interaction term specification and modeling the conditionality, I use another method to test hypotheses 2 and 3 by running multivariate regressions on a specification similar to the one above but without the interaction term, and I run them on split samples consisting either of pure Left or pure Right governments. Within the scope of the dataset in question, I assume a pure Left government is one with partisanship score less than or equal to the 33rd percentile value of the continuous partisanship variable, while a pure Right government is one with score larger than the 66th percentile value of continuous partisanship variable[38]. The main independent variable will be the union centralization, and the expectations are that when there are pure Left governments, union centralization will not have significant influence on ILM levels; when there are pure Right governments, union centralization will have positive and significant influence on ILM levels. The usual control variables are also included. The model specification for the split sample tests is as follows:

$$Mobility_{it} = \alpha + \beta_1(union\_centralization_{it}) + \beta_2(pop\_over65_{it}) + \beta_3(unempl\_rate_{it})$$
$$+ \beta_4(GDP\_pc_{it}) + \beta_5(GDP\_growth_{it}) + \beta_6(openness_{it}) + \beta_7(cpi\_index_{it}) + \beta_8(Time_t) + u_i + \varepsilon_{it}$$

---

[37] Except for panel (g), which narrowly misses the 5% significance level.

[38] I choose to divide governments into three even parts in order that those governments in the middle of the ideological spectrum will not dilute the predictions. Moderate governments are to the right of Left governments so they have more union pressure for high ILM than the Left governments, but they are to the left of Right governments so they are less heavily constrained. The result is diminished predictive power when it comes to the moderate governments and I choose to avoid them in the split sample tests.

Table 4.8 reports the regression results according to the preceding specification when there are pure Left governments. Models 9 and 10 use elasticity of labor supply as the measurement for ILM, model 9 uses feasible GLS as the estimation method and model 10 applies OLS with PCSEs. Models 11 and 12 use COV of wages as the measurement of ILM, with model 11 using FGLS and model 12 using PCSE. Across all models in table 4.8, coefficients for the union centralization variable are statistically insignificant. This result support the claim in hypothesis 2 that levels of ILM will not significantly change with higher levels of union centralization when there are Left governments.

[Table 4.8 about here]

Table 4.9 reports the statistical results when there are pure Right governments. Models 9'-12' similarly replicate the estimations alternating between measurements of ILM and the estimation methods. Across all models in table 4.9, coefficients for the union centralization are statistically significant (model 12' at the 10% level). Using elasticity measure where higher value means higher labor mobility, the coefficients are positive; using COV of wages where higher value means lower labor mobility, the coefficients are negative. Hence the results in table 4.9 strongly support the claim in hypothesis 3 that levels of ILM will be higher with higher levels of union centralization when there are Right governments.

[Table 4.9 about here]

4.1.4. Summary

Based on the analyses of the statistical and graphical evidence in this section, we can establish the close relationship between government partisanship and levels of interindustry labor mobility. Other things being equal, the levels of ILM under different types of partisan governments tend to be conditioned by the institutional environment of union centralization. Three conditional hypotheses describe the patterns of partisan correspondence with labor mobility and the union moderation. The empirics presented in this section confirm these conditional hypotheses.

4.2. Government policies and interindustry labor mobility

This section will empirically show that certain public policies can affect levels of interindustry labor mobility. By showing that certain government policies do have labor mobility changing effects, we can infer that there are viable policy instruments at the governments' disposal should they become motivated to influence ILM levels. There is no doubt that governments can engage in the full gamut of policies if they elect to influence interindustry labor mobility, and by selecting some but not other policies I may miss important aspects of what governments do. Yet the purpose here is not to conduct an exhaustive survey on labor mobility changing policies, rather, I seek to reveal that some government endeavors can have significant and substantively big impact on levels of interindustry labor mobility, and in so doing indicating some possible causal mechanisms through which interindustry labor mobility may be endogenously shaped by government policy interventions.

4.2.1. What government policies and a simple causal argument

Following the discussion in the theory chapter, I include the government policies in this empirical analysis that fulfill at least one of the following criteria: 1) such government policies should be related to labor market institutions in general; 2) such government policies may aim at influencing the equilibrium prices of labor factor; and 3) such government policies may directly stipulate the movement of workers across industries, thus manipulating the regulatory barriers for interindustry labor movement. In view of the relationship between policies and labor mobility, such policies should contribute to the general improvement in that the given wage levels of workers must be justified by the given levels of their labor market skills. Public social spending programs could thus be the pertinent candidates for this analysis because, first, they have been used in the literature as important policy instruments to intervene into the economy (Burgoon and Hiscox 2000; Martin and Swank 2004); second, their definitions indicate that they focus on certain important aspects of labor market I just mentioned; and third, there exist systematic data of public social spending programs over the years that enable cross-country comparison among the OECD countries[39].

From these criteria, I include the following seven public social spending programs: public expenditure on health, public expenditure on unemployment benefits, and five component programs of the generally termed active labor market programs (ALMP), these are: labor market training, subsidized employment, employment services and administration, special programs for youth, and special programs for the disabled. The formal definitions of these programs are collected in the appendix to this chapter.

The statistical analysis that follows will attempt to reveal the possible causal links between the resources spent on each public policy and the corresponding marginal impact on labor mobility levels in a time-series-cross-country setting.

4.2.2. Variables and sources

As an initial attempt to show the existence of the hypothesized relationship and also due to the concern of data availability, I will again focus on OECD countries in the analysis here. Most of the original data come from United Nations Industrial Development Organization (UNIDO) and OECD. Measures of interindustry labor mobility are derived from UNIDO Industrial Statistics Database at 3-digit level of ISIC (Rev.2) (UNIDO 2005). The database covers manufacturing sector that comprises 29 categories, and it contains data on all countries or equivalent political entities of the world (217 countries as of 2005) from 1961 to 2003 (43years). Just as in the last section I use two measures of interindustry labor mobility as my dependent variables: the elasticity of cross-industry labor movement upon changes of interindustry wages and the coefficient of variation among interindustry wages. The main independent variables on public social expenditure are from OECD Social Expenditure Database (SOCX) and Source OECD. OECD began systematically reporting their member countries' public social spending since 1980, and starting 1999 (included), 12 OECD members switched their currencies to Euro. The time coverage of these public social programs is from 1980 to 2001, and the

---

[39] Public spending on Education may also be a pertinent policy instrument of the governments. But I could not find systematic data on this subject for OECD countries prior to 1997; hence it is not included in the analysis.

coverage varies depending on the countries and the specific programs in question. The best data available on public social programs are in national currencies, which are used as the bases whenever derivation of additional variables becomes desirable[40]. To enable cross-country comparison, I convert all the countries' spending into purchasing power parity in current international dollars on a per capita basis; I then normalize spending in each public policy area by expressing them as percentage of PPP GDP per capita. The data of PPP conversion rate and per capita current PPP GDP are from Penn World Table 6.1 and World Development Indicators respectively. Primarily because data on public social expenditure are only available after 1980, the final dataset compiled in this analysis will span 22 years (between 1980 and 2001) and cover 30 OECD countries. In comparison with the dataset used in last section, the critical difference is that the dataset in this section uses country-year as the basic unit of analysis, while the dataset in last section uses country-administration as the basic unit. Data availability problem makes the dataset in this section an unbalanced panel.

The same sets of control variables as in the last section are included in the analysis to control for their possible independent influence on levels of ILM. In addition, I include an institutional control of *union density* for its important role in labor market. Trade unions work to insure workers against labor market risks, and workers join unions to seek some form of social protection (Iversen and Soskice 2001). Higher levels of union density are usually associated with stronger labor movement in the country (Garrett 1998); in fact, in my dataset the correlation between union density and union centralization is rather high at 0.54. The discussions in the last section indicate that stronger labor movement will likely be associated with higher ILM, especially when the government is Right-leaning,

---

[40] Where possible, I used data from SourceOECD, which runs from 1980 to 1999. SourceOECD reports all its data in national currencies and importantly for Euro-zone countries prior to 1999, data denominated in their old national currencies. While SOCX also reports data in national currencies, for Euro-zone countries, it converted all data prior to 1999 into Euro as well, using a fixed conversion rate for each country, even though Euro was not in circulation back then. Hence I suspect SOCX data may artificially change the real value of public spending and decide to use for all countries SourceOECD data prior to 1999 and SOCX data only after 1999 (included).

so one may expect positive impact on ILM by trade union density. Yet other theories in the literature, such as the insider-outsider argument, contend that unions may evolve into special interests of their own such that stronger unions may hinder cross-industry labor mobility. The empirical result consequently can shed some light on such differentiating expectations. The data of union density come from the OECD Corporate Data Environment on labor market statistics. The data used in the analysis are mostly the administrative data on trade union density[41]. I also include an indicator of *Year* to control for time trend.

4.2.3. Operationalization and estimation methods

Unlike in the previous section where the basic time unit is administration, the basic time unit in the analysis is year. The rationale for doing this is that if the effects of policy intervention on labor mobility levels will only manifest in the next administration, governments may not have the incentive to engage such policies since they may not be in office by then to reap the benefits. Spending level for each public social program tends to vary from year to year, and the research design should be able to capture such variation and its impact on corresponding levels of ILM.

Obviously, policy variables may not instantaneously affect levels of labor mobility because the policy effects either on the market equilibrium factor prices or on the real or perceived labor movement barriers usually take time to develop. I lag the policy variables by one period to allow time for their effects to reflect in labor mobility levels. Public social spending levels, however, tend to be in a dynamic data generating process and

---

[41] There is also a series of survey data on trade union density. Administrative data is used because it has the most available observations. But for some key countries, such as US, only survey data is available, so that US will be dropped from the regression analysis if only administrative union data were used. To avoid this and also to maximize the number of observations in regression, I substitute the survey values into the missing administrative values for years when administrative data is missing but survey values are not, and create a combined series on trade union density. Before the combining, the pair wise correlation between administrative and survey trade union density is 0.9973, and after the procedure the correlation between the combined and administrative series is 1.0000, between the combined and survey is 0.9978.

that the actual amounts tend to be highly correlated with the previous period's amounts. I add lagged dependent variable to the right-hand side to deal with the persistent influence of the independent variables. The rationale for doing so have been extensively discussed in Keele and Kelly (2006). Using an LDV obviates the need to use further lags of policy variables. Using an LDV also helps overcome the simultaneity between policies and levels of labor mobility, since it is possible that levels of public social spending may be shaped by the current labor mobility levels while the model argues that the current public social spending may have an impact on labor mobility levels of the next period. Following suggestions by Keele and Kelly, I test whether the dependent variable of ILM is stationary. Since stationary time-series tend to have constant estimation result, if the data are nonstationary, OLS with LDV will be incorrect and first differencing of the dependent and main independent variables will be needed (Keele and Kelly 2006). I test the stationarity of the dependent variable using two tests. The first is the Im-Pesaran-Shin panel unit root test, (or -ipshin- in STATA), which assumes that all series are non-stationary under the null hypothesis (Im et al. 2003). This test shows that the balanced dependent variable (measured either as elasticity or as COV of wages) has p-values low enough to reject the null hypothesis when only one lag is permitted. The second is the Levin-Lin-Chu panel unit root test, (or -levinlin- in STATA), which assumes the null hypothesis of non-stationarity (Levin et al. 2002). For both ILM measures, this test also yields low p-values to reject the null hypothesis when only one lag is permitted[42].

As robustness checks against sudden increase or decrease of public social spending levels, I use the lagged moving average of all policy variables over the previous 3 or 5 years; so that in any given year, labor mobility level is hypothesized to be affected by the cumulative effect of public social policies over the past 3 or 5 years. All other controls are in the same time period as the yearly measure of labor mobility to show their contemporaneous constraints.

---

[42] Both unit root tests require balanced panels. My data violate this because some countries do not have ILM values for many years; I recode the missing values as zeros to make for the balanced panel.

I specify the baseline model in this analysis as follows:

$$Mobility_{it} = \alpha + \beta_0(Mobility_{i,t-1}) + \beta_1(health\_spending_{i,t-1}) + \beta_2(unemployment\_comp_{i,t-1})$$
$$+ \beta_3(labor\_training_{i,t-1}) + \beta_4(subsidized\_empl_{i,t-1}) + \beta_5(empl\_services_{i,t-1}) + \beta_6(youth\_almp_{i,t-1})$$
$$+ \beta_7(disabled\_almp_{i,t-1}) + \beta_8(pop\_over65_{it}) + \beta_9(unempl\_rate_{it}) + \beta_{10}(GDP\_pc_{it})$$
$$+ \beta_{11}(GDP\_growth_{it}) + \beta_{12}(openness_{it}) + \beta_{13}(political\_rights_{it})$$
$$+ \beta_{14}(democracy_{it}) + \beta_{15}(union\_density_{it}) + \beta_{16}(cpi\_index_{it})$$
$$+ \beta_{17}(year_i) + u_i + \varepsilon_{it}$$

I include "year" variable to control the possible trend of labor mobility changes that simply occur overtime. According to Beck (2001), fixed effects are the appropriate specification for time-series cross-section data. To make sure fixed effects are warranted, I run models in random effects and then perform a Breusch and Pagan Lagrangian multiplier test to make sure the test rejects the null hypothesis of no country-specific variance. When a specific model passes the test, I will control for country-specific fixed effects.

I check whether there is cross sectional heteroskedasticity in the model by running fixed-effects OLS regressions first and then apply a modified Wald test for groupwise heteroskedasticity, which will indicate whether I should reject the null hypothesis of homoskedasticity. If the test indicates I should reject the null, then I will control for heteroskedasticity in estimations. I check whether there is first order serial autocorrelation in the model by performing a Wooldridge test for autocorrelation according to the model specification and the test indicates whether I could reject the null hypothesis of no first-order autocorrelation. If the test shows that I should reject the null, then I will control for first-order autocorrelation (AR1) in the estimations.

The dataset in this analysis has about 30 units (countries) and 22 time periods (years), ordinary least squares (OLS) technique may be consistent in estimating the correlation coefficients, but because it cannot control for the possible disturbances in error structure, there may be bias in estimations based only on OLS. Feasible generalized least squares (FGLS) can control for possible panel heteroskedasticity, contemporaneous correlation, and panel specific serial correlation in the errors process, but FGLS correction of contemporaneously correlated errors is only valid as long as the time period T is at least as big as the units N (Beck and Katz 1995; Beck et al. 1993), which this dataset clearly violates. OLS with panel corrected standard errors (PCSEs) can remedy the problems associated with panel heteroskedastic and contemporaneously correlated errors, and it does not require T to be larger than N (Beck and Katz 1995, 1996). Therefore I adopt OLS with PCSE as the estimation method in this analysis.

As before, I use both versions of interindustry labor mobility measures as the dependent variable, namely, the elasticity of labor supply upon interindustry wage differentials and the coefficient of variation among interindustry wages.

4.2.4. Findings

For the dataset of OECD countries from 1980 to 2001, the summary statistics of all variables used in the analysis in this section are presented in table 4.10.

Table 4.10: Summary statistics of variables used in the analysis					
Variable	Obs	Mean	Std. Dev.	Min	Max
Independent variables					
Public social expenditure on health (normalized)	532	5.36	1.34	1.00	8.56
Unempl compensation (nml)	469	1.13	.90	.00	3.91
Labor market training (nml)	440	.19	.19	0	1.06
Subsidized employment (nml)	416	.21	.22	.00	1.01
Employment service and administration (nml)	438	.11	.07	0	.29
Youth measures (nml)	380	.09	.10	0	.50
Disabled measures (nml)	402	.13	.18	0	.80
Controls					
Over 65 years old (log)	552	14.31	1.58	10.00	17.39
Unemployment (%)	534	7.34	4.29	.2	23.9
Per capita GDP (thousand current PPP)	552	17.57	7.48	2.25	58.81
GDP growth	552	2.77	2.53	-7.49	11.14
Openness	552	71.32	42.83	15.92	285.46
Political rights	552	1.17	.61	1	5
Democracy	552	9.71	.95	2	10
Trade union density (combined)	511	41.79	21.08	7.4	96.4
Inflation/CPI index	413	8.47	29.12	-.76	567.88
Dependent variables					
ILM (estimated elasticity)	418	-.03	1.30	-3.98	3.95
ILM (COV)	432	30.93	22.95	10.40	181.24

4.2.4.1. Empirical results

Table 4.11 presents the estimation results of the baseline specification. The first column uses elasticity measure of labor mobility as the dependent variable and it includes the lagged dependent variable. Three policies, unemployment compensation, labor market training, and subsidized employment, are shown to have statistically significant impact on levels of ILM. For example, one standard deviation increase of unemployment compensation, which is 0.90, meaning the per capita amount spent on unemployment compensation program expressed as the percentage of GDP per capita increases by 0.90 percent, will lead to an increase of interindustry labor mobility by 0.36, which is more than a quarter of the standard deviation of ILM measured by elasticity. The reason unemployment compensation program can increase ILM measured by elasticity may be that unemployment compensation encourages the excessive labor supply be taken off the labor market so that for the remaining labor forces in the market, their wage levels will better reflect their labor market skills than previously.

Spending on labor market training and subsidized employment, on the other hand, will significantly lower labor mobility as measured by elasticity. These programs may primarily have been designed to effectively fight unemployment. For example, labor market training has been provided to both unemployed adults and those at risk of unemployment, or employed adults alike (OECD 2002). And subsidized employment may take any of the three stylized types: a) an employer subsidy for hiring an individual on welfare, b) relief jobs in the public sector for individuals on welfare, and c) training programs in the public sector for individuals on welfare (Jongen et al. 2003). OECD employment outlook in 2005 finds that in terms of easing the pains of the unemployed and sustaining certain levels of employment within the economy, subsidized employment programs and especially the private hiring subsidies frequently have positive impact on participation in employment (OECD 2005). However, both these programs may have the effect of subsidizing the excessive workers, or those without the requisite skill sets, to continue staying in the labor market, thus worsening the economy-wide fitness between wage levels and justifiable productivity levels.

The other policy variables do not have influences within the statistical significance of 5% level.

From the first column in table 4.11, we can also tell that higher unemployment rate tends to depress the level of labor mobility domestically, so does the increase of GDP per capita. Improving political rights levels (meaning the lower values of political rights variable) will increase domestic labor mobility levels. Higher strength of labor movement as measured by increases in trade union density will have insignificant impact on labor mobility levels.

[Table 4.11 about here]

The second column of table 4.11 uses the COV of wages as the dependent variable; however, no policy variables attain statistical significance, except the unemployment compensation variable at 10% level. This may be due to the fact that COV of wages are based solely on interindustry wage differentials, and it is known that there is considerable stickiness in wage levels, so that COV of wages may not be as sensitive to policy interventions as the elasticity measure, which considers wage and employment structure simultaneously.

4.2.4.2. Robustness tests

As a first set of robustness tests, I use the main independent variables in their lagged three or five year moving averages. I employ the moving averages to prevent the possibility that the results have been driven by some sudden increase or decrease of certain policy in some countries. The results are reported in table 4.12.

The first two columns use the elasticity as the ILM measure. The results strongly corroborate the first column in table 4.11. Whether using the three-year or five-year moving average, unemployment compensation will increase the labor mobility as measured by elasticity while labor market training will decrease labor mobility. In addition, when the key independent variables take the forms of moving average, health expenditure turns out to positively affect labor mobility while employment service expenditure will negatively affect labor mobility, and subsidized employment will lose its statistical significance. The controls variables will maintain their direction of influence and statistical significance when using the moving average. And as before, when the dependent variable is the COV of wages, using the key independent variables in moving averages will generate generally insignificant results, except that subsidized employment will increase interindustry wage differentials while ALMP programs for the disabled will decrease the wage differentials.

[Table 4.12 about here]

In addition to varying the length of time over which I calculate the moving average of policy variables, I employ several other checks to examine the robustness of the finding that certain key government policies can have substantive and significant impact on labor mobility levels, especially when measured as the elasticity of labor supply upon intersectoral wage differentials.

I first use jackknife. This is a technique that takes random samples from the full sample, the difference being that the random samples leave one observation out, so that jackknife procedure "shaves" one observation off each time and then runs the same regression on the random samples. Jackknife estimator of a population (here it means the full sample) parameter is the mean of the estimates from all random samples; jackknife variance calculates the variability between the random sample estimates. The first column in table 4.13 shows the jackknife results when the dependent variable is elasticity. The results strongly corroborate those in the previous two tables; therefore the results using jackknife to shave off one observation at a time are robust to influences from possible outlier observations.

[Table 4.13 about here]

It could be possible that the source of outlier influences come not from a single observation, but a cluster of observations, for example one particular country might have particularly high social spending and high labor mobility that this country alone could be driving the results. To check the robustness against this possibility, I re-run the jackknife estimation but "shave" off one country at a time instead of one observation. The second column in table 4.13 reports the finding. The results are very similar to the first column in table 4.13, and they also closely track those in the previous two tables. So that the relationship that certain public social policies significantly affect levels of labor mobility is robust against the possible outlier country effects as well.

Since the dataset in this analysis spans from 1980 to 2001, and Euro as a currency began to denominate the economy of 12 of the countries within the dataset since 1999; to preclude the possibility that the relationship identified before was simply due to converting to another currency, I exclude those observations that use Euro. The third column in table 4.13 reports the results considering the Euro effect. They show that all policy variables have about the same substantive effects and significance levels as those in tables 4.11 and 4.12.

Finally, I consider the possibility that Scandinavian countries are primarily responsible for the relationship that policies affect ILM levels, since the literature has shown that Scandinavian countries usually have high provision of welfare state and extensive labor market policies (Golden and Pontusson 1992; Pontusson 2005). I do this by taking off from the dataset those observations from the five countries: Norway,

Sweden, Finland, Iceland, and Denmark. And run the baseline regressions on non-Scandinavian countries only. The last column in table 4.13 reports the results. The results show that the gist of the relationship that certain government policies can affect ILM levels in major ways remains for non-Scandinavian countries. Unemployment compensation continues to positively affect ILM as measured by elasticity and labor market training negatively affects mobility. Furthermore, in the non-Scandinavian sample the spending on employment services and the program for the disabled tends to have substantive and significant effects on ILM levels, with more expenditure on employment services decreasing and more expenditure on the disabled measures increasing labor mobility. All signs are the same as before.

In all estimations and robustness checks, interindustry labor mobility as measured by elasticity tends to trend upwards over time, which may mean there has been an exogenous rising of labor mobility levels, which possibly may be due to overtime technological improvement that facilitates cross-industry labor movement.

4.2.5. Summary

From the empirical findings and robustness checks, we can make the following inferences. First, government policies can have statistically significant while substantive impact on levels of interindustry labor mobility as measured by elasticity method, but their impact on interindustry wage differentials has been inconsequential. Second, different policies can have differentiating impact: some may increase interindustry labor mobility while others may depress labor mobility. Third, it has been found that two policies consistently have significant impact on ILM levels: unemployment compensation and labor market training. More spending on the unemployment compensation tends to increase labor mobility while more spending on the labor market training tend to decrease labor mobility. This finding is robust to the various checks reported in this section. Last, the finding that certain government policy makes a difference in the labor mobility levels is a general one, as when I limit the sample to non-Scandinavian countries, the finding still holds.

4.3. A discussion of possible endogeneity

Given the previous literature that argues that levels of interindustry factor mobility may have shaped the types of domestic political coalitions and have constrained the policy space available to partisan governments (Alt and Gilligan 1994; Hiscox 1999, 2002; Magee 1980; Mukherjee et al. 2007), there may be concerns that the government partisanship of a country may not be independent from the level of interindustry labor mobility at the time, so that the regressions I ran in section 4.1 may have suffered from endogeneity where my main independent variable of government partisanship may also be determined by the current level of interindustry labor mobility.

This concern can first be assuaged by the clarification of different time frames used in those studies that I just mentioned and my current study. Previous studies usually look for the determining effects of interindustry factor mobility on politics through a long-run perspective, and they found in the long-term time frame that factor mobility levels indeed shape various political patterns. My empirical results in figure 4.1 and table 4.1 help confirm this, where I aggregate the labor mobility levels and partisanship score over four decades and find the two are closely correlated.

However, the theory, hypotheses, and the bulk of empirical evidence in my current study deal with the possible partisan manipulation of interindustry labor mobility in the short-term, usually no longer than the duration of an administration. It may be stretching to the limits to apply theories that purport to explain the long-run phenomena to understand the short-term dynamics. And this study argues that in the short-term, partisanship of governments and the consequent partisanship motivated policy interventions can have significant impact on current levels of interindustry labor mobility. This study further assumes that in the short run, levels of interindustry labor mobility cannot affect the partisanship of the governments at the current period.

Second, I address the concern of endogeneity statistically by testing reverse causality on the key models. Because government partisanship variable will have greater variation when measured as a continuous variable, I test the reverse causality on models 1, 3, 7, and 7'. In these reverse causality models, named R1, R3, R7, and R7' respectively, the dependent variable becomes the continuous measure of government partisanship, and the interindustry labor mobility becomes one independent variable. All other independent variables remain as in the original models except for the interaction term (partisanship*union centralization), which is dropped from the reverse causality models since it will cause collinearity problem. The expectation is that in all the reverse causality models, the coefficients for the interindustry labor mobility variables will be statistically insignificant, meaning current levels of labor mobility will have no impact on partisanship of the contemporary governments.

Table 4.14 reports the results of the reverse causality models, and it is clear from all columns that when current interindustry labor mobility levels are used as the independent variables, they tend to have no statistically significant impact on the contemporary government partisanship.

[Table 4.14 about here]

I have also tried to use the instrument variable approach to further address the endogeneity concern, however, the problem then shifts to finding a good instrument that is highly correlated with the government partisanship variable yet uncorrelated with interindustry labor mobility. Using a country's neighbors' partisanship to instrument for the country's partisanship seemed a good instrument, yet my calculation reveals that it is only weakly correlated with partisanship variable (with correlation coefficient below 0.10), so that estimation using this instrument variable will not return valid results.

4.4. Conclusion

This chapter presents the empirical evidence in support of the argument that interindustry labor mobility can be endogenous within the domestic political process. The first section shows that levels of labor mobility within a country can be fundamentally shaped by the partisanship of the government, and such relationship is moderated by the levels of domestic union centralization. The second section presents some time-series cross-national evidence that certain public policies at the disposal of governments can significantly and substantively affect labor mobility levels. Combining the two parts of evidence, it is natural to conclude that interindustry labor mobility levels we observe can be caused by political manipulations of the governments, whose motivation to doing so may be due to their partisan ideologies. I will further substantiate the partisan manipulation of labor mobility levels through two case studies of Sweden and the U.S in the next two chapters.

Appendix to Chapter 4: Definition of various public social expenditure programs

Public Social Expenditure

Public social expenditure is the provision by public institutions of benefits to, and financial contributions targeted at, households and individuals in order to provide support during circumstances which adversely affect their welfare, provided that the provision of the benefits and financial contributions constitutes neither a direct payment for a particular good or service nor an individual contract or transfer. Such benefits can be cash transfers, or can be the direct ('in-kind') provision of goods and services (OECD 2004).

Public social expenditure on health

Social expenditure data in the health policy area is taken from the OECD Health database (OECD 2003). All public expenditure on health is included (not total health expenditure): current expenditure on health (personal and collective services (HC.1 to HC.7 in the ICHA) and investment (HC.R.1). Expenditure in this category encompasses, among other things, expenditure on in-patient care, ambulatory medical services and pharmaceutical goods. Individual health expenditure, insofar as it is not reimbursed by a public institution, is not included. As already noted, cash benefits related to sickness are recorded under sickness benefits (OECD 2004).

Public Expenditure on Unemployment

This category includes all cash expenditure to people compensating for unemployment. This includes redundancy payments out of public resources as well as pensions to beneficiaries before they reach the 'standard' pensionable age if these payments are made because they are out of work or otherwise for reasons of labor market policy (OECD 2004). According to OECD Social Expenditure Database, public expenditure on unemployment contains three programs: unemployment compensation, early retirement for labor market reasons, and severance pay (OECD 2004). Among the three, unemployment compensation has the largest number of available observations and in many countries is the sole content of unemployment expenditure.

Active Labor Market Programs

The category active labor market programs (ALMP) contains all social expenditure (other than education) which is aimed at the improvement of the beneficiaries' prospect of finding gainful employment or to otherwise increase their earnings capacity. This category includes spending on public employment services and administration, labor market training, special programs for youth when in transition from school to work, labor market programs to provide or promote employment for unemployed and other persons (excluding young and disabled persons), and special programs for the disabled (OECD 2004).

Public Employment Services and Administration

The following services are included: placement, counseling and vocational guidance; job-search courses and related forms of intensified counseling for persons with difficulties in finding employment; support of geographic mobility and similar costs in connection with job search and placement. In addition, all administration costs of labour market agencies (at central and decentralized levels), including unemployment benefit agencies (even if these are separate institutions) as well as administrative costs of other labour market programs are included (OECD 2007).

Labor Market Training

Training measures undertaken for reasons of labor market policy, other than special programs for youth and the disabled. Expenditures include both course costs and subsistence allowances to trainees, when such are paid. Subsidies to employers for enterprise training are also included, but not employers' own expenses.

- Training for unemployed adults and those at risk: Programs aimed mainly, though not always exclusively, at the unemployed and those at risk of losing their jobs, or other disadvantaged groups such as the poor (especially in the United States). Mostly in training centers, but often also in enterprises.
- Training for employed adults: training supported for reasons of labour market policy other than the need to help the

unemployed and those at risk. Most frequently, grants to enterprises for staff training in general (OECD 2007).

Youth Measures

They only include special programs for youth in transition from school to work. Thus they do not cover young people's participation in programs that are open to adults as well.

• Measures for unemployed and disadvantaged youth: Remedial education, training or work practice for disadvantaged youth to facilitate transition from school to work. The principal target group usually consists of those who do not follow regular upper-secondary or vocational education and are unsuccessful in finding jobs.

• Support of apprenticeship and related forms of general youth training: it covers many forms of training and work practice in enterprises for young people. Access is not restricted to persons with employment problems (OECD 2007).

Subsidized Employment

Targeted measures to promote or provide employment for unemployed persons and other groups specified as labour market policy priorities (other than youth or the disabled).

• Subsidies to regular employment in the private sector: wage subsidies for the recruitment of targeted workers or, in some cases, for continued employment of persons whose jobs are at risk. Grants aiming primarily to cover enterprises' capital costs are not included, nor are general employment subsidies or subsidies paid for all workers in certain regions. • Support of unemployed persons starting enterprises: the support can consist of unemployment benefits or special grants.

• Direct job creation (public or non-profit): temporary work and, in some cases, regular jobs in the public sector or in non-profit organizations, offered to unemployed persons (OECD 2007).

Measures for the Disabled

Only special programs for the disabled are included. The category does not cover the total policy effort in support of the disabled.

• Vocational rehabilitation: ability testing, work adjustment measures and training other than ordinary labour market training.

• Work for the disabled: sheltered work and subsidies to regular employment (OECD 2007).

Graphical Appendix to Chapter 4:

In this appendix, I show the time series graphs of the annual interindustry labor mobility levels for every one of the OECD countries, and I use the three main methods used in the empirics: elasticity of labor supply upon wage signals and without the endogeneity control; the interindustry wage differentials (COV of wages); and the compensate employment changes. Figures 4.A.1-3 report the graphs.

[Figures 4.A.1-3 about here]

Table 4.3. Estimation of the partisan influence on levels of ILM, using FGLS

	Model 1 DV=Elasticity	Model 2 DV=Elasticity	Model 3 DV=COV of wages	Model 4 DV=COV of wages
Gov Partisanship (continuous)	-0.016**		0.049	
	(0.007)		(0.033)	
Gov Partisanship (Dummy)		-0.526**		3.093**
		(0.247)		(1.407)
Union Centralization	-0.117	0.244	0.942	0.004
	(0.211)	(0.149)	(0.921)	(0.651)
Partisanship*Centralization	0.014***	0.434***	-0.032*	-1.718**
	(0.004)	(0.154)	(0.018)	(0.731)
Population over 65	0.254	-0.288	12.175***	13.722***
	(0.792)	(0.805)	(3.840)	(3.319)
Unemployment	0.088***	0.096***	-0.058	-0.114
	(0.027)	(0.027)	(0.092)	(0.079)
GDP PPP per capita	0.076***	0.075***	-0.199**	-0.230***
	(0.026)	(0.027)	(0.090)	(0.073)
Openness	0.014	0.019**	-0.020	-0.024
	(0.009)	(0.009)	(0.033)	(0.029)
GDP Growth	-0.080***	-0.075***	-0.054	-0.071
	(0.027)	(0.027)	(0.094)	(0.083)
Inflation	-0.015	0.000	-0.084	-0.139*
	(0.022)	(0.023)	(0.091)	(0.076)
Time period	-0.103*	-0.068	0.388**	0.343***
	(0.058)	(0.057)	(0.184)	(0.130)
Constant	-5.201	1.570	-150.080***	-169.527***
	(11.116)	(11.373)	(54.552)	(47.675)
Observations	123	123	125	125
# of Countries	16	16	16	16
Wald chi2	933.637	851.497	1403.853	2724.373
Prob>chi2	.	.	.	.

Estimated using feasible GLS, country fixed effects, all models assume heteroskedastic panels and AR(1)

Standard errors in parentheses, country effects not reported

* p<.10, ** p<.05, *** p<.01

Table 4.4. Estimation of the partisan influence on levels of ILM, using OLS with PCSEs

	Model 1' DV=Elasticity	Model 2' DV=Elasticity	Model 3' DV=COV of wages	Model 4' DV=COV of wages
Gov Partisanship (continuous)	-0.016**		0.059	
	(0.008)		(0.049)	
Gov Partisanship (Dummy)		-0.448		2.588
		(0.273)		(2.147)
Union Centralization	-0.002	0.339**	1.019	0.921
	(0.229)	(0.161)	(1.700)	(1.346)
Partisanship*Centralization	0.012***	0.352**	-0.022	-1.480
	(0.004)	(0.169)	(0.028)	(1.231)
Population over 65	0.430	-0.086	21.398***	22.274***
	(0.863)	(0.885)	(6.643)	(6.287)
Unemployment	0.096***	0.100***	0.096	0.097
	(0.030)	(0.029)	(0.214)	(0.209)
GDP PPP per capita	0.101***	0.105***	-0.408*	-0.407*
	(0.030)	(0.031)	(0.226)	(0.214)
Openness	0.007	0.009	-0.099	-0.088
	(0.009)	(0.010)	(0.084)	(0.079)
GDP Growth	-0.053*	-0.049	0.142	0.107
	(0.031)	(0.031)	(0.213)	(0.223)
Inflation	-0.003	0.010	0.012	-0.030
	(0.025)	(0.026)	(0.194)	(0.197)
Time period	-0.138**	-0.115*	0.565	0.512
	(0.066)	(0.067)	(0.475)	(0.457)
Constant	-7.842	-1.332	-282.167***	-293.211***
	(12.134)	(12.528)	(94.970)	(90.621)
Observations	123	123	125	125
# of Countries	16	16	16	16
Wald chi2	910.171	813.941	1400.953	2727.620
Prob>chi2	0.00	0.00	0.00	0.00
R-squared	0.806	0.779	0.674	0.702

Estimated using OLS with PCSEs, country fixed effects, all models assume heteroskedastic panels and AR(1)

Panel corrected standard errors in parentheses, country effects not reported

* p<.10, ** p<.05, *** p<.01

Table 4.6. Estimation of the partisan influence on levels of ILM measured by Elasticity, using FGLS

	Model 5 Cont Par, With PR DEM	Model 6 Dum Par, With PR DEM	Model 7 Cont Par, No Controls	Model 8 Dum Par, No Controls
Gov Partisanship (continuous)	-0.017**		-0.006	
	(0.007)		(0.004)	
Gov Partisanship (Dummy)		-0.581**		-0.154
		(0.244)		(0.156)
Union Centralization	-0.160	0.229	-0.154	0.017
	(0.207)	(0.146)	(0.142)	(0.095)
Partisanship*Centralization	0.015***	0.483***	0.005*	0.123
	(0.004)	(0.154)	(0.003)	(0.104)
Population over 65	0.014	-0.585		
	(0.793)	(0.809)		
Unemployment	0.059**	0.067**		
	(0.028)	(0.027)		
GDP PPP per capita	0.058**	0.056**		
	(0.026)	(0.026)		
Openness	0.014*	0.020**		
	(0.009)	(0.009)		
GDP Growth	-0.077***	-0.070***		
	(0.027)	(0.026)		
Political Rights	-0.458**	-0.457**		
	(0.227)	(0.219)		
Democracy	0.249	0.286		
	(0.332)	(0.343)		
Inflation	-0.013	0.004		
	(0.022)	(0.023)		
Time period	-0.055	-0.016	0.086***	0.087***
	(0.058)	(0.057)	(0.013)	(0.013)
Constant	-3.706	3.441	-1.407***	-1.616***
	(11.415)	(11.725)	(0.434)	(0.435)
Observations	123	123	227	227
# of Countries	16	16	16	16
Wald chi2	989.873	894.393	153.451	137.729
Prob>chi2	.	.	.	.

Estimated using feasible GLS, country fixed effects, all models assume heteroskedastic panels and AR(1)

Standard errors in parentheses, country effects not reported

* p<.10, ** p<.05, *** p<.01

Table 4.7. Estimation of the partisan influence on levels of ILM measured by COV of wages, using FGLS

	Model 5' Cont Par, With PR DEM	Model 6' Dum Par, With PR DEM	Model 7' Cont Par, No Controls	Model 8' Dum Par, No Controls
Gov Partisanship (continuous)	0.071**		0.063***	
	(0.030)		(0.018)	
Gov Partisanship (Dummy)		3.584***		1.769***
		(1.151)		(0.667)
Union Centralization	0.734	-0.278	1.067**	-0.100
	(0.847)	(0.587)	(0.521)	(0.399)
Partisanship*Centralization	-0.047***	-2.310***	-0.039***	-1.099***
	(0.016)	(0.650)	(0.010)	(0.377)
Population over 65	16.146***	18.404***		
	(3.686)	(3.341)		
Unemployment	0.062	0.081		
	(0.100)	(0.099)		
GDP PPP per capita	-0.227**	-0.239***		
	(0.089)	(0.085)		
Openness	-0.044	-0.063*		
	(0.037)	(0.035)		
GDP Growth	0.043	0.012		
	(0.109)	(0.111)		
Political Rights	2.169	2.866**		
	(1.364)	(1.299)		
Democracy	-6.671***	-6.296***		
	(1.610)	(1.515)		
Inflation	-0.013	-0.073		
	(0.101)	(0.106)		
Time period	0.440**	0.327	0.208***	0.202***
	(0.191)	(0.201)	(0.032)	(0.032)
Constant	-143.374***	-176.889***	20.008***	21.951***
	(54.030)	(49.276)	(1.537)	(1.286)
Observations	125	125	234	234
# of Countries	16	16	16	16
Wald chi2	1457.277	2008.665	799.710	758.378
Prob>chi2	.	.	.	.

Estimated using feasible GLS, country fixed effects, all models assume heteroskedastic panels and AR(1)

Standard errors in parentheses, country effects not reported

* p<.10, ** p<.05, *** p<.01

Table 4.8. Estimation of the influence of centralized unions on ILM levels, when there are Left governments

	Model 9 DV=Elasticity, Method=FGLS	Model 10 DV=Elasticity, Method=PCSE	Model 11 DV=COV of wages, Method=FGLS	Model 12 DV=COV of wages, Method=PCSE
Union Centralization	0.149	0.104	0.749	0.415
	(0.190)	(0.236)	(0.760)	(1.361)
Population over 65	0.196	0.895	30.539***	31.916***
	(1.344)	(1.816)	(7.342)	(12.346)
Unemployment	0.018	0.056	0.350	0.740*
	(0.061)	(0.068)	(0.245)	(0.435)
GDP PPP per capita	0.148***	0.133**	-0.134	-0.315
	(0.053)	(0.061)	(0.197)	(0.350)
Openness	0.011	0.030	-0.012	-0.141
	(0.018)	(0.026)	(0.089)	(0.164)
GDP Growth	-0.108**	-0.040	0.600***	0.704
	(0.051)	(0.060)	(0.230)	(0.580)
Inflation	-0.002	0.025	0.115	0.271
	(0.038)	(0.047)	(0.187)	(0.448)
Time period	-0.219**	-0.160	-0.129	-0.064
	(0.104)	(0.129)	(0.477)	(0.905)
Constant	-3.613	-15.188	-416.319***	-432.983***
	(19.237)	(26.216)	(106.999)	(178.231)
Observations	40	41	40	41
# of Countries	9	10	9	10
Wald chi2	914.473	1437.257	750.668	3717.374
Prob>chi2	.	0.000	.	0.000
R-squared		0.860		0.826

Estimated using feasible GLS or OLS with PCSEs as indicated, country fixed effects, all models assume heteroskedastic panels and AR(1)

Standard errors in parentheses, country effects not reported

* p<.10, ** p<.05, *** p<.01

Table 4.9. Estimation of the influence of centralized unions on ILM levels, when there are Right governments

	Model 9' DV=Elasticity, Method=FGLS	Model 10' DV=Elasticity, Method=PCSE	Model 11' DV=COV of wages, Method=FGLS	Model 12' DV=COV of wages, Method=PCSE
Union Centralization	0.865***	0.925***	-2.495***	-3.002*
	(0.175)	(0.261)	(0.748)	(1.618)
Population over 65	-3.388***	-3.412**	22.862***	16.526*
	(1.018)	(1.618)	(5.427)	(8.482)
Unemployment	-0.057*	-0.065	-0.352	-0.808**
	(0.032)	(0.062)	(0.233)	(0.397)
GDP PPP per capita	0.042	0.066	-0.287*	-0.427*
	(0.041)	(0.050)	(0.167)	(0.247)
Openness	0.031***	0.031***	-0.055	-0.088*
	(0.008)	(0.011)	(0.034)	(0.050)
GDP Growth	-0.145***	-0.106**	0.396***	0.721***
	(0.026)	(0.042)	(0.153)	(0.255)
Inflation	-0.016	-0.001	-0.156	-0.336
	(0.035)	(0.047)	(0.145)	(0.281)
Time period	0.114*	0.104	-0.196	0.020
	(0.069)	(0.106)	(0.360)	(0.516)
Constant	45.204***	44.972**	-290.435***	-193.828
	(14.120)	(22.724)	(76.620)	(119.895)
Observations	48	50	50	52
# of Countries	12	14	12	14
Wald chi2	4391.254	27335.251	3066.253	7003.390
Prob>chi2	.	0.000	.	0.000
R-squared		0.903		0.955

Estimated using feasible GLS or OLS with PCSEs as indicated, country fixed effects, all models assume heteroskedastic panels and AR(1)

Standard errors in parentheses, country effects not reported

* p<.10, ** p<.05, *** p<.01

Table 4.11. Estimation of the policy impact on levels of interindustry labor mobility		
	DV=Elasticity IDV=Lag1	DV=COV of wages IDV=Lag1
Lagged Elasticity	0.611***	
	(0.064)	
Lagged COV		0.536***
		(0.173)
Health Expenditure-Lag1	0.072	1.711
	(0.107)	(1.773)
Unemployment Compensation-Lag1	0.398**	7.067*
	(0.166)	(4.132)
Labor Market Training-Lag1	-1.086**	9.981
	(0.431)	(9.215)
Subsidized Employment-Lag1	-0.732**	6.818
	(0.337)	(7.634)
Employment Service & Administration-Lag1	-1.649	7.000
	(1.183)	(25.216)
ALMP Youth Program-Lag1	-0.498	4.346
	(0.865)	(12.446)
ALMP Program for the Disabled-Lag1	0.330	5.906
	(1.186)	(14.581)
Population over 65	-1.542	62.951*
	(1.230)	(34.063)
Unemployment	-0.088**	-3.735***
	(0.034)	(1.224)
GDP PPP per capita	-0.079***	-0.647
	(0.028)	(0.458)
GDP Growth	-0.021	-0.694**
	(0.021)	(0.328)
Openness	0.007	0.219*
	(0.007)	(0.130)
Political Rights	-0.376**	1.557
	(0.151)	(2.786)
Democracy	0.457	0.987
	(0.836)	(7.404)

Table 4.11. Estimation of the policy impact on levels of interindustry labor mobility (continued)

	DV=Elasticity IDV=Lag1	DV=COV of wages IDV=Lag1
Trade Union Density	0.021	0.196
	(0.016)	(0.462)
Inflation	0.000	0.016
	(0.002)	(0.011)
Year	0.131***	-0.157
	(0.041)	(0.616)
Constant	-243.468***	-592.458
	(70.224)	(1082.090)
Observations	189	196
# of Countries	17	17
Wald chi2	6588.061	728.454
Prob>chi2	0.000	0.000
R-squared	0.872	0.517

Estimated using OLS with PCSEs, country fixed effects, all models control for heteroskedastic panels and AR(1)

Panel-corrected standard errors in parentheses, country effects not reported

* p<.10, ** p<.05, *** p<.01

Note: MA denotes moving average. For example, "Health Expenditure-MA5" means the lagged Health Expenditure averaged over the previous five years; ditto for MA3.

Table 4.12. Estimation of the policy impact on levels of interindustry labor mobility, robustness check

	DV=Elasticity IDV=MA3	DV=Elasticity IDV=MA5	DV=COV of wages IDV=MA3	DV=COV of wages IDV=MA5
Lagged Elasticity	0.610***	0.528***		
	(0.062)	(0.063)		
Lagged COV			0.914***	1.016***
			(0.104)	(0.081)
Health Expenditure-MA3	0.228**		2.024	
	(0.111)		(1.588)	
Unemployment Compensation-MA3	0.494***		2.322	
	(0.140)		(2.233)	
Labor Market Training-MA3	-1.229**		2.315	
	(0.525)		(7.636)	
Subsidized Employment-MA3	-0.082		19.071**	
	(0.400)		(8.150)	
Employment Service & Administration-MA3	-2.637*		-58.202	
	(1.549)		(37.223)	
ALMP Youth Program-MA3	-1.363		1.224	
	(1.022)		(13.437)	
ALMP Program for the Disabled-MA3	1.613		-31.299**	
	(1.350)		(12.989)	
Health Expenditure-MA5		0.440***		1.409
		(0.123)		(1.119)
Unemployment Compensation-MA5		0.513***		1.862
		(0.138)		(1.682)
Labor Market Training-MA5		-2.022***		5.634
		(0.719)		(7.921)
Subsidized Employment-MA5		0.573		10.262*
		(0.464)		(5.900)
Employment Service & Administration-MA5		-4.233**		-48.245
		(2.002)		(29.743)
ALMP Youth Program-MA5		-1.660		-2.786
		(1.319)		(10.703)
ALMP Program for the Disabled-MA5		3.375**		-22.157**
		(1.681)		(10.772)
Population over 65	-1.486	-1.496	0.188	0.174
	(1.291)	(1.388)	(1.902)	(1.421)
Unemployment	-0.083***	-0.062***	-0.603	-0.370
	(0.025)	(0.021)	(0.572)	(0.402)
GDP PPP per capita	-0.057**	-0.038	-0.534	-0.392
	(0.029)	(0.029)	(0.343)	(0.255)
GDP Growth	-0.035	-0.035*	-0.090	0.064
	(0.021)	(0.021)	(0.268)	(0.285)

Table 4.12. Estimation of the policy impact on levels of interindustry labor mobility, robustness check (continued)

	DV=Elasticity IDV=MA3	DV=Elasticity IDV=MA5	DV=COV of wages IDV=MA3	DV=COV of wages IDV=MA5
Openness	0.002	-0.004	0.024	0.023
	(0.007)	(0.007)	(0.053)	(0.040)
Political Rights	-0.345***	-0.401***	2.778	2.469
	(0.145)	(0.164)	(2.242)	(1.923)
Democracy	0.284	0.273	6.384***	4.598***
	(0.847)	(0.848)	(2.629)	(1.751)
Trade Union Density	0.013	0.013	-0.197	-0.123
	(0.016)	(0.016)	(0.184)	(0.134)
Inflation	0.000	0.000	0.015	0.012
	(0.002)	(0.001)	(0.012)	(0.011)
Year	0.105***	0.086*	0.925*	0.735***
	(0.045)	(0.048)	(0.510)	(0.369)
Constant	-190.339**	-153.542*	-1897.710*	-1507.993**
	(76.696)	(82.529)	(1041.805)	(753.904)
Observations	189	189	196	196
# of Countries	17	17	17	17
Wald chi2	2667.505	3069.487	496.774	1071.473
Prob>chi2	0.000	0.000	0.000	0.000
R-squared	0.881	0.882	0.368	0.510

Estimated using OLS with PCSEs, country fixed effects, all models control for heteroskedastic panels and AR(1)

Panel-corrected standard errors in parentheses, country effects not reported

* p<.10, ** p<.05, *** p<.01

Note: MA denotes moving average. For example, "Health Expenditure-MA5" means the lagged Health Expenditure averaged over the previous five years; ditto for MA3.

Table 4.13. Robustness tests of the policy impact on levels of interindustry labor mobility; DV= elasticity measure of labor mobility, IDV= policy variables lagged one period

	Jackknife (one obs at a time)	Jackknife (one country at a time)	Euro effect	Scandinavian effect
Lagged Elasticity	.612	.603	0.594***	0.557***
	.064	.067	(0.068)	(0.070)
Health Expenditure-Lag1	.073	.071	0.082	0.129
	.107	.111	(0.111)	(0.130)
Unempl Compensation-Lag1	.399	.386	0.460***	0.512*
	.166	.174	(0.175)	(0.276)
Labor Market Training-Lag1	-1.085	-1.091	-1.090***	-1.556***
	.432	.457	(0.441)	(0.735)
Subsidized Employment-Lag1	-.732	-.699	-0.916***	-0.325
	.337	.352	(0.348)	(0.399)
Employment Service & Administration-Lag1	-1.653	-1.667	-2.064*	-2.818***
	1.186	1.247	(1.213)	(1.419)
ALMP Youth Program-Lag1	-.500	-.479	-0.683	-0.113
	.867	.914	(0.945)	(1.367)
ALMP Program for the Disabled-Lag1	.331	.322	0.019	3.916***
	1.189	1.242	(1.185)	(1.408)
Population over 65	-1.540	-1.500	-0.990	-3.016*
	1.233	1.297	(1.326)	(1.659)
Unemployment	-.088	-.0860	-0.121***	-0.090***
	.034	.036	(0.039)	(0.042)
GDP PPP per capita	-.079	-.074	-0.098***	-0.047
	.028	.031	(0.032)	(0.030)
GDP Growth	-.021	-.021	-0.020	-0.034
	.021	.021	(0.022)	(0.023)
Openness	.007	.007	0.009	-0.000
	.007	.007	(0.007)	(0.007)
Political Rights	-.375	-.372	-0.394***	-0.539***
	.151	.159	(0.151)	(0.186)
Democracy	.325	-.756	0.462	0.506
	.866	1.165	(0.825)	(0.779)
Trade Union Density	.021	.021	0.028**	0.026
	.016	.016	(0.016)	(0.016)
Inflation	.000	6.44e-06	-0.000	0.001
	.002	.003	(0.002)	(0.002)
Year	.131	.128	0.147***	0.148***
	.041	.044	(0.047)	(0.051)
Constant	-242.166	-226.131	-282.130***	-255.713***
	70.038	72.379	(81.491)	(84.420)
Observations	189		175	157
# of Countries	17	16	17	15
R-squared			0.874	0.884

Estimated using OLS with PCSEs, country fixed effects, all models control for heteroskedastic panels and AR(1); standard errors beneath coefficients; country effects not reported

* p<.10, ** p<.05, *** p<.01

Table 4.14. Reverse causality tests on labor mobility, using FGLS

DV= Gov Partisanship (continuous)	Model R1 IDV=Elasticity	Model R3 IDV=COV of wages	Model R7 IDV=Elasticity	Model R7' IDV=COV of wages
ILM-Elasticity	-0.705		0.351	
	(2.078)		(1.355)	
ILM-COV		0.342		0.286
		(0.258)		(0.198)
Union Centralization	6.403*	5.887*	3.308	3.947*
	(3.504)	(3.313)	(2.228)	(2.132)
Population over 65	-6.892	-15.405		
	(20.648)	(21.116)		
Unemployment	0.998	1.095*		
	(0.688)	(0.655)		
GDP PPP per capita	0.438	0.641		
	(0.535)	(0.561)		
Openness	-0.081	-0.090		
	(0.205)	(0.204)		
GDP Growth	0.623	0.464		
	(0.707)	(0.704)		
Inflation	-1.302**	-1.193**		
	(0.519)	(0.526)		
Time period	-1.777	-2.013	0.933***	1.012***
	(1.279)	(1.332)	(0.236)	(0.209)
Constant	154.151	267.552	40.342***	31.847***
	(288.825)	(295.010)	(7.622)	(8.862)
Observations	123	125	227	234
# of Countries	16	16	16	16
Wald chi2	195.605	178.748	107.130	125.670
Prob>chi2	.	.	.	.

Estimated using feasible GLS, country fixed effects, all models assume heteroskedastic panels and AR(1)

Standard errors in parentheses, country effects not reported

* p<.10, ** p<.05, *** p<.01

Figure 4.1: Scatter plots of the relationship between government partisanship and ILM
Averages from 1960-1999

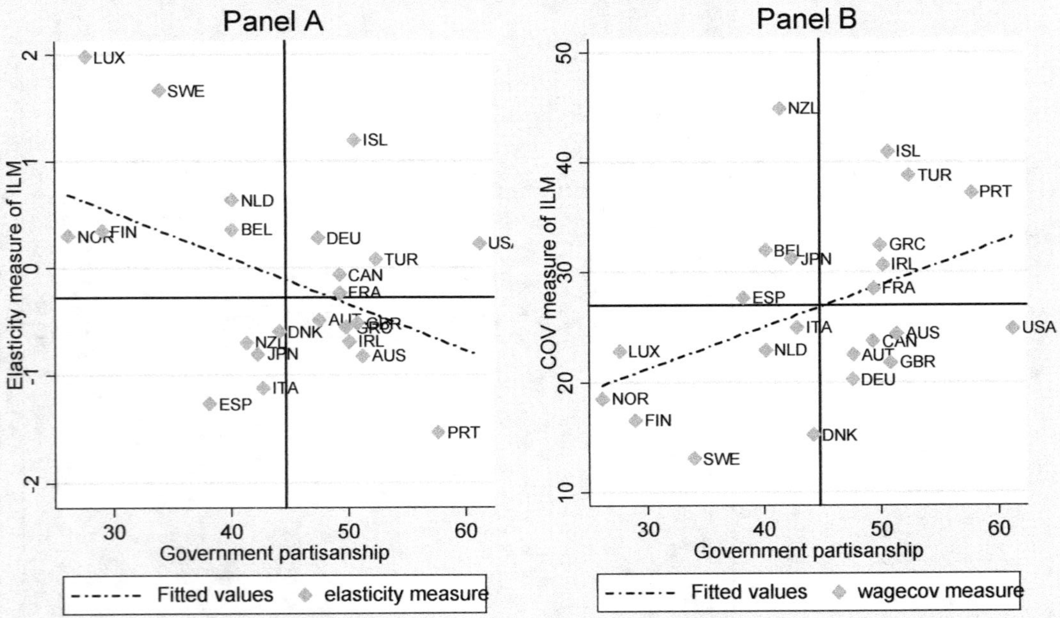

The solid lines are the mean values along the X, and Y axis

Figure 4.2: Estimated marginal partisan influence on levels of ILM Conditional on Union Centralization and using FGLS

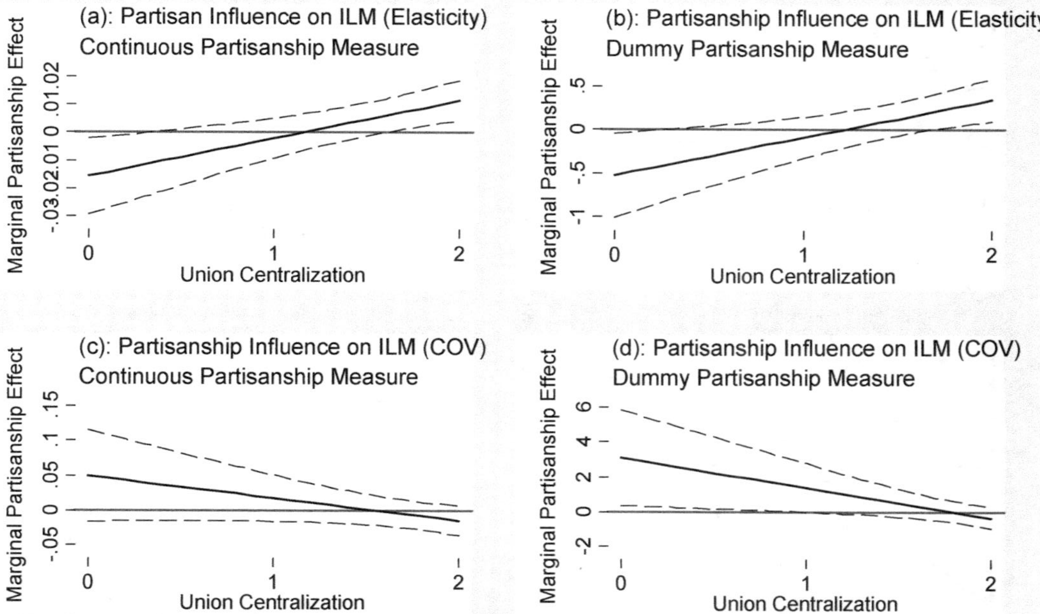

The solid lines denote estimated coefficients, dashed lines are the 95% confidence intervals

Figure 4.3: Influence of Union Centralization on ILM Levels Conditional on Various Government Partisanship

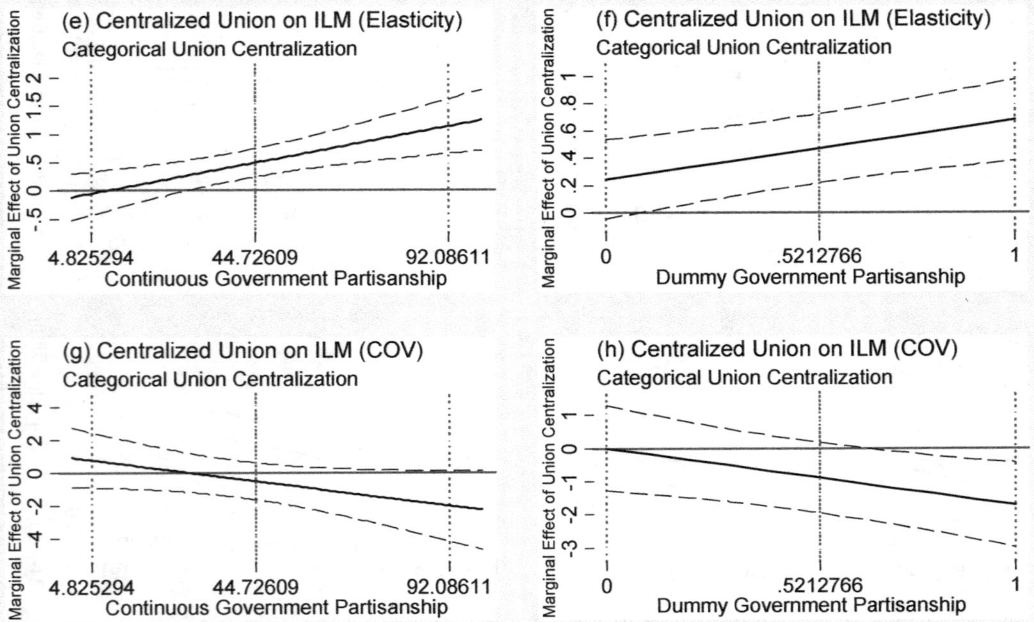

The dotted lines are the min, mean and max values of government partisanship

Figure 4.A.1. Country Specific Variance of Interindustry Labor Mobility
ILM=Elasticity

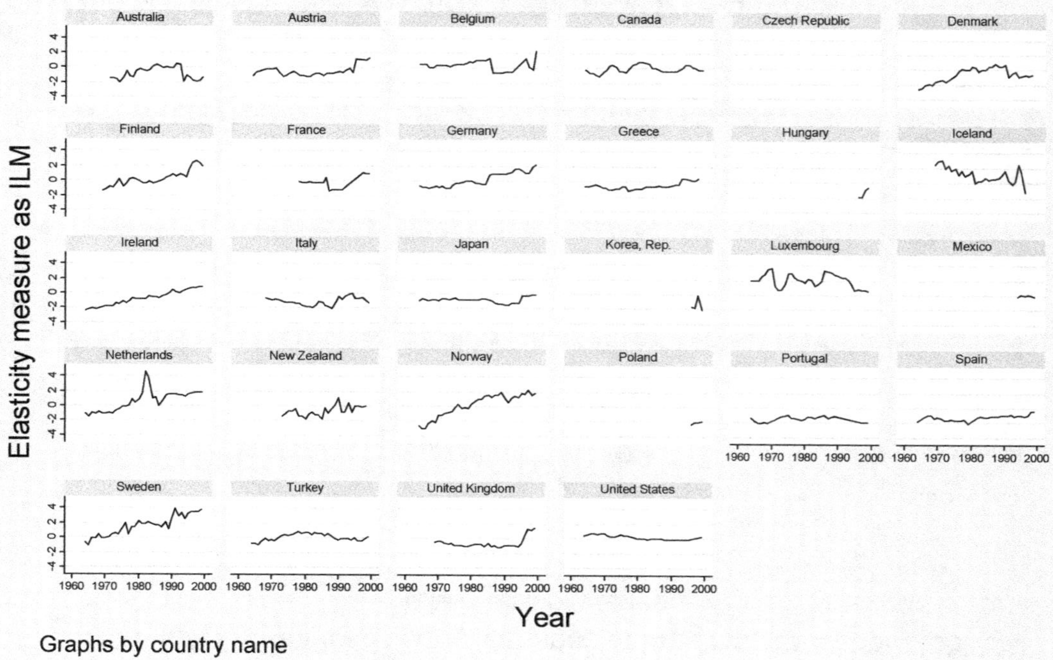

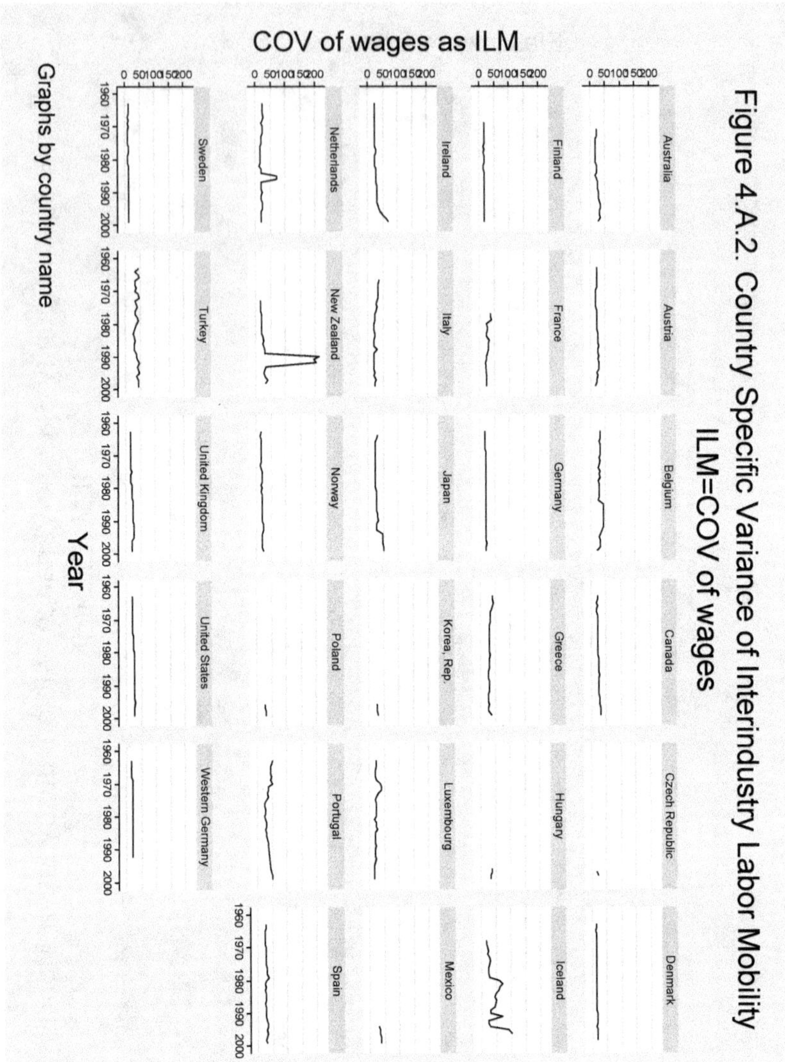

Figure 4.A.2. Country Specific Variance of Interindustry Labor Mobility
ILM=COV of wages

Figure 4.A.3. Country Specific Variance of Interindustry Labor Mobility
ILM=Compensated employment changes

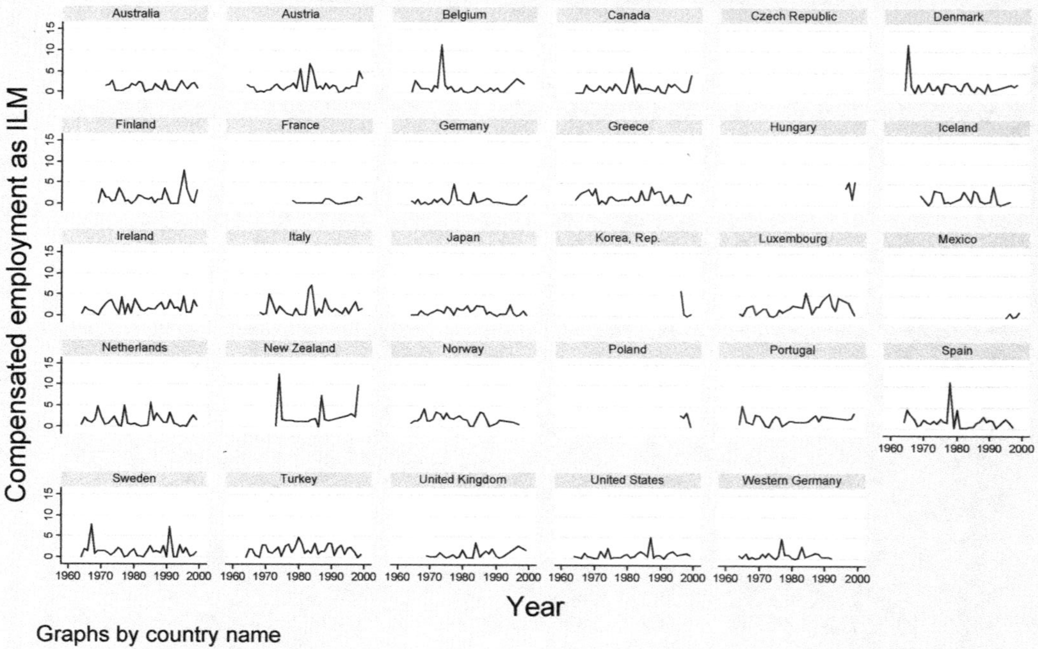

Chapter 5
A Case Study of Sweden

5.1. Theory and predictions about Sweden

Having presented the cross national time series empirical evidence, in this chapter I embark on a brief case study on Sweden to see if my theory can travel beyond the cross national setting and find support in a specific country. Sweden is the choice of country case study because first, my large N empirical analysis has shown that internationally, Sweden stands out as an archetypical country with high levels of interindustry labor mobility; second, a distinguishing feature of the Swedish political economy in the post-WWII era has been a strong labor movement coupled with long dominance of the Swedish Social Democratic Party (SAP), and for decades the labor movement and SAP had been committed to wage solidarity and pro-mobility policies. Such a context makes it particularly interesting to probe further the development within Sweden in search of the suspected causal linkage between government interventions, their interactions with centralized labor organizations, and the corresponding levels of labor mobility.

Recall that my theory argues that other things being equal and when there are low levels of domestic union centralization, ILM levels tend to be higher under the Left governments than under the Right governments; and when unions become more centralized, levels of ILM may evince different patterns depending on the partisanship of the governments. In specific for Left governments, because they want to implement labor-friendly policies and want to foster social conditions that favor the achievement of these policies, they prefer to have cohesive labor forces. Both high ILM levels and strong centralized labor unions can make labor owners across industries become more coherent within the structure of the economy; hence in a functionalist view for the sake of cohesive labor forces, the two are essentially substitutable. When union centralization is low, labor solidarity or cohesiveness will largely be shaped by the economy's ILM levels, so I expect Left governments under this situation to strongly favor high ILM level and to take policy actions for this end. When union centralization is high, however, the strong centralized labor organizations on their own can to a large extent sustain high degree of labor solidarity/cohesiveness, and Left governments will lose their direct incentives for high ILM levels; nevertheless their policy actions toward ILM levels may be similar in the effect of maintaining high levels of ILM due to the prodding from centralized unions.

Conversely for Right governments, due to their instincts to implement capital-friendly policies and to create social conditions favorable to the passage of such policies, they prefer to have cohesive capital and less cohesive labor, which low ILM levels can help bring about. When union centralization is low, various labor organizations are only loosely coordinated and effective collective actions among labor for a common political goal are hard to orchestrate, unconstrained Right governments are then more likely to implement policies that are conducive to limiting labor mobility. Highly centralized labor union, on the other hand, would most likely constitute a domestic constraint on the Right governments' pursuit of low ILM levels. As a result, for Right governments and when there exists a centralized union movement, the ILM levels tend to be significantly higher than when the "same" governments were facing a weak and loosely organized union movement.

Applying this theory to the specific case of Sweden, from the literature we know that Sweden has had the quintessential strong centralized labor union in much of its modern history and long time Social Democratic dominance in its politics, thus we should expect that for a long time after the Second World War the strong centralized labor organizations in Sweden (chiefly the LO) tend to be primarily responsible for the sustaining of high labor solidarity and that their political representatives (mainly the Swedish Social Democratic Party) tend to give deference to LO and rarely take initiatives in formulating policies that are mobility-enhancing in nature. And when the Right/bourgeois coalitions manage to wring power from the Social Democrats, they tend to be heavily constrained by both the Left coalitions in the parliament and the labor movement in society, that their attempts at manipulating labor mobility will be severely limited. The historical evidence shows that for much of the post-war period, Swedish economic policies under the Social Democrats can be described as featuring mobility-enhancing policies, and the origins of these policies can be traced to the consensus among Swedish labor unions. Furthermore, the occasional bourgeois governments in Sweden can barely challenge those policies that have mobility-enhancing implications.

5.2. Trends of ILM, government partisanship and union centralization in Sweden

Figures 5.1.A to D give us a graphical presentation of the levels of interindustry labor mobility, government partisanship and union centralization in Sweden during most of the post WWII period. Figure 5.1.A compares the levels of interindustry labor mobility measured by elasticity in Sweden with the average ILM levels in all other OECD countries. The graph shows that, comparing with its OECD counterparts, Sweden has almost always had higher labor mobility levels throughout the post WWII era. And as far as the data permit, we can also detect a rise of ILM levels from early 1960s to 1980, and a slight decline from 1980 to 1985, then a rise again from 1985 to 2000.

[Figures 5.1.A through D about here]

Using a different measure of interindustry labor mobility, in figure 5.1.B we also find ILM measured by coefficient of variations of wages are consistently higher in Sweden than in another average OECD country[43]. However, the degrees of wage dispersion in Sweden tend to be very narrow, so that COV of wages tend to be quite flat throughout the post WWII era in Sweden.

In figure 5.1.C, I plot the government partisanship in Sweden since 1945. I use two gauges of government partisanship. The first is a continuous measure computed by Kim and Fording, which is also used in the empirical analysis in previous chapter[44]. Higher values mean more Right-leaning in this Kim-Fording measure. Next, I create a simple dummy variable that equals zero if Swedish Social Democratic Party

[43] In this graph I have inversed values of COV of wages by multiplying all original COV values with "-1". This is to facilitate the graphical presentation. In the original COV of wages measure, higher values mean lower levels of ILM.

[44] For details of this measure, please consult section 4.1.1.2 in chapter 4.

was leading the governments, and equals one if the non-socialist coalitions were in charge of the governments. The two measures corroborate each other well, and we can easily tell that for most of the post WWII era, Social Democrats were dominant in Swedish politics.

Figure 5.1.D shows the degrees of union centralization in Sweden since 1950. I first use the Golden, Lange and Wallerstein measure of union centralization, which is the same measure I used in empirical analysis before. This measure shows that from 1950 to 1955, Swedish union centralization had fluctuate between highly centralized and moderately centralized, but from 1955 to 1982 union centralization in Sweden had been highly centralized, and from 1983 to 2000 union centralization in Sweden again fluctuated between highly centralized and moderately centralized. This development of union centralization in Sweden was corroborated using another measure by Kenworthy on the wage setting coordination (Kenworthy 2001). The scores of wage setting coordination according to Kenworthy are similar to the Golden, Lange and Wallerstein measure, with higher values denoting higher degree of centralized wage bargaining. The only difference between the two measures for the case of Sweden is that according to Kenworthy measure, highly centralized wage bargaining never returned to Sweden after 1983.

5.3. From the end of WWII to the Golden Age of the Rehn-Meidner model

As has been shown, in most of the post-WWII period, Swedish politics has been dominated by the Swedish Social Democratic Party, SAP, so much so that the SAP has led the government for 65 of the 76 years since 1932; the 2006 election ended its most recent term of 12 consecutive years in office (USDOS 2008). The Swedish Social Democrats have historically had close ties with the Swedish Trade Union Confederation, commonly known as LO, which represents blue-collar workers in private as well as public sectors.

To give some institutional context in Sweden, currently there are three major trade union confederations in Sweden, ranking from the biggest, these are the Swedish Trade Union Confederation (*Landsorganisationen i Sverige* or *LO*), the Swedish Confederation of Professional Employees

(*Tjänstemännens Centralorganisation* or *TCO*), and the Swedish Confederation of Professional Associations (*Sveriges Akademikers Centralorganisation* or *SACO*). LO is the most influential in the Swedish labor movement. This is an umbrella organization or a national trade union center for 15 affiliated unions (as of 2007) for blue-collar workers covering all of the labor market. In 2006, its total membership was over 1.8 millions, compared with TCO's 1.3 millions and SACO's 0.58 million (LO 2007), and to put this in some perspective, the population in Sweden as of 2007 is about 9 millions (SAP 2007). Historically, LO had been the consummation of the labor movement in Sweden. In the 1950s for example, the total number of wage and salary earners in Sweden eligible for trade union membership is slightly over 2 millions, and LO had about 1.3 million members in 40 affiliated industrial unions (LO 1953). LO has also maintained friendly relationship and cooperation at various levels with the other major labor organizations. More significantly, LO has had deep links with the Swedish social democratic party. When the Swedish Social Democratic Party was founded in 1889, the trade unionists were in the majority. And when in 1898 the LO was founded by members of social democratic party, it was expressly stated that trade unionists expected the social democratic party to look after their political interests in Parliament (LO 1953). LO members have been the core electoral support base for the Swedish Social Democratic Party, as SAP readily acknowledges. The LO president is always in the 7-member SAP party executive committee; and at regional and local level, LO members hold positions as members of SAP and have considerable influence (LO 2007; SAP 2007). By contrast, the other two major labor organizations, TCO and SACO, do not have official connections with any political parties in Sweden. As of mid-1980s, about 40 percent of LO members belong to the Social Democratic Party through their local unions, and such collective affiliation accounts for more than two-thirds of the total Social Democratic membership (Heclo and Madsen 1987).

From the end of the WWII to the end of the 1950s Swedish fiscal policy was countercyclical, so too was monetary policy from the mid-1950s, but with a tendency to expansionism (Erixon 2008). In a variety of occasions, there had been growing discontent with Swedish economic policies, even within the LO, such as toward the consecutive freezing of wages in 1949 and 1950, and the 1949 Swedish devaluation of krona. Two trade union economists – Gosta Rehn and Rudolf Meidner – developed an alternative to the Keynesian post-war model. Rudolf Meidner was the head of LO's research department 1946-1966 and Gosta Rehn the department's leading macroeconomist 1941-1952. The Rehn-Meidner model involves the wage policy of solidarity to achieve wage stability and structural change, restrictive fiscal policy and active labor market policy to reduce overall profits and promote labor mobility. It seeks to combine full employment with fair wages, price stability and high economic growth (Erixon 2008). The Rehn-Meidner program was presented in the 1951 report to the Congress of LO (LO 1953).

From late 1950s to early 1970s was the Golden Age for Rehn-Meidner model in Sweden, as the ideas and policies advocated in the Rehn-Meidner program were largely incorporated into economic policy making by the Social Democrats; among the most significant proponents of the Rehn-Meidner model was the Minister of Finance Gunnar Strang, whom Rehn praised for having met the tendency toward increased unemployment with an active labor market policy and not with an expansionary fiscal policy (Erixon 2008, pp.14-15). But the main reason for the breakthrough of Rehn-Meidner model in Sweden would have to do with the strong position of LO in Swedish politics, its economists, and LO's influence in the discourse of economic policy-making.

During this period, the typical Swedish way of dealing with industrial relations was through centralized bargaining between labor and employer's confederations, with the possibility of government interventions in case of failure to reach agreement. The main counterpart to LO on the employers side is the Confederation of Swedish Enterprise (SAF). Through a variety of channels and contacts, the two organizations sought to settle on an aggregate wage rate figure that did not threaten the foreign markets for Swedish goods and that were also compatible with the government's economic policy. Once the LO-SAF settlement was in sight, the white-collar employees who were primarily in trades that were sheltered from foreign competition began their bargaining with employers, and their negotiations were guided by the pending LO-SAF agreements (Heclo and Madsen 1987, pp.118-119). It was against this broad institutional backdrop that the Rehn-Meidner plan must operate.

One of the chief instruments of the expansion of Swedish labor market policy has been the National Labor Market Board (AMS), which administers many of the active labor market policies advocated in the Rehn-Meidner program that have implications for vocational mobility, such as matching (labor market information, geographical mobility and investigation costs), training (labor market education), job creation (youth teams, in-plant training to avoid lay-offs, trainee replacement scheme, relief work and trainee programs, etc.), and programs for disabled persons (special work-adjustment measures, vocational rehabilitation and public sheltered work) (Erixon 2008, pp.74-75). Figure 5.2 shows the amount spent by AMS and its affiliates on several active labor market policies as well as the total expenditure on these labor market policies as a share of GDP. One impression from this graph is that during the Golden Age of Rehn-Meidner model, total expenditure on labor market programs had been rising up to 1973 when the First Oil Crisis hit the world economy; spending on the component labor market policies was typically increasing over time, especially for policies that target labor supply and adjustment, which is the sum of spending on matching and training.

[Figure 5.2 about here]

To better achieve LO's underlying goal of full employment, Rehn-Meidner model argued for the principle of wage solidarity, that is, equal work across industries should receive equal pay, any wage differentials must be justified by the degrees of difficulty of the work, the nature and contents of the work, whether considerable training is required, whether it involves the risk of accidents, insecurity of tenure, seasonal unemployment, etc.; and wage differentials should not be based on various profitableness of firms and industries. Such principle can be summarized in the phrase of "equal pay for equal work", as has been used in (Hibbs and Locking 2000). The proposed wage solidarity policy should necessarily ensure that wages in the low paid industries would rise, which would put pressure on the firms in these industries to rationalize and adopt labor-saving technologies. And if the firms and the industries cannot keep up with the rationalization pressure, they should go to the other trades altogether or go under, unless the State provide these industries with subsidies for national defense seasons. There would be employers who may be able to pass the wage increases into prices or for other reasons able to afford wage increases to their workers, but if these wage leaders were easily granted their wishes, there would be a lack of uniformity in wage developments that tended to lead to general rate of increase in wages exceeding what the increase in productivity would warrant, and consequently to destroy the price stability. To curb such uncoordinated wage increases, Rehn-Meidner model argued that the maintenance of full employment would be the necessary condition to implement the wage solidarity policies, and at the same time the retention of low profit margins would also be a necessary condition to allow the increase of wages to be slow enough so as not to cause a steady rise in prices (LO 1953, pp.94-99).

The SAF saw distinct advantage in the harmonization of wage settlements; the few big employers that constitute the core of SAF leadership were also big exporters, hence a policy of wage restraint and wage solidarity helped their international competitiveness (Heclo and Madsen 1987). For this reason SAF was not particularly critical of wage solidarity and centralized bargaining during this period.

Inspired by the Rehn-Meidner model, Swedish governments put in place a set of active labor market policies to help the workers adjust with the transitions, such policies can be divided into four main groups:

(1) Forecasting, and planning measures against unemployment, e.g. the collection and working up of statistics and planning suitable work projects.

(2) Unemployment insurance and unemployment relief.

(3) Measures to create employment, e.g. emergency works, the placing of orders with firms experiencing employment difficulties to enable them to maintain production during a difficult period, and the provision of work for handicapped workers.

(4) Measures to stimulate geographical mobility, through the labor exchanges, including the granting of removal and family allowances, starting allowances, and various financial inducements to increased geographical mobility; and

occupational mobility, through vocational training, further training and re-training.

These labor market policies are the central part of the whole framework of Swedish economic policies in this period, which also consisted of international trade, credit, and tax policies (LO 1963). Those mobility-enhancing labor market policies had the effect of counteracting the sector-based labor resistance to restructuring and adjustment, a case in point was about the protectionist-leaning textile workers: having experienced a boom in the 1930s, the textile industry in Sweden was facing the need to adjust in the late 1950s, and after some soul-searching, the textile workers chose to retrain for better employment elsewhere rather than to preserve their declining and underpaid industry (Magnusson 2000; Milner 1989).

The success of Rehn-Meidner model contributed to a favorable macroeconomic outcome of economic stability, full employment, rising standard of living and low budget deficits in Sweden. The Swedish economy, however, was severely affected by the global economic downturns triggered by the Oil Crisis in 1973, and for the first time since the landmark election of 1932, Social Democrats lost control of government in 1976.

5.4. First Social Democratic loss of power from 1976 to 1982

The first loss of power for the SAP in many decades might be due in no small part to a controversial Meidner plan of 1975, which proposed to divert a proportion of the profits of each company to purchase shares that would be owned by a union-managed fund. Over many years, ownership would pass into the hands of that fund, which would use the ownership collectively, in trust for the work force. As an indirect nationalization plan in a different guise, the Meidner plan of 1975 provoked antagonism among business groups and white-collar unions and helped bring together an electoral majority among the bourgeois coalitions in Sweden: the Conservatives (with the name of Moderate Party), Liberals and Center Party (Gourevitch 1986; Hiscox 2002).

Not coincident with this development was the shift to what Hibbs and Locking called the Phase II solidarity wage policy, which transformed the idea of "equal pay for equal work" to "equal pay for all work" (Hibbs and Locking 2000, p762). Both the LO and other private white-collar unions led the push for equality, which was marked by a concerted drive to improve the relative wages of the low paid and which was reflected in the distributional profiles of the central wage agreements negotiated by LO with SAF (Hibbs and Locking 1996). Contrast to Phase I solidarity policy that was associated with compressions of wage differentials between industries and plants, Phase II policy promoted dramatic leveling of relative wages within plants and industries and across occupations and skills grades. Such radicalization of union wage policy prompted the SAF to abandon its historical support of central bargaining and to launch campaigns to dismantle such a system (Hibbs and Locking 2000, p763). The Meidner plan of 1975 could be deemed as the consummation of the wage equality drive that contributed to the first government turnover in many decades in Sweden.

But the non-socialist three-party coalition faced political constraints that the government could neither alter nor escape, that the coalition could make little economic policy change when they were in power from 1976 to 1982 (Heclo and Madsen 1987). First of all, the three-party coalition had to struggle to maintain coalition unity to make any government action, with Center Party representing rural and small business interests, the Conservatives representing larger business interests and the Liberals representing middle-class with a mix of concerns, it was very difficult for the coalition to achieve any clear sense of economic priorities; and the safest course was to try to give a little something to everyone. Secondly, the bourgeois coalition came to power with a general commitment to reduce taxes and other claims on industry, and to reduce governmental presence in business decisions, so it became very awkward for the government to play a big role in typical Swedish agreements between labor and capital that imposed costs on employers in return for wage restraints and other tax adjustments. But the third and most important constraint on the non-socialist coalition came from the Social Democrats and the union movement. For two generations preceding 1976, the SAP and union movement had warned the public about the dismantling of social commitments if a bourgeois government came to power; the post-1976 governments of the Right were under immense pressure to prove such a prediction wrong (Heclo and Madsen 1987).

The bourgeois governments accepted the upward momentum of public spending, business subsidies and labor market programs to try to contain the increase of unemployment, which in traditionally full employment Sweden was a politically explosive issue. A good part of the bourgeois governments' calculation to continue the social policy spending was their prediction that global economy would improve soon, but the economic upswing the governments had hoped for did not materialize; instead, Sweden's economy by the early 1980s seemed to be drifting toward permanent decline. In the face of growing public sense of crisis the bourgeois governments began to take a more aggressively conservative stance and proposed modest restraints in social policy spending, such as cutting food subsidies, reintroducing unpaid sick days, and cutting grants to local governments. Yet these measures were quite unpopular. Politically the governments also could not avoid the spending on labor market programs (Heclo and Madsen 1987). The miserable record of Swedish economy combined with growing discontent with the government among the union movement and in the public led to the non-socialist parties' electoral defeat in 1982.

5.5. Adjustment of Social Democratic economic policies in the 1980s

Within the Social Democrats, the feelings were originally that the election loss in 1976 was a temporary aberration that would be corrected when voters experienced the failures of the bourgeois government. Yet the 1979 election loss shocked the Social Democrats into searching for a new economic program[45]. Young economists within the Social Democratic Party, led by Kjell-Olof Feldt, began to advocate an economic program that would hold back both private and public consumption in order to increase investment in internationally competitive sectors of Swedish economy. When Social Democrats won the 1982

[45] Many factors may have contributed to the Social Democratic loss in 1979, including for example the unconstructive way the Social Democrats appealed to voters as an opposition party in 1979, and importantly the issue of developing nuclear energy in Sweden to cope with the 1979 Oil Crisis and the nuclear referendum. For more, see (Heclo and Madsen 1987).

election and formed a government under Olof Palme, Feldt became the finance minister. The Social Democratic government put much of the new economic program into actions. It imposed several budget constraints to hold back public spending, such as greatly reducing subsidies to declining industries such as textiles, announcing a freeze of any new major social reforms, and closing of many inefficient plants; it also implemented a sudden and drastic devaluation of krona by 16 percent. All these measures would be beyond the wildest imagination of the nonsocialist governments had not the labor movement come along (albeit reluctantly) with the Social Democrats. Leading LO officials complained that it was difficult to distinguish the new government's policies from the standard bourgeois agenda (Heclo and Madsen 1987). Nevertheless, these measures helped the Swedish economy, which was also aided by favorable improvement of the global economy, to rebound and grow robustly; and Social Democrats won elections in 1985 and 1988.

A seismic change of Swedish industrial relations happened in 1983 when the historical centralized wage bargaining in Sweden underwent a dramatic transformation. It formally broke when the employer's association for engineering and fabricated metals negotiated separate wage agreements with labor unions in metal industry. The 1983 metal industry agreement provided for much wider wage differentials, and it did not contain the earnings guarantee as in previous agreements that contributed to wage leveling within industries or plants (Heclo and Madsen 1987; Hibbs and Locking 2000). Wider interindustry wage differentials were also tolerated, as the remaining negotiations proceeded from the precedent of the metal industry contract. Since then, the Swedish centralized wage bargaining was replaced by a system of sector-based bargaining.

The dissolution of central bargaining in Sweden may due in no small part to the increasing tension between the private workers unions (especially the blue-collar unions) and the public employees unions. Over the previous decades, economic growth and increasing political clout of the public sector unions made them more inclined to deviate from the LO-SAF agreement framework and to often propose positions that undercut such wage settlements. This is particularly evident in the first labor crisis in Sweden from the fall of 1979 to 1980. In the midst of the 1979 Oil Crisis, the LO and SAF were engaged in hard negotiations of the wage agreement and a central bargaining resulting in an "SAF's zero offer", where the previous wage agreement would simply be extended one more year, was about to emerge. At the same time, the public employee unions entered a new collaborative arrangement and demanded for a 12 percent raise, defying the pleadings from LO's chairman. LO and other union confederations had to follow suit, but the episode reflected the deep division of the interests between public-sector unions and LO. When in 1983, after the new LO chairman was chosen from the metal industries union, Metall, the new wage norm of sector-based bargaining with leading industrial unions as the benchmark setters emerged and was tacitly supported by LO's industrial unions, SAF, and the Social Democratic government, and the public employment unions were not in a position to challenge it (Heclo and Madsen 1987).

Following the decentralization of wage bargaining in Sweden, the prevailing principle transformed yet again to "different pay for different work", with extra compensation for the high skilled and wage formation process beginning to be shaped by earnings based on company profitability. Hibbs and Locking reported finding higher variance of relative wages among LO-SAF workers since 1983 (Hibbs and Locking 2000). In figure 5.1.B we can also notice the downward tilt of inversed interindustry wage differentials in Sweden since the early 1980s.

5.6. Sweden in the 1990s

By 1990, after a decade of struggle, the SAF dismantled its central bargaining unit and subsequently withdrew from central boards of various manpower programs. SAF's chairman, Ulf Laurin, declared that "The course for our wage policy is totally clear. It is focused upon decentralization – with the intent of providing a dominant role for firm level bargaining" (Wood 2001). The splits between trade unions, especially between the public and private sector unions, were wider than before. Decades of expanding the public consumption have given rise to a large public sector and its employees, whose wage increases are contractual and may not be in sync with global economic fluctuations as the wages increases in private sectors usually do. Meanwhile, labor unions in the export-oriented engineering industries had grown increasingly discontent with centralized wage bargaining (Hiscox 2002). As union demands become more diversified, it becomes harder for the social democratic party to represent a "generalized working-class interest" (Kitschelt 1994). At the same time, the once very low level of unemployment rate in Sweden began to rise quickly in the 1990s, it rose from 1.6 percent in 1989 to 9.3 percent in 1993, and stayed high ever since.

After the 1991 election, a four-party minority center-right coalition under Carl Bildt came to power. The minority government was severely hampered by internal divisions, yet it was able to enact some budget cuts and moderate reforms. The government cut sick pay compensation and work injury pay in 1991 and 1992. Between 1993 and 1995 the unemployment benefit replacement rate was reduced from 90 to 75 percent, and a five-day period of uncompensated unemployment was introduced. Absenteeism was effectively attacked by varying sickness benefit rates and making employers financially responsible for the first few weeks of an employee's absence from work. Compensation to participants of ALMP programs was linked to unemployment benefit replacement rates, rather than to market wages as it had been since 1933 (Wood 2001). Compared with the previous bourgeois governments, the nonsocialist coalition from 1991 to 1994 was helped by the weakening of LO/SAF consensus and the decline of union centralization. As the argument in this study would predict, highly centralized union movement can exert strong restraints on the Right-leaning governments while less centralized labor movement may invite interventions from the Right governments for the sake of disrupting the labor cohesiveness and lowering levels of interindustry labor mobility. In the case of Sweden, given the empirically established positive relationship between unemployment compensation and ILM levels, it would be no surprising that the Right governments in Sweden during this period chose to embark on cutting unemployment benefits.

Such welfare retrenchment initiated by the Conservative government was put to a stop after the SAP under Ingvar Carlsson returned to power in 1994. Social Democratic government proposed "Halving Unemployment" program and returned the unemployment benefit replacement rates to 80 percent of wages (Wood 2001), opposite to what governments on the Right would do. The Social Democrats responded to the newfound problem of unemployment in three ways. First, they restructured the active labor market programs (ALMP), including introducing two new programs of "Youth Practice Placement" and "Working Life Development Projects" on far less generous terms than their predecessor programs. Second, job search activity has been refocused towards constructing individual strategies for re-employment, rather than mass loading on to state training schemes. Third, the widening gap between rates of unemployment among workers of different skill levels has led the government to emphasize formal education more and ALMP less, so the state has been reducing its role in vocational training for the unemployed, and increasing its role in education for the pre-employed (Wood 2001). As far as the erosion of collective wage bargaining is concerned, despite the seemingly neoliberal rhetoric of SAF, Swedish employers remained committed to institutions of collective bargaining, although the location of such institutions moved from national to sectoral level, with Metall often playing the role of leader in wage negotiations. This pattern can be seen from figure 5.1.D, where the degree of Swedish union centralization since mid-1980s has decidedly moved away from very high centralization to moderate centralization.

5.7. Discussion and conclusion

The evolvement of interindustry labor mobility levels, government partisanship, and degrees of labor union centralization in Sweden from the Second World War to the turn of the century generally follows the predictions based on the theory I had proposed earlier. Early in this period, Swedish economy was still recovering from the turmoil of World War II, the governing Social Democratic Party readily accepted the labor union backed Rehn-Meidner model and among other things implemented the wage solidarity policies and a host of active labor market policies aimed at increasing the labor mobility levels. The result was the increasing labor mobility during this so-called Golden Age of Rehn-Meidner model up to early 1970s.

When economic crisis of the early 1970s helped bring non-socialist governments in Sweden, Swedish union centralization had become quite advanced, consequently the Right governments tended to have very limited room for maneuver and they had to submit to the constraints imposed by the strong union movement and its usual companion of strong Left legislative opposition. In terms of interindustry labor mobility manipulations, these Right governments were under pressure to not do what they would like to do, which was to cut spending on labor market intervention policies and to reduce social commitments in general. Figure 5.1.A shows that there was even a rebound of levels of labor mobility during the tenure of Right governments from 1976 to 1982.

The rest of the 1980s saw the Social Democrats in power again, and this generation of Social Democratic leaders was reform-minded and was open to adjustment of the Rehn-Meidner model. Coupled with incipient and concomitant declining of centralized union movement, the policy-making of the Social Democratic governments at this time may appear somewhat inconsistent. They scaled back the overall social commitments, as shown in figure 5.2 by the declining percent of GDP devoted to active labor market policies, and the spending for job creation was slashed. However, they kept investing more on the programs for the disabled, and more relevantly, continually increased the spending on services related to labor supply and adjustment, which may be more directly linked to labor mobility. The levels of interindustry labor mobility throughout this period continued to be high, as figure 5.1.A and B show, but with a slight downward trend. Interestingly, from figure 5.1.A, we can see an upward tick of labor mobility just before 1991, an election year in Sweden, as if the Left government was propping up labor mobility levels in preparation for the upcoming election.

Since the mid-1980s and throughout the 1990s, the degree of union centralization in Sweden has been in decline, as the location of collective wage bargaining gradually shifted from national level to sector level. As the theory argues, less centralized labor unions may not have sufficient sanction power or coordinating capacity to orchestrate effective collective actions among various unions to constrain the government. We can observe that when from 1991 to 1994 the non-socialist coalitions formed the government; the government was more assertive compared with the 1976-82 period; despite the internal divisions, the government attacked labor market programs that might have mobility-enhancing implications as much as they could and where politically feasible. Figure 5.2 shows that starting from services on labor supply and adjustment and the programs for the disabled, government social spending declined during the tenure of the non-socialist government, and the decline spread to job creation programs and overall spending on active labor policies later in the term of this Right government. And from figure 5.1.A in particular, we can discern a sharp drop of labor mobility levels coinciding with the tenure of the Right government.

Labor mobility levels started rising again later in the 1990s, as shown in figure 5.1.A, which roughly follows the change of government partisanship back to the Social Democratic. The pattern conforms to the theoretical prediction, because when the locus of collective wage bargaining in Sweden has moved from national toward sector level, Left governments are expected to compensate for the loss of labor cohesiveness from highly centralized unions through the pursuit of higher labor mobility levels. Increasing the resources available to unemployment benefits and labor supply and adjustment services can be the effective instruments for Swedish Social Democrats; figure 5.2 shows that spending on labor supply and adjustment services as well as on the programs for the disabled increased during the late 1990s, even against the backdrop of declining share in the GDP of overall expenditure on active labor market policies.

Figure 5.1.A. Swedish Labor Mobility from 1963 to 2000
Using Elasticity as ILM measure

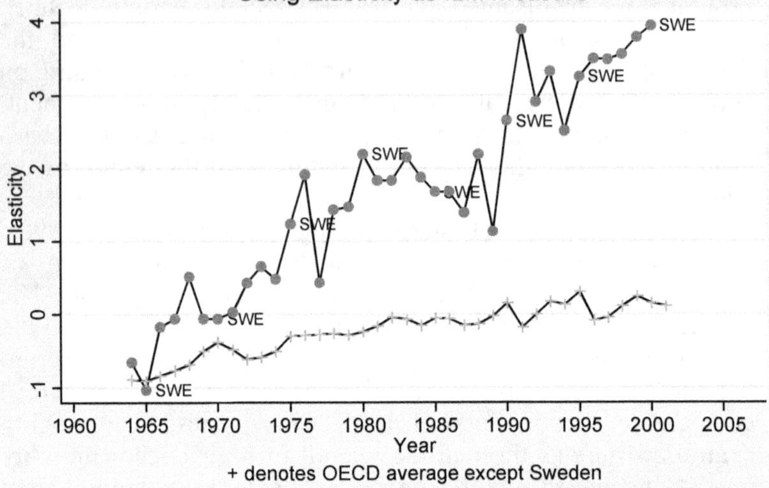

Figure 5.1.B. Swedish Labor Mobility from 1963 to 2000
Using COV of Wages as ILM measure

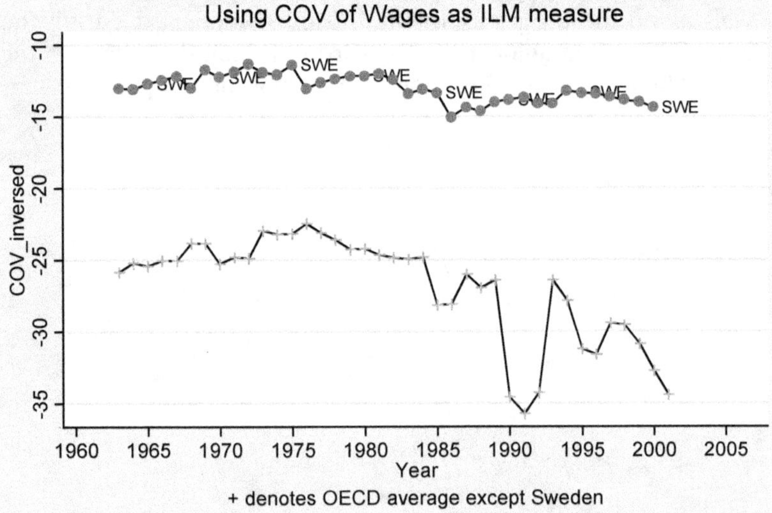

Figure 5.1.C. Swedish Government Partisanship since 1945

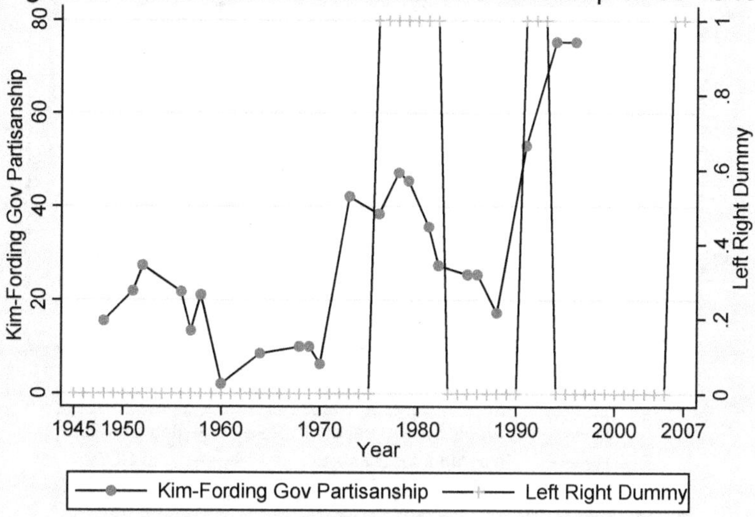

Figure 5.1.D. Swedish Union Centralization since 1950

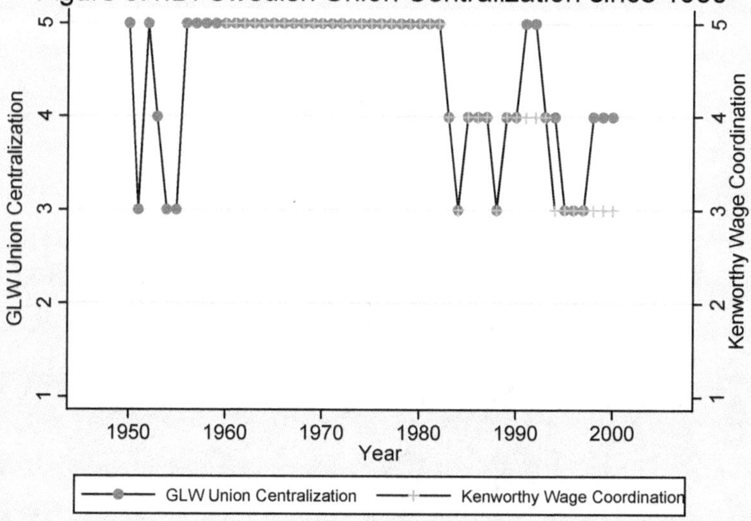

Figure 5.2. Expenditures by National Labor Market Board (AMS) and its Affiliates on Various Active Labor Policies in Sweden

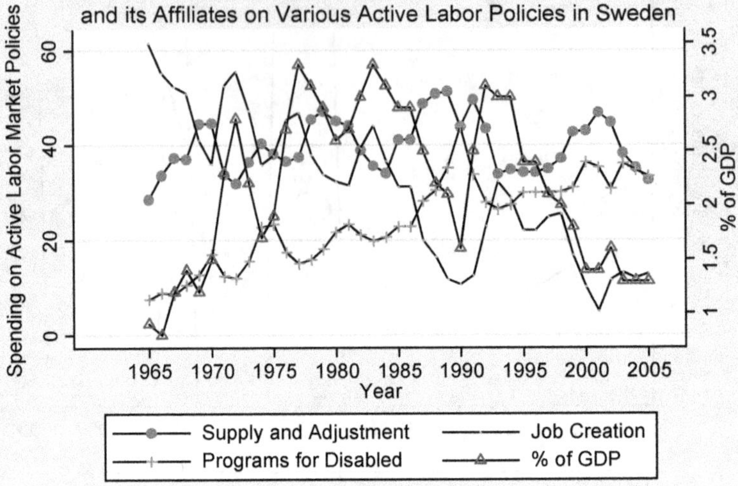

Data from Erixon 2008, table 1

Chapter 6
A Case Study of the United States

6.1. Theory and predictions about US

After the discussions about Sweden, whose welfare state provision is well above the average internationally, whose centralized union movement is the epitome of what a strong labor movement should look like, and whose Social Democratic dominance has been extraordinary, it is interesting to see how the theoretical predictions will travel in another country with less expansive state welfare provision, less centralized labor movement, and with more regular partisanship shifts in the governments. The United States is a good choice for such a comparison. First, although there have been numerous studies on the US and this one surely benefits from them, there exists little research on the US linking its partisan politics with the underlying (and changing) levels of interindustry labor mobility. This study can make a modest contribution in this respect. Second, the US contrasts neatly with Sweden. Welfare program provisions are often lagging in the US compared with other OECD countries; union movement has never been strong in the US and has been declining further in the past decades, according to some accounts (Golden et al. 2006; Golden and Pontusson 1992; Kenworthy 2001); and judged by the control of Presidency, in the post WWII era partisanship in the US shifts between Left-leaning Democratic and Right-leaning Republican rather regularly. For example, in a study on the politics of adjustment assistance in the US, Burgoon and Hiscox described that, "Since the 1950s, Sweden has provided one of the deepest and broadest adjustment assistance efforts, while U.S. policies have provided perhaps the shallowest and most specific assistance (Burgoon and Hiscox 2000)." Finally and needless to emphasize more, as the most powerful state in the current international system, study of the US labor market and the relationship between government partisanship and economy-wide labor mobility levels in the US can be important in its own sake.

My theoretical argument is that Left governments generally prefer and pursue higher levels of interindustry labor mobility than Right governments, and such partisan bias toward labor mobility is mediated by the domestic development of union movement. Both Left and Right governments prefer to have friendly and internally cohesive constituencies in order to facilitate the implementation of their favored policies. On one hand, higher levels of interindustry labor mobility can give rise to a working class that is more economically solidified, while at the same time lead to a business class with more diverging economic interests. On the other hand, more centralized labor union movement also facilitates the coordination among labor groups and helps increase the cohesiveness among working class, thus may be a functional substitute for high labor mobility levels in terms of their effect on working class solidarity. More centralized labor movement may also act as organizational constraint on the behavior of the Right governments. So I expect to observe diverging patterns when partisan governments confront either a centralized or a less centralized labor union movement. When there are low levels of union centralization, Left governments tend to have strong incentive to prefer a high level of interindustry labor mobility and Right governments are expected to prefer a low level of labor mobility, so that the labor mobility levels associated with Left governments will be significantly higher than the levels associated with Right governments. And when there are higher levels of union centralization, the incentive for Left governments to prefer high labor mobility levels diminishes while the constraint on Right governments increases when it comes to policy interventions that may have labor mobility implications, hence observationally we may not discern a clear pattern of different partisan governments being associated with different levels of labor mobility.

The political economy literature on the US indicates the US fits the scenario when the union centralization is low for most of the post WWII era. The theoretical expectations for the US would generally be that there would be significant partisan divergence in the governments' attitude toward labor mobility, Left-leaning Democratic governments are expected to favor higher levels of labor mobility than the Right-leaning Republican governments, and we should consequently expect to observe policy manipulations by different governments in order to influence labor mobility levels.

6.2. Trends of ILM, partisanship and union centralization in the US

Parallel to the discussions about Sweden, I first present graphically the trends of labor mobility, partisanship and union centralization in the US. Figures 6.1.A and B show the levels of interindustry labor mobility in the US from early 1960s to 2000 using two measures of interindustry labor mobility. Using elasticity to measure mobility, figure 6.1.A plots the trend of labor mobility in the US against the average of OECD countries except the US. The graph shows that labor mobility in the US has generally been declining since the early 1960s, but with periodical fluctuations over time; this is in contrast to the rest of OECD countries, where the average labor mobility levels have generally been rising throughout the same period. Using coefficient of variation among wages to measure mobility[46], figure 6.1.B shows the same trend for the US, that labor mobility levels in the US have been declining since the early 1960s, but the periodical fluctuations of labor mobility levels are not as manifest as using the elasticity measure; for the rest of OECD countries, labor mobility as measured by COV of wages had remained relatively stable up to mid-1980s, but have since taken some dramatic swings during the 1990s. As a general impression from these two graphs, US tended to have higher labor mobility levels than the rest of OECD before the late 1970s but tended to have lower ILM levels than the rest of OECD since the late 1970s.

[Figures 6.1.A through D about here]

In terms of the dominant partisanship, the US experienced rather regular oscillations; this is shown in figure 6.1.C using two measures of partisanship. First, I use a continuous measure of dominant partisanship, and to ensure comparison, the measure also came from Kim and Fording[47]. Since they didn't measure the government partisanship in the US directly, I use

---

46 To reiterate how the graph got drawn, in this graph I have inversed values of COV of wages by multiplying all original COV values with "-1" in order to facilitate the visual presentation. In the original COV of wages measure, higher values mean lower levels of ILM.

47 Again for details of this measure, please consult section 4.1.1.2 in chapter 4.

their measure of the median voter ideology published in *Mapping Policy Preferences* in substitute of the dominant partisanship in the US (Kim and Fording 2001). Likewise, higher values mean more Right-leaning. Second, I generate a dummy variable that equals zero if there was a Democratic President, and equals one if there was a Republican President. As can be seen from figure 6.1.C, these two measures of dominant partisanship in the US corroborate with each other very well during the post WWII era.

Finally, figure 6.1.D presents the levels of union centralization in the US since 1950. It is quite obvious using both the Golden, Lange and Wallerstein measure of union centralization and the Kenworthy measure of the wage setting coordination that labor unions in the US have remained fragmented throughout the post WWII era. The only aberration happened in 1972-73 when there was a spike of centralization using both measures, that is because the U.S. briefly imposed wage-price controls accompanied by a peace clause – a form of state-imposed coordination (Kenworthy 2001)[48].

Equipped with some basic predictions, let me now turn to a recount of post WWII interactions among various political forces in the US and between them and the important labor and business groups, and what those can tell us about the validity of the predictions.

6.3. A brief legislative history of the US labor market policies since 1945

Since I have shown that levels of interindustry labor mobility can be susceptible to labor market interventions by the governments, it seems pertinent to focus on the politics of labor market policies in the United States.

By the end of the Second World War, Democrats had managed job creation during the depression and production during the war, and they were confident that they could eliminate peacetime unemployment. The 1944 Democratic Party platform proposed to "guarantee full employment". The Democrats introduced the Murray-Wagner Full Employment Act in the Senate on January 22, 1945. Initially labor had split

[48] Internationally, Canada experienced the same spike in union centralization score from 1976-78 for the same reason.

opinions toward this bill. The Congress of Industrial Organizations (CIO) supported it while the American Federation of Labor (AFL) opposed it due to their different agendas toward social rights and passive labor market policies[49]. Despite the initial differences, labor leaders testified in support of the bill and supplied amendments. Employers were opposed to this bill. The National Association of Manufacturers (NAM) was vehemently against the bill while the Chamber of Commerce also opposed the bill but it did not testify at the hearings because its head, Eric Johnston, was running for president and did not want to go on record as opposing full employment (Bailey 1950). When the Murray-Wagner bill went to the House, the conservative House managed to force a compromise that replace "full employment" with "maximum employment" balanced with minimum inflation. The final Employment Act of 1946 set up the Council of Economic Advisers to the president, but it contained no other operative provisions (Janoski 1990).

American labor completed its consolidation and entered Democratic politics during the 1950s; meanwhile after the Republican resurgence since mid-1940s the Democrats began to regain political clout in the 1958 congressional elections. Labor friendly Senators such as Eugene McCarthy recommended "a nationwide vocational training program through federal grants-in-aid to the states" (Robertson 1981). When Kennedy became president, he order the Department of Labor, the Bureau of the Budget, and Senator Joseph Clark to produce a new training bill giving training and manpower planning to the Department of Labor. The proposed bill would ask the employment services to promote On-the-Job Training (OJT) and contract with public and private schools for training, and it would give organized labor and the Department of Labor control over vocational education. However, the American Vocational Association (AVA), representing vocational educators and with a main constituency of instructors in public skills centers and community colleges, was strongly opposed to the bill. AVA wanted in-school training run by AVA instructors and it deployed its connections in Washington to thwart the proposal. Despite the seeming mismatch of the AVA versus the

[49] The two union confederations did not merge until 1955.

administration and AFL-CIO, AVA lobbyist M. D. Mobley had connections to a Southern Democrat on the House Rules Committee, which gave AVA, a minor service delivery interest group, veto power to the training bill. The final compromise, the Manpower Development and Training Act of 1962 (MDTA), was far less than what the administration had hoped for; it offered job training in schools financed with state distribution formulas and matching funds, rather than extensive OJT under the Department of Labor (Janoski 1990).

One pillar of President Lyndon Johnson's Great Society programs and central to his reelection campaign was the War on Poverty. Introduced on March 16, 1964, the Economic Opportunity Act of 1964 would create a powerful Office of Economic Opportunity to oversee a variety of community-based antipoverty programs. Aided by surging Democratic Party power and two activist presidents as well as labor movement pressure for employment and training programs, the bill passed both chambers of the Congress relatively easily and was signed by Johnson on August 20, 1964. The act included programs such as the Job Corps, Operation Mainstream, Neighborhood Youth Corps, and the Concentrated Employment Program (Janoski 1990). These proactive labor market policies were likely conducive to the steady rise of labor mobility levels in the US up to the late 1960s. However, despite the legislative success of the act at the time, the community action programs in the act suffered from two fundamental problems. First, they were based on the grass-roots democratic theory that assumes bureaucracies are to be avoided because of their inherent vices, and that power should come from and always stay in the bottom lest the protest groups and their leaders be co-opted by higher level leadership and elites; such radical but anti-state stance alienated both conservatives and local Democratic leaders and failed to make the program an integral part of the state. Second, these programs oriented toward community consumption rather than organizational production, hence they could hardly foster the development of stable neo-corporatist labor institutions in terms of control of capital, and they were vulnerable to future conservative backlashes and changes in funding priorities. In fact, after the Democrats lost the Presidency in 1968, the succeeding Nixon and Ford administrations dismantled most of the community action programs, decentralized the others, and terminated the Office of Economic Opportunity (Janoski 1990).

When it comes to active labor market policies, Nixon stressed revenue sharing with reorganization, management reform, and the consolidation of categorical employment programs. He was against job creation programs such as public service employment and also wanted to decentralize such programs to state and local levels. Based on such criteria Nixon vetoed a Democratic emergency employment act on December 16, 1970. However, as unemployment rose to more than 6 percent in 1971, even some Republicans were joining Democrats to push for emergency employment that included some public service employment. The cities as well as AFL-CIO testified strongly for the proposal in both Senate and House, and the final Emergency Employment bill that emerged from the conference committee would provide emergence public service employment along with other manpower services for two years. Nixon signed the act on July 12, 1971.

In 1973, the Congress was facing the expirations of MDTA and the Emergency Employment Act. Once again, Nixon, who had just won reelection by landslide, demanded decentralized manpower programs to the state and local governments and large power to the secretary of labor to reduce funds for programs not meeting specific transition targets. But his stance was softened by the Watergate scandal and rising unemployment, and intense negotiations between the House and Senate produced the Comprehensive Employment and Training Act of 1973 (CETA), which contained a few programs on public service employment but was essentially decentralized and revenue-sharing as Nixon envisioned. Nixon signed it in December 1973.

When Carter came to the While House in 1977, he pledged to fight unemployment. He managed to extend active labor market policies through the Economic Stimulus Act of 1977, the Youth Employment and Demonstration Projects Act of 1977, the Revenue Act of 1978, and most significantly the CETA Reauthorization Act of 1978. The AFL-CIO and other unions strongly endorsed the extension of CETA, while government employee unions expressed serious concerns about the substitution effects of the CETA programs to their labor standards, wages, and job security. State and local governments wanted more expenditure and local control, while most Republicans and business groups opposed CETA and public service jobs. President Carter had wanted to have a reauthorized CETA that would redouble measures toward structural and youth unemployment and increase auditing to eliminate substitution effects, but his bill was heavily compromised after undergoing criticism from both Democrats and Republicans in the Congress and the final CETA Reauthorization Act reduced both structural and cyclical job creation funds and limited individual participation to eighteen months in five years on public service employment, it also had a $7000 national average for CETA earnings. The downsized CETA could not offer enough help to the unemployed when the oil crisis hit in 1979, and the restrictions and targeting on the disadvantaged caused local governments to reduce participation in CETA and thus leaving many community-based organizations withering with little political clout. Furthermore, the reauthorized CETA did not address the substitution effects that were the main source of its unpopularity (Janoski 1990).

When Reagan became the president in 1981, he cut CETA job creation programs by 75 percent in 1981-82. When CETA came up for reauthorization again in 1982, Reagan wanted to eliminate job creation programs altogether. He proposed the Job Training Partnership Act (JTPA) of 1982, which would create business-dominated private industry councils, give power to the states, and make few guarantees for wages and employment standards. Democrats in the House fought in vain to enact their version of employment and training bill to replace CETA, despite the AFL-CIO support behind them; Senators Daniel Quayle and Edward Kennedy proposed a bipartisan compromise that came very close to Reagan's proposal except for slightly more expenditure. In the end, Reagan got what he wanted, the Job Training and Partnership Act of 1982 replaced CETA; it gave the states control of the programs, provided no OJT programs, spent meager amounts, and severely limited trainee wages (Janoski 1990; Robertson 1988).

Reagan's relationship with organized labor turned confrontational at times. In August 1983 Reagan fired all 11,400 striking members of the Professional Air Traffic Controllers Organization (PATCO) and decertified the union, despite the ironic fact that the PATCO had endorsed Reagan for president. More consequential, however, was his covert effort to make institutional changes to the National Labor Relations Board (NLRB). Historically, the board of NLRB was drawn from business, labor, and the wider public and exhibited a pro-labor bias. Reagan appointees to the board began to constitute a majority in 1983, and once the majority was obtained, "within 150 days, the new majority … reversed eight major precedents, and recast forty percent of the decisions made since the 1970s that conservatives found objectionable" (Blyth 2002; Moe 1987).

But more far-reaching in its consequences to the general level of government social spending was the huge federal deficit run up by the Reagan administration. With the combination of income-tax cuts, increases in military spending, and the indexation of tax brackets, Reagan both eliminated the resources that would otherwise have been used for increased social outlays and focused attention on deficit spending. For advocates of public provision, the result was disastrous as they were forced to make the case for social programs against escalating pressure to bring the federal deficit under control without raising taxes. Moderates in both parties joined the right in demanding a balanced budget, making the deficit issue the top priority in the national agenda while crowding out calls for more government spending on growing social needs (Blyth 2002; Noble 1997).

To some extent, Clinton relived the policy dilemma that Reagan faced, that is, how to increase the government spending without increasing the deficit. Under this backdrop, he could have little done during most of his first term besides marginal increases in the minimum wage, the extension of the earned income tax credit, and the family leave bill (Blyth 2002). During the heat of his reelection campaign in 1996, Clinton signed the Personal Responsibility and Work Opportunity Reconciliation Act (PRWORA), which abolished Aid for Families with Dependent Children (AFDC), replacing it with the Temporary Assistance for Needy Families program (TANF), which established a five-year time limit for the receipt of welfare benefits, and which established the "work-first" principle underlying new welfare-to-work programs. The bill was submitted by Congressional Republicans with the anticipations that it would be vetoed since Clinton had already vetoed a similar version of the bill early in 1996. The bill was mostly designed to serve a political rather than policy function, as Republican National Committee strategist Eddie Gillespie explained "They tried to write a bill where [Clinton would] be hurt either way – that if he signed it he would make his base crazy and if vetoed it he would be going against the mainstream" (Drew 1997). On the Democratic side, Clinton was concerned about how this bill would affect his reelection chances, especially after he had made the campaign pledge to "end welfare as we know it". His signing of the bill was out of pure political calculation and he was able to convince the Democratic convention that it was the lesser of two evils to pass this bill and let a Democratic president to tinker with it later on than to veto the bill and elect a Republican president (Lafer 2002).

The main focus of the TANF programs was to get the people on welfare into the labor market. This was done through imposing a five-year lifetime limit on cash assistance, requiring states to see to it that those who do receive assistance are working, looking for work or participating in unpaid work experience or "job readiness" training. Because of the emphasis of the TANF programs was to place welfare recipients into the first available job – any job, at any wage, and because many of the training programs were exposed to have only deplorable skill content and seemed unable to increase the upward mobility of their participants, there have been laments that this bill turned the hardest-line vision of Reagan Republicans into reality (Blyth 2002; Lafer 2002).

6.4. Discussion and conclusion

From the brief recount of the legislative history in the US on labor market programs, we can clearly discern differing partisan preferences toward ALMP programs in particular and labor-business relations in general in America. The Democratic presidents and members of Congress tended to prefer and promote the increases in social spending generally and more active labor market programs in specific; in contrast, the Republican presidents and members of Congress wanted to limit increases or even to orchestrate decreases in social spending and active labor market programs. The root cause of such differences clearly lies in differing ideologies and different core constituencies who have fundamentally different economic interests.

Unlike in Sweden where there exists a powerful, well-organized, and national labor unions confederation in the LO, in the US, the counterpart national labor confederation in AFL-CIO lacks the centralized sanctioning power, is unable to effectively coordinate various union actions and has been incoherent in articulating a class-based labor demand in social policies. As a result, the Democratic Party has often been in the lead in proposing key programs benefiting labor and facilitating labor market. In the early years after the Second World War, serious attempts had been made by the Democratic Party and administrations to enact full employment in the US. The MDTA under Kennedy and the Great Society programs under Johnson, though fell short of what their proponents had hoped for, were able to devote substantial resources into the labor market and especially to helping the people at the very bottom of the labor market; and they represented a high point in the Democratic power in post war America. It is worth noting that, from figures 6.1.A and B, we could not only see the rising levels of interindustry labor mobility in the US up to the late 1960s, but also discern the fact that the levels stayed high and were the peak of labor mobility levels throughout the post war period.

When the Presidency shifted to the Republican, it became hard for programs that provide assistance to labor and facilitated labor markets to pass the president's desk. Only after persistent pressure from Congress members from both parties, coupled with the hard economic reality of high unemployment, did Nixon agree to the Emergency Employment Act and the CETA. These bills however tended to be decentralized, under-funded, and too transient. It should come as no surprise, one can argue, given the hostile altitudes of the executive authorities toward labor market programs that labor mobility levels measured in both elasticity and COV of wage would decline during the tenure of Nixon, as figures 6.1.A and B show. During most of the Ford's presidency however, the two measures diverge, with the COV of wages measure indicating a continuing decline that would level off in the 1980s, while the elasticity measure picking up more subtle changes in the labor market over time in that there was a bounce-up of labor mobility levels coinciding with most of Ford's presidency, which may be attributed more to exogenous shocks than to the domestic policies[50].

Not quite conforming to the theory was the observation that labor mobility levels declined during Carter's presidency, when we would expect that under a Left administration and with weakly centralized unions, the Left executive would strive to enhance labor mobility. However, the labor market legislations during the Carter presidency tended to be timid, restrictive, and providing only insufficient resources for the needs of labor market. Since interindustry labor mobility should ultimately reflect how labor market participants respond to economic incentives, limited resources would yield only limited effects. A significant part of the explanation as to why the Carter administration was reluctant to devote more resources to labor market policies could be due to Carter's penchant for blaming inflation on the deficit. By making this linkage, Carter essentially discredited the demand-side compensatory economic ideas that had been adopted during the previous Democratic administrations (Blyth 2002).

Since the inception of Reagan revolution, the US would enter a long period of stagnant (and low) levels of interindustry labor mobility. Thanks in no small part to Reagan's effort to bust unions, re-regulate labor and deregulate business, slash social expenditures, as well as dry up resources that may possibly be used for social programs, labor mobility levels during the tenures of Reagan and Bush Sr. tended to be low and stayed low. From figure 6.1.A, we can see that compared with any other periods from the early 1960s to 2000, the period of Reagan retrenchment witnessed the lowest levels of labor mobility. Figure 6.2.A shows the per capita social expenditure by the US government on unemployment compensation and active labor market programs; figure 6.2.B shows the per capita US government spending on the key components of the active labor market programs[51]. The data come from OECD's social

[50] Note that during the period between 1970 and 1975, there was an OECD wide upswing of labor mobility levels, as indicated in figures 6.1.A and B, which hinted that movement of labor mobility during this period might have more to do with exogenous changes than to political manipulations. Most likely, technological innovations during the period in response to the first oil shock of 1973 and concurrent depression could have played a big role.

[51] Except for TANF payment; this is a part of unemployment compensation.

expenditure database. Both figures confirm that at the height of the Reagan revolution, i.e., from 1981 to 82, total spending on ALMP as well as the key components of it all fell sharply. ALMP spending mounted a comeback in 1985-86, primarily due to the passage of Perkins Act that dealt with vocational and technical education. As a result of the Act, labor market training spending per member of the labor force increased by almost $15. Unfortunately for advocates of labor interests, the previous large-N empirical analyses have shown that more labor market training, net of the impact from other labor market policies, would tend to decrease labor mobility[52]. Hence as figures 6.1.A and B show, labor mobility levels in fact declined slightly in the US after 1985.

[Figures 6.2.A and B about here]

Clinton's TANF programs, though roundly criticized as being the reincarnation of the Reagan approach and for its "tough love" for welfare recipients, may be responsible for finally curbing the declining trend of labor mobility levels since Reagan and even induced an upswing of labor mobility, as figures 6.1.A and B show. In addition to vocational training, skills training, OJT, or school attendance requirement, the programs emphasis on actual job placement may in reality help hasten the associations between workers with gradations of labor market skills and jobs requiring just such credentials, thus contributed to an improvement of interindustry labor mobility. Figure 6.2.B shows the increase in the appropriations to the TANF programs, as well as the increases in general, though slightly, for all components of ALMP during the second term of the Clinton administration.

Another observation emerges from the study of the US legislative history is that the character of the US political system as well as other institutional factors may also shape the outcome of labor market legislation in ways unique from the other countries. For example, the US presidents, though not completely immune to the Congress, can to a large extent

---

[52] This may be that labor market training programs tend to enroll workers in training programs in schools or job centers for a small amount of compensation. Such earning tends to be smaller than what the workers made prior to the training program, which necessarily translates to decreasing interindustry labor mobility according to its definition. For a critical view of such labor training programs in the US, see (Lafer 2002).

pursue their own political agenda independent from the Congress. For another instance, particular members in the legislative process may also exhibit outsize influence, thanks to the US institution of Congressional Committees. This had allowed a minor service provider association of the American Vocational Association (AVA), to find access to veto the determined drive by the Kennedy administration to broaden the vocational training in the labor market.

Figure 6.1.A. United States Labor Mobility from 1964 to 2000
Using Elasticity as ILM measure

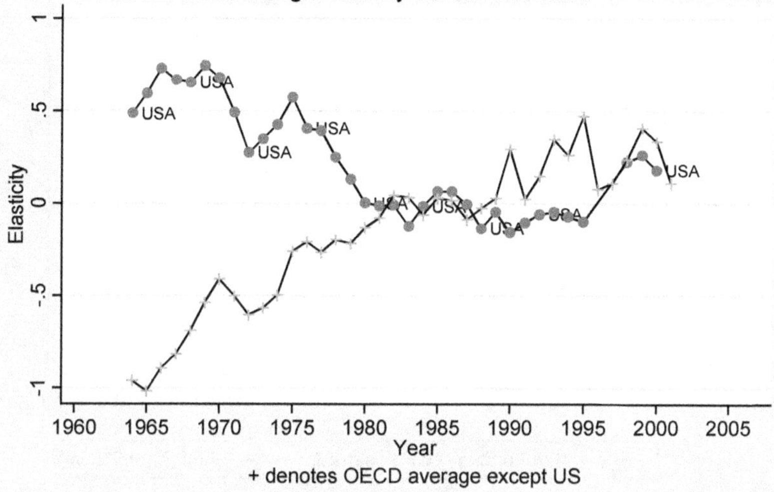

Figure 6.1.B. United States Labor Mobility from 1963 to 2000
Using COV of Wages as ILM measure

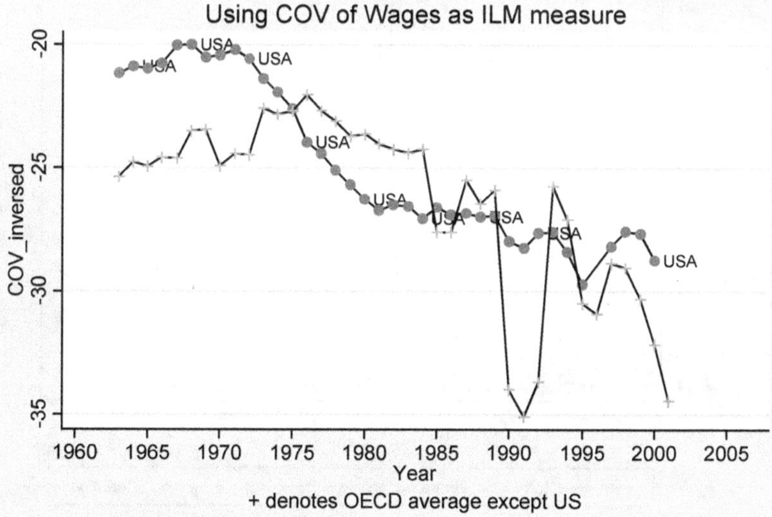

Figure 6.1.C. United States Dominant Partisanship since 1945

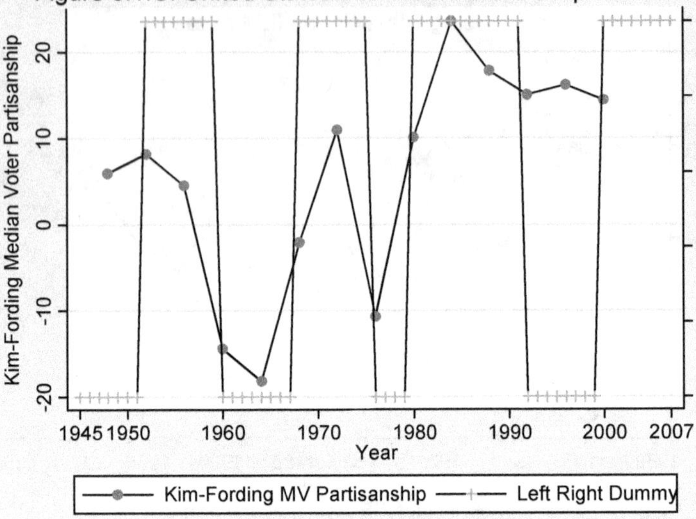

Figure 6.1.D. United States Union Centralization since 1950

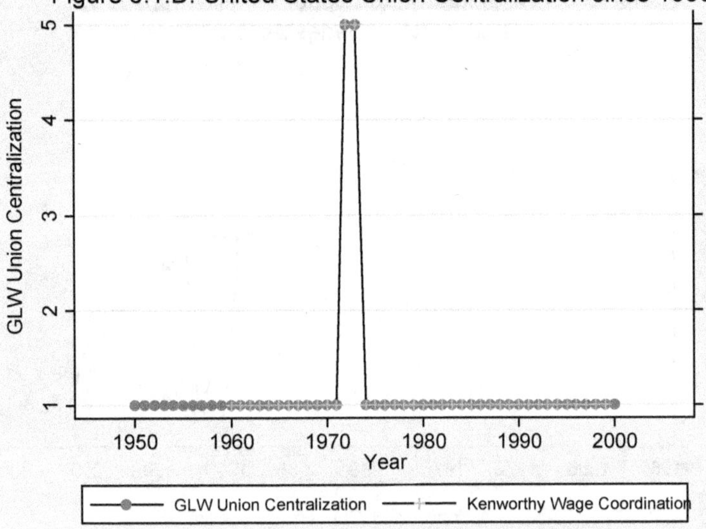

Figure 6.2.A. U.S. Social Expenditures on Unemployment and Aggregate ALMP

Data from SourceOECD Social Expenditure Database

Figure 6.2.B. U.S. per capita Social Expenditures on Key Labor Market Programs

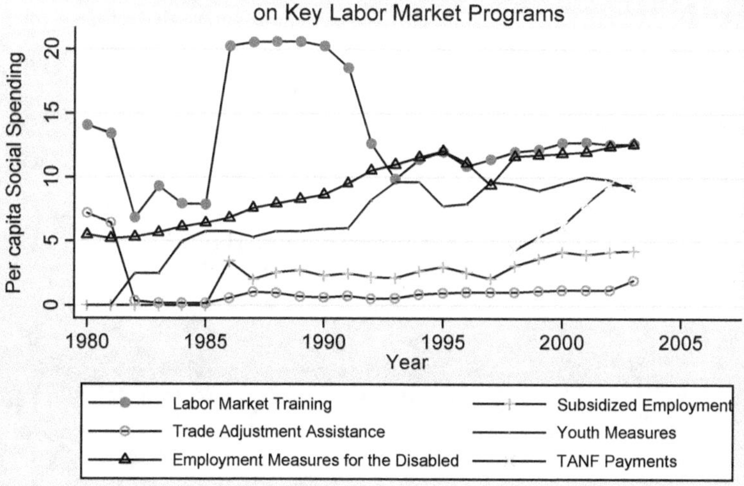

Data from SourceOECD Social Expenditure Database

Chapter 7
Conclusion

It is now possible to summarize the argument and findings in this dissertation, and to elaborate how this study of endogenous interindustry labor mobility can be connected to existing theories in international and comparative political economy as well as IR/Comparative literature at large. I discuss some policy implications of this study in the end.

7.1. What have we learned so far?

This dissertation argues that interindustry labor mobility can be shaped by domestic political process and thus become endogenous to domestic politics. In chapter 2 I develop a theory that argues that levels of interindustry labor mobility may subject to partisan influence from the governments. Left governments are generally associated with higher labor mobility while Right governments are generally associated with lower labor mobility. And this relationship is conditioned by the degree of domestic union centralization. Chapter 4 empirically tests the conditional hypotheses derived based on arguments in chapter 2, the empirics confirms the expectations that when there are low union centralization levels, Left governments are associated with higher levels of labor mobility than Right governments. And it confirms the moderation effects of centralized unions depending on the partisanship of governments. When there are Left governments, centralized unions will not push the governments for higher labor mobility levels; when there are Right governments, centralized unions will constrain the governments so that levels of labor mobility will be higher with higher levels of union centralization.

In chapter 4 I also explore the policy instruments through which governments can interfere with labor mobility levels. Among the public social spending policies I find unemployment compensation will consistently increase labor mobility and labor market training program will consistently decrease labor mobility. In the empirical analysis, I use two measures of interindustry labor mobility, the first is the elasticity of labor supply upon interindustry wage differentials, which is based on formal definition of interindustry labor mobility in economic literature and which I construct in detail in chapter 3; the other is a measure of interindustry wage differentials as in the coefficient of variation among interindustry wages, which many political economists have used in their studies.

In chapters 5 and 6, I conduct two country case studies on Sweden and the US. In the Swedish case, there was extremely high union centralization up to 1982, and during this period, the governments were mostly Social Democratic, and the evidence was that labor unions initiated and promoted the Rehn-Meidner plan to maintain high levels of labor mobility. And in post-1982 Sweden, governments increasingly took the initiatives and evinced partisan biases toward labor mobility changing policies. In the US case, because there has been no centralized union movement, the expectation is that Left and Right governments will exhibit dramatically different approaches toward labor mobility, and the legislative history in the US seems to back up this claim. The Democrats tend to be associated with upswings of labor mobility levels and increases of labor market spending, and Republicans do the opposite.

7.2. The connections with existing IPE/CPE literature and beyond

The current study can be linked with existing IR and Comparative Politics literature in a variety of ways, and because the core argument here is that interindustry labor mobility can be endogenous to domestic politics, it can either supplement some or further develop other political economy theories.

7.2.1. Variety of capitalism and international trade

This dissertation can help combine the Variety of Capitalism (VoC) literature with the international trade theories. As I have reviewed before, VoC literature argues there are important institutional complementarities within different groups of countries. In coordinated market economies or CMEs, many institutions are intertwined and any one institution is in the symbiosis relationship with other institutions. The workers in CMEs are "guaranteed" by their employers to keep their jobs and maintain their real wage levels, this "guarantee" make the workers willing to make the necessary investment into industry-specific skills that cannot be readily transferred to another industry without losses. The workers are backed by the employee's associations that negotiate with employers and when necessary support the workers through hardship. The employers and their associations make the implicit or explicit bargains with employee's associations so that in return for their guarantee for worker's wages and jobs, they get highly trained work forces that enable them to specialize and get competitive edges in international markets. The relationship is also sustained by long term finance provided by banking sectors that are not bound by short term profit goals. Such symbiotic relationships help sustain the CME model within the country.

The opposite can be said for the liberal market economies or LMEs, where market is the ultimate source of income and risks. Workers will derive their income primarily from the market alone, no guarantee or effective support from employee's associations can be expected. As a result, workers tend not to make industry-specific investment in human capital, and they invest in general skills instead. The employers in LMEs cannot expect highly skilled work forces and their best market strategy is to invest in technologies that use mostly general education and that can be fit for mass production. They, and the banking sector that finance them, are subject to short term profitability constraint from the market so they expect quick results and liquidity of assets (Estevez-Abe, Iversen, and Soskice 2001; Hall and Soskice 2001; Mares 2001).

Consequently different types of institutional complementarities will have labor mobility implications. Workers who invest in industry-specific skills in CMEs tend to have less transferable human capital so that interindustry labor mobility levels tend to be low in CMEs. Conversely, workers in LMEs who invest in general skills would possess more transferable human capital so that ILM levels would be high in LMEs.

This observation hints that institutional complementarities may influence the distributional consequences of international trade. Recall that according to Stolper-Samuel theory, which assumes perfect interindustry factor (labor and capital) mobility, exogenous easing of international trade will benefit the locally abundantly endowed factor while hurt the locally scarcely endowed factor, and that according to Specific factors theory, which assumes immobile factors, opening to international trade will benefit the exporting industries while hurt the import-competing industries, regardless of factor types. Hence varying level of interindustry factor mobility will determine the varying distributional consequences of international trade and whether the subsequent trade coalitions will form along the class or industry fault lines.

Based on the central argument in this dissertation that interindustry labor mobility can be endogenous to domestic politics, in addition to drawing the conclusions that institutional complementarities may have shaped levels of interindustry labor mobility, we can push the VoC literature further to analyze exactly how the different domestic institutional configurations have influenced the formation of domestic trade coalitions and the outcomes of trade or trade-related economic policies; we can even explore the role of partisan governments in facilitating the formation of a particular set of institutional complementarities over another throughout the course.

7.2.2. Redistribution and inequality

Another area of study this dissertation can shed light on concerns redistribution and inequality. Some have argued that increasing internationalization of national economies have made the expansion of public economy and providing social safety nets more necessary within these economies, and such welfare provision requires profound changes in governments' role in the economy as well as induces potential societal backlashes. For example, Cameron argues governments have become more influential as providers of social services and income supplements, and even investors of capital in advanced industrial countries, and a substantial part of the explanation for this development is due to the governments' attempts to shelter their economies from the competitive risks of the international economy (Cameron 1978); using case studies and extensive empirical analysis, Rodrik confirms this relationship, and he further points out the danger that international economic integration may contribute to social disintegration, and warns that "winners" have as much at stake from the possible consequences of social instability as the "losers" (Rodrik 1997); Benabou argues redistribution policies command less political support in an unequal society than in a more homogeneous one, hence we may have two types of societies that are not Pareto rankable yet are in steady states: one with high inequality and low redistribution, as in the United States; the other with low inequality and high redistribution, as in Western Europe (Benabou 2000); Persson and Tabellini show that there is a negative correlation between inequality and subsequent growth, and argue it is due to the politico-economic equilibrium from overlapping generation economic agents making the investment and voting decisions under the prevailing inequality levels (Persson and Tabellini 1994).

However, different levels of interindustry labor mobility may also have redistribution effects: high labor mobility levels facilitate the convergence of wage levels toward those justified by labor market skills and low labor mobility levels themselves imply the existence of such mismatches, so improving labor mobility levels can be welfare-enhancing for certain groups while at the same time ridding off other groups of their super-industry rents. In this sense, labor mobility policies can have redistributive effects and in many circumstances they can be used in lieu of the traditional redistributive policies such as transfers or various kinds of public spending programs. And to push the consequence of labor mobility further, it becomes logical to suggest that sustained levels of interindustry labor mobility can help shape the domestic inequality levels. This dissertation argues that interindustry labor mobility levels can be shaped by domestic political process and it substantiates this claim with empirical analyses of the causal impact of certain public spending programs on labor mobility levels, hence it can lead to further analysis as to what labor mobility policies have been used to achieve redistributive results and how these policies are engaged, as well as what political calculations motivate the employment of labor mobility policies instead of the traditional redistributive policies. Such studies will help us better understand the politics of domestic income inequality and redistribution.

7.2.3. Insider-outsider debate

This dissertation can help us better understand the insider-outsider debate. Rueda argues that labor is divided into insiders and outsiders, and the interests of insiders and outsiders are fundamentally different. Insiders are those workers whose jobs are sufficiently protected so as not to feel greatly threatened by increases in unemployment; on the other hand, outsiders are either unemployed or hold jobs characterized by low levels of protection and employment rights. For insiders, their main interest is job protection; for outsiders, their main interest is lower unemployment and job precariousness (Rueda 2005). The current study can contribute to this debate in that higher levels of interindustry labor mobility will blur the division between insiders and outsiders, so that insider-outsider problem will become less and less salient with the increases of labor mobility levels. The implication of this study for the insider-outsider model may be that the researchers should explicitly state their assumption of fixed interindustry labor mobility and acknowledge the comparative static nature of the model. Furthermore, for a more complete understanding of the insider-outsider issue, we may have to take into account of the potentially endogenously determined labor mobility levels and directly model such feedback effects. For example, the very ALMP policies that Rueda argues reflect the insider-outsider division may also help shape the levels of interindustry labor mobility and thus determine the insider-outsider division.

7.2.4. Interindustry vs. international factor mobility

This study of endogenous **interindustry** labor or factor mobility can also supplement the studies on **international** factor mobility. One area of international factor mobility, i.e., the international capital mobility, has received much attention and academic treatment. Andrews argues that international capital mobility has become a fact of life and it exerts a structural constraint on the behavior of states participating in the global economy (Andrews 1994). Whereas Garrett argues that increased international capital mobility may not always lead to the same global economy as prescribed by the neoclassical economics, that the left-labor power and the macroeconomic policy regime they espouse have shown remarkable resilience in face of heightened international capital mobility (Garrett 1995; Garrett 1998). Other scholars have worried about the race to the bottom effect brought about by the increasing internationalization of national economies, where international trade, international capital mobility, and to a lesser extent international labor movement, help bring down wage levels in developed countries for the unskilled workers, or contribute to the worsening labor conditions in developing countries where labor regulations may be lax (Bhagwati 2004;

Borjas 2005; Freeman 2000; Rodrik 1997). In short, the international capital mobility thesis has generally presented a picture where domestic labor owners are most likely the receiving ends of the negative impact from international factor mobility. The insight this dissertation can bring to the study of the political economy of international factor mobility is that increasing levels of international factor mobility need not necessarily lead to the political outcomes as described in the current theories, and one of the critical variables that can also help shape the political outcomes is the level of domestic interindustry labor mobility. The predictions of current theories on the consequences of increasing international factor mobility often depend on the implicit assumption that the interindustry factor, and especially labor, mobility is perfect, so that globalization of production factors would often pit one domestic factor against another, often in the form of internationally immobile labor retreat in terms of their social and political demands in the face of internationally mobile capital. When this implicit assumption is relaxed, i.e., interindustry factor and labor mobility is less than perfect, as is almost always the case, the consequences of international factor mobility need to be rethought. For example, if capital is internationally and domestically mobile across industries, while labor is internationally immobile and domestically specific to the industries, then international capital mobility will benefit both the capital and the specific industries that receive the capital inflows, as productivity and wages will rise in these industries. Due to interindustry labor immobility, the rest of labor forces within the host countries cannot share the benefits from foreign capital but will have to endure relative income loss comparing to those industries receiving foreign capital. In this sense, labor in both the home and the host countries will not uniformly be negatively affected and be opposed to international capital mobility as the current theories on international capital mobility suggest, since labor owners' interests will depend on the fortune of their industries, labor may evince varied preferences toward international capital mobility and affect the politics on this issue accordingly. Furthermore, this dissertation also suggests that governments may also have engaged in interindustry labor mobility manipulations in order to attain favorable political environment to facilitate the implementation of their desired policies.

7.2.5. Other fronts

This study can have many other implications to the development of political economy literature. It can deepen our understanding of the origin of the social cleavages such as class. Based on the relationship established in this study that high levels of interindustry labor mobility can contribute to high levels of labor class solidarity, which can help distinguish labor's interests from those of the capital's more clearly, we can hypothesize that part of the explanation as to the origin of the class cleavage may be that past governments may have had intentionally or unintentionally manipulated labor mobility policies to keep labor mobility levels high enough for prolonged period, so that the consequent dominant social cleavage took the shape of labor versus capital. And in those countries where the past governments had not engaged in much of the labor mobility manipulations, the dominant social cleavage may be less along the class line but along other fault lines where the past political battles were fought.

And this dissertation can immediately shed light on the debate within the international trade literature over whether the mobile factor Stolper-Samuelson model or the Specific factors model more accurately describes the dynamics following the opening to international trade. This study conveys the understanding that not only the initial conditions may differ thus dictate the fitness of one model over another at a particular juncture of time, but also the subsequent development of domestic politics can result in different arrays of policies hence different levels of interindustry labor mobility levels, which may reinforce or alter the fitness of one particular model due to the fundamental role of interindustry factor mobility in these models. Therefore this study can enrich our understanding in when and why should we put our faith in industry-based or class-based theories.

7.2.6. Paths to future improvement

In no small ways, however, this dissertation can benefit from incorporating more nuanced theories in international relations and comparative politics. Currently, this dissertation assumes a rather simplistic partisan model where Left and Right governments adopt pro-labor or pro-capital policies automatically. However, upon closer scrutiny, we have observed much more varied realities where, for instance, Left governments may adopt policies that favor some segments of labor instead of the general labor forces. In the future research, I can draw on the insights from CPE theories such as the insider-outsider model to analyze the political implications for the Left governments when their critical constituency constitutes only some segments of the labor owners, and how will the different constituent bases influence the Left governments' altitudes toward interindustry labor mobility levels.

Another frontier in which this study can be pushed further is to acknowledge that in modern advanced industrial countries, there are not only Left and Right parties but also the Christian Democratic parties, which may be conservative in social issues but radical in others, especially the economic issues. Analyzing and incorporating the Christian Democratic preferences toward interindustry labor mobility can undoubtedly improve the empirical purchase of the current study and provide a more nuanced partisan model.

7.3. Policy implications

Armed with the added knowledge that interindustry labor mobility levels may be endogenous to domestic politics, for partisan governments the policy implications become straightforward.

First, an assessment of the consequences to labor mobility levels should henceforth enter into the governments' calculation before they enact any new policies, especially those concerning the labor market.

Second, depending on the goals of respective partisan governments, a conscientious effort to prioritize certain labor mobility policies over other policies may become necessary to help foster the political support among their core constituency or correct the wrong committed by the previous governments.

Finally, the governments of whatever ideology may find it in their interests to identify other policies that can have labor mobility changing effects, and furthermore, to try to devise new ones to better suit their purpose.

Bibliography:

Alesina, Alberto, and Howard Rosenthal. 1989. "Partisan Cycles in Congressional Elections and the Macroeconomy." *American Political Science Review* 83 (2):373-98.

Alesina, Alberto, and Howard Rosenthal. 1995. *Partisan Politics, Divided Government, and the Economy* New York, NY: Cambridge University Press.

Alesina, Alberto, Nouriel Roubini, and Gerald D. Cohen. 1997. *Political Cycles and the Macroeconomy*. Cambridge, Massachusetts: The MIT Press.

Alt, James E., and Michael Gilligan. 1994. "The Political Economy of Trading States: Factor Specificity, Collective Action Problems, and Domestic Political Institutions." *Journal of Political Philosophy* 2 (2):165-192.

Alvarez, R. Michael, Geoffrey Garrett, and Peter Lange. 1991. "Government Partisanship, Labor Organization and Macroeconomic Performance." *American Political Science Review* 85 (2):541-56.

Andrews, David M. 1994. "Capital Mobility and State Autonomy: Toward a Structural Theory of International Monetary Relations." *International Studies Quarterly* 38 (2):193-218.

Bailey, Stephen Kemp. 1950. *Congress Makes a Law: the story behind the Employment Act of 1946*. New York: Columbia University Press.

Beaulieu, Eugene. 2002. "The Stolper-Samuelson Theorem Faces Congress." *Review of International Economics* 10 (2):343-360.

Beck, Nathaniel. 2001. "TIME-SERIES–CROSS-SECTION DATA: What Have We Learned in the Past Few Years?" *Annual Review of Political Science* 4:271-93.

Beck, Nathaniel, and Jonathan N. Katz. 1995. "What To Do (And Not To Do) With Time-Series Cross-Section Data." *American Political Science Review* 89 (3):634-47.

Beck, Nathaniel, and Jonathan N. Katz. 1996. "Nuisance vs. Substance: Specifying and Estimating Time-Series-Cross-Section Models." *Political Analysis* 6:1-36.

Beck, Nathaniel, Jonathan N. Katz, R. Michael Alvarez, Geoffrey Garrett, and Peter Lange. 1993. "Government Partisanship, Labor Organization, and Macroeconomic Performance: A Corrigendum." *American Political Science Review* 87 (4):943-8.

Benabou, Roland. 2000. "Unequal Societies: Income Distribution and the Social Contract." *The American Economic Review* 90 (1):96-129.

Bhagwati, Jagdish N., and T. N. Srinivasan. 1983. *Lectures on International Trade*. Cambridge, MA: The MIT Press.

Bhagwati, Jagdish. 2004. *In Defense of Globalization*. New York: Oxford University Press.

Blyth, Mark. 2002. *Great Transformations: Economic Ideas and Institutional Change in the Twentieth Century*. New York: Cambridge University Press.

Boix, Carles. 1997. "Political Parties and the Supply Side of the Economy: The Provision of Physical and Human Capital in Advanced Economies, 1960-90." *American Journal of Political Science* 41 (3):814-45.

Borjas, George J. 2005. Globalization and Immigration. In *Globalization: What's New?*, edited by M. M. Weinstein. New York: Columbia University Press.

Brambor, Thomas, William Roberts Clark, and Matt Golder. 2006. "Understanding Interaction Models: Improving Empirical Analyses." *Political Analysis* 14:63-82.

Braumoeller, Bear F. 2004. "Hypothesis Testing and Multiplicative Interaction Terms." *International Organization* 58:807-20.

Brawley, Mark R. 2006. Adjustment, Ambiguity, and Policy Interventions: A Political Approach to the Domestic Politics of Trade. In *First meeting of International Political Economy Society*. Princeton University.

Bretcher, Richard A. 1992. "An Efficiency-Wage Model with Explicit Monitoring: Unemployment and Welfare in an Open Economy." *Journal of International Economics* 32:179-91.

Burgoon, Brian, and Michael J. Hiscox. 2000. Trade Openness and Political Compensation: Labor Demands for Adjustment Assistance. In *Annual Meeting of the American Political Science Association*. Washington DC.

Calvert, Randall L. 1985. "Robustness of the Multidimensional Voting Model: Candidate Motivations, Uncertainty, and Convergence." *American Journal of Political Science* 29 (1):69-95.

Cameron, David R. 1978. "The Expansion of the Political Economy: A Comparative Analysis." *American Political Science Review* 72 (4):1243-61.

Davidson, Carl, Lawrence Martin, and Steven Matusz. 1988. "The Structure of Simple General Equilibrium Models with Frictional Unemployment." *Journal of Political Economy* 96 (6):1267-93.

Davidson, Carl, Lawrence Martin, and Steven Matusz. 1991. "Multiple Free Trade Equilibria in Micro Models of Unemployment." *Journal of International Economics* 31:157-69.

Davidson, Carl, Lawrence Martin, and Steven Matusz. 1999. "Trade and search generated unemployment." *Journal of International Economics* 48:271-99.

Davis, Steve, John Haltiwanger, and Scott Shuh. 1996. *Job Creation and Destruction*. Cambridge, MA: MIT Press.

Drew, Elizabeth. 1997. *Whatever It Takes: The Real Struggle for Political Power in America*. New York: Penguin Books.

Dutt, Pushan, and Devashish Mitra. 2002. "Political Ideology and Endogenous Trade Policy: An Empirical Investigation." In *National Bureau of Economic Research Working Paper (9239)*.

Dutt, Pushan, and Devashish Mitra. 2005. "Political Ideology and Endogenous Trade Policy: An Empirical Investigation." *The Review of Economics and Statistics* 87 (1):59-72.

Edin, Per-Anders, and Johnny Zetterberg. 1992. "Interindustry Wage Differentials: Evidence from Sweden and a Comparison with the United States." *The American Economic Review* 82 (5):1341-9.

Erixon, Lennart. 2008. "The Rehn-Meidner model in Sweden: its rise, challenges and survival." Stockholm: Department of Economics, Stockholm University.

Esping-Andersen, Gosta. 1990. *The Three Worlds of Welfare Capitalism*. Cambridge, UK: Polity Press.

Estevez-Abe, Margarita, Torben Iversen, and David Soskice. 2001. Social Protection and the Formation of Skills: A Reinterpretation of the Welfare State. In *Varieties of Capitalism: The Institutional Foundations of Comparative Advantages*, edited by P. A. Hall and D. Soskice. New York, NY: Oxford University Press.

Flanagan, Robert J. 1987. "Efficiency and Equality in Swedish Labor Markets." In *The Swedish Economy*, ed. B. P. Bosworth and A. M. Rivlin. Washington, D.C.: The Brookings Institution.

Fox, Justin. 2007. Why Denmark Loves Globalization. *Time*, Thursday, Nov. 15, 2007.

Franzese, Robert J. 2006. "Political Business Cycles." In *Oxford Handbook of Political Economy*, ed. B. Weingast and D. Wittman. New York, NY: Oxford University Press.

Freeman, Richard B. 2000. Are Your Wages Set in Beijing? In *International Political Economy: Perspectives on Global Power and Wealth*, edited by J. A. Frieden and D. A. Lake. New York: Bedford/St. Martin's.

Frieden, Jeffry. 1991. *Debt, Development, and Democracy: Modern Political Economy and Latin America, 1965-1985*. Princeton, NJ: Princeton University Press.

Garrett, Geoffrey. 1995. "Capital Mobility, Trade, and the Domestic Politics of Economic Policy." *International Organization* 49 (4):657-687.

Garrett, Geoffrey. 1998. *Partisan Politics in the Global Economy*. New York: Cambridge University Press.

Golden, Miriam. 1993. "The Dynamics of Trade Unionism and National Economic Performance." *American Political Science Review* 87 (2):439-54.

Golden, Miriam, Peter Lange, and Michael Wallerstein. 2006. "Union Centralization among Advanced Industrial Societies: An Empirical Study."

Golden, Miriam, and Jonas Pontusson. 1992. *Bargaining for Change: Union Politics in North America and Europe*. Ithaca and London: Cornell University Press.

Golder, Matt. 2006. "Presidential Coattails and Legislative Fragmentation." *American Journal of Political Science* 50 (1):34-48.

Gourevitch, Peter. 1986. *Politics in Hard Times: Comparative Responses To International Economic Crises*. Ithaca: Cornell University Press.

Grossman, Gene M. 1983. "Partially Mobile Capital." *Journal of International Economics* 15:1-17.

Grossman, Gene M., and Elhanan Helpman. 1994. "Protection for Sale." *The American Economic Review* 84 (4):833-850.

Hainmueller, Jens, and Michael J. Hiscox. 2007. "Being Specific: Measuring Asset Specificity For Political Economy." In *Annual APSA Meeting*. Chicago.

Hall, Peter A., and Robert J. Franzese. 1998. "Mixed Signals: Central Bank Independence, Coordinated Wage Bargaining, and European Monetary Union." *International Organization* 52 (3):505-35.

Hall, Peter A., and David Soskice. 2001. An Introduction to Varieties of Capitalism. In *Varieties of Capitalism - The Institutional Foundations of Comparative Advantage*, edited by P. A. Hall and D. Soskice. New York: Oxford University Press.

Hall, Peter A., and David Soskice. 2001. *Varieties of Capitalism: The Institutional Foundations of Comparative Advantage*. New York: Oxford University Press.

Heclo, Hugh, and Henrik Madsen. 1987. *Policy and Politics in Sweden: Principled Pragmatism*. Philadelphia: Temple University Press.

Hibbs, Douglas A. 1977. "Political Parties and Macroeconomic Policy." *American Political Science Review* 71 (4):1467-87.

Hibbs, Douglas A. 1987. *The American Political Economy*. Cambridge: Harvard University Press.

Hibbs, Douglas A. 1994. "The Partisan Model of Macroeconomic Cycles: More Theory and Evidence for the United States." *Economics and Politics* 6 (1):1-23.

Hibbs, Douglas A. 2006. "Brief Essay on "Political Parties and Macroeconomic Policy"." *American Political Science Review* 100 (4):670-71.
Hibbs, Douglas A., and Hakan Locking. 1996. "Wage Compression, Wage Drift and Wage Inflation in Sweden." *Labour Economics* 3:109-41.
Hibbs, Douglas A., and Hakan Locking. 2000. "Wage Dispersion and Productive Efficiency: Evidence for Sweden." *Journal of Labor Economics* 18 (4):755-82.
Hill, John K., and Jose A. Mendez. 1983. "Factor Mobility and the General Equilibrium Model of Production." *Journal of International Economics* 15:19-25.
Hiscox, Michael J. 1999. "The Magic Bullet? The RTAA, Institutional Reform, and Trade Liberalization." *International Organization* 53 (4):669-698.
Hiscox, Michael J. 2001. "Class Versus Industry Cleavages: Inter-Industry Factor Mobility and the Politics of Trade." *International Organization* 55 (1):1-46.
Hiscox, Michael J. 2002. "Commerce, Coalitions, and Factor Mobility: Evidence from Congressional Votes on Trade Legislation." *American Political Science Review* 96 (3):593-608.
Hiscox, Michael J. 2002. "Interindustry Factor Mobility and Technological Change: Evidence on Wage and Profit Dispersion Across U.S. Industries, 1820-1990." *The Journal of Economic History* 62 (2):383-416.
Hiscox, Michael J. 2002. *International Trade and Political Conflict : Commerce, Coalitions, and Mobility*. Princeton, N.J.: Princeton University Press.
Hiscox, Michael J., and Stephanie J. Rickard. 2002. Birds of a Different Feather? -- Varieties of Capitalism, Factor Specificity, and Interindustry Labor Movements: Harvard University and University of California, San Diego.
Hoon, Hian Teck. 1991. "Comparative Advantage and the Equilibrium Rate of Unemployment." *Economics Letters* 37:299-304.
Huber, Evelyne, Charles Ragin, and John D. Stephens. 1993. "Social Democracy, Christian Democracy, Constitutional

Structure, and the Welfare State." *American Journal of Sociology* 99 (3):711-49.

Huber, Evelyne, and John D. Stephens. 2001. *Development and Crisis of the Welfare State: Parties and Policies in Global Market*. Chicago and London: The University of Chicago Press.

Im, Kyung So, M. Hashem Pesaran, and Yongcheol Shin. 2003. "Testing for Unit Roots in Heterogeneous Panels." *Journal of Econometrics* 115 (1):53-74.

Iversen, Torben, and David Soskice. 2001. "An Asset Theory of Social Policy Preferences." *American Political Science Review* 95 (4):875-93.

Iversen, Torben. 2006. "Class Politics is Dead! Long Live Class Politics! A Political Economy Perspective on the New Partisan Politics." *APSA-CP Newsletter*, Summer, 1-6.

Janoski, Thomas. 1990. *The Political Economy of Unemployment: Active Labor Market Policy in West Germany and the United States*. Berkeley and Los Angeles: University of California Press.

Jones, Ronald W. 1965. "The Structure of Simple General Equilibrium Models." *Journal of Political Economy* 73 (6):557-72.

Jones, Ronald W. 1971. A Three-Factor Model In Theory, Trade, and History. In *Trade, Balance of Payments and Growth: Papers in International Economics in Honor of Charles P. Kindleberger*, edited by J. N. Bhagwati, R. W. Jones, R. A. Mundell and J. Vanek. Amsterdam: North-Holland Publishing Co.

Jongen, Egbert L.W., Edwin van Gameren, and Johan J. Graafland. 2003. "Exploring the Macroeconomic Impact of Subsidized Employment." *De Economist* 151 (1):81-118.

Katzenstein, Peter. 1985. *Small States in World Market*. Ithaca, N.Y.: Cornell University Press.

Keele, Luke, and Nathan J. Kelly. 2006. "Dynamic Models for Dynamic Theories: The Ins and Outs of Lagged Dependent Variables." *Political Analysis* 14:186–205.

Kenworthy, Lane. 2001. "Wage-Setting Measures: A Survey and Assessment." *World Politics* 54 (1):57–98.

Kim, Hee-Min, and Richard C. Fording. 2001. "Extending Party Estimates to Governments and Electors." In *Mapping Policy Preferences: Estimates for Parties, Electors, and Governments 1945-1998*, ed. I. Budge, H.-D. Klingemann, A. Volkens, J. Bara and E. Tanenbaum. New York: Oxford University Press.

Kim, Hee-Min, and Richard C. Fording. 2002. "Government Partisanship in Western Democracies, 1945-1998." *European Journal of Political Research* 41:165-84.

Kitschelt, Herbert. 1994. *The Transformation of European Social Democracy*. New York: Cambridge University Press.

Krueger, Alan B., and Lawrence H. Summers. 1988. "Efficiency Wages and the Inter-Industry Wage Structure." *Econometrica* 56 (2):259-93.

Ladewig, Jeffrey W. 2006. "Domestic Influences on International Trade Policy: Factor Mobility in the United States, 1963 to 1992." *International Organization* 60:69-103.

Lafer, Gordon. 2002. *The Job Training Charade*. Ithaca: Cornell University Press.

Laver, Michael J., and Ian Budge, eds. 1992. *Party Policy and Government Coalitions*. London: Macmillan.

Leamer, Edward E. 1984. *Sources of International Comparative Advantage: Theory and Evidence*. Cambridge, Mass.: MIT Press.

Levin, Andrew, Chien-Fu Lin, and Chia-Shang James Chu. 2002. "Unit Root Tests in Panel Data: Asymptotic and Finite Sample Properties." *Journal of Econometrics* 108 (1):1-24.

Lilien, David M. 1982. "Sectoral Shifts and Cyclical Unemployment." *Journal of Political Economy* 90 (4):777-93.

LO. 1953. Trade Unions and Full Employment. Stockholm: The Swedish Confederation of Trade Unions.

LO. 1963. *Economic Expansion and Structural Change: A Trade Union Manifesto*. Translated by T. L. Johnston. Edited by T. L. Johnston. London: George Allen & Unwin LTD.

LO. 2007. "The Swedish Trade Union Confederation - Facts and History." Stockholm LANDSORGANISATIONEN I SVERIGE.

Magee, Stephen P. 1980. Three simple tests of the Stolper-Samuelson theorem. In *Issues in International Economics* edited by P. Oppenheimer. Boston: Oriel Press.

Magnusson, Lars. 2000. *An Economic History of Sweden*. New York: Routledge.

Mares, Isabela. 2001. Firms and the Welfare State: When, Why, and How Does Social Policy Matter to Employers? In *Varieties of Capitalism: The Institutional Foundations of Comparative Advantage*, edited by P. A. Hall and D. Soskice. New York: Oxford University Press.

Martin, Cathie Jo, and Duane Swank. 2004. "Does the Organization of Capital Matter? Employers and Active Labor Market Policy at the National and Firm Levels." *American Political Science Review* 98 (4):593-611.

McLaughlin, Kenneth J., and Mark Bils. 2001. "Interindustry Mobility and the Cyclical Upgrading of Labor." *Journal of Labor Economics* 19 (1):94 -- 135.

McLure, Charles E. 1970. "Taxation, Substitution, and Industrial Location." *Journal of Political Economy* 78 (1):112-32.

Milner, Helen V., and Benjamin Judkins. 2004. "Partisanship, Trade Policy, and Globalization: Is There a Left-Right Divide on Trade Policy?" *International Studies Quarterly* 48:95-119.

Milner, Henry. 1989. *Sweden: Social Democracy in Practice*. New York: Oxford University Press.

Moe, Terry. 1987. "Interests, Institutions, and Positive Theory: The Politics of the NLRB." *Studies in American Political Development* (2):236-99.

Morrissett, Irving. 1952. "Criticism Invited." *Econometrica* 20 (3):515-6.

Mukherjee, Bumba, Dale Smith, and Quan Li. 2007. Labor (Im)mobility and the Politics of Trade Protection in Majoritarian Democracies. Princeton, NJ.

Muller, Wolfgang C., and Kaare Strom, eds. 1999. *Policy, Office, or Votes? How Political Parties in Western Europe*

Make Hard Decisions. New York: Cambridge University Press.
Noble, Charles. 1997. *Welfare As We Knew It: A Political History of the American Welfare State*. New York: Oxford University Press.
OECD. 2002. "OECD Employment Outlook." Paris: OECD.
OECD. 2003. "OECD Health Data 2003." Paris: OECD.
OECD. 2004. "Social Expenditure Database (SOCX), 1980-2001." Paris: OECD.
OECD. 2005. "OECD Employment Outlook." Paris: OECD.
OECD. 2007. "The Social Expenditure Database: An Interpretative Guide." Paris: OECD.
Parai, Amar K., and Eden S. H. Yu. 1989. "Factor Mobility and Customs Unions Theory." *Southern Economic Journal* 55 (4):842-52.
Persson, Torsten, and Guido Tabellini. 1994. "Is Inequality Harmful for Growth?" *The American Economic Review* 84 (3):600-621.
Pierson, Paul. 1996. "The New Politics of the Welfare State." *World Politics* 48 (2):143-79.
Polak, J. J. 1950. "Note on the Measurement of Elasticity of Substitution in International Trade." *The Review of Economics and Statistics* 32 (1):16-20.
Pontusson, Jonas. 2005. *Inequality and Prosperity: Social Europe vs. Liberal America*. Ithaca and London: Cornell University Press.
Pontusson, Jonas, David Rueda, and Christopher R. Way. 2002. "Comparative Political Economy of Wage Distribution: The Role of Partisanship and Labor Market Institutions." *British Journal of Political Science* 32:281-308.
Przeworski, Adam, and John Sprague. 1986. *Paper Stones: An History of Electoral Socialism*. Chicago: Chicago University Press.
Przeworski, Adam. 2007. Political Rights, Property Rights, and Economic Development. In *Democracy and Development Seminars*. Princeton University.
Rickard, Stephanie J. 2004. Asset Specificity, Domestic Institutions and Policy Choice: Explaining the Form of

Compensatory Policies: Department of Political Science, University of California, San Diego.
Rickard, Stephanie J. 2005. Broad versus Narrow: Explaining the Form of Redistributive Policies. In *Annual Meeting of the American Political Science Association*. Washington, D.C.: the American Political Science Association.
Robertson, David. 1981. Politics and Labor Markets. Ph.D. dissertation, Department of Political Science, Indiana University, Bloomington, IN.
Robertson, David Brian. 1988. "Governing & Jobs: America's Business-Centered Labor Market Policy." *Polity* 20 (3):426-56.
Rodrik, Dani. 1997. *Has Globalization Gone Too Far?* Washington, D.C.: Institute of International Economics.
Rogowski, Ronald. 1987. "Political Cleavages and Changing Exposure to Trade." *American Political Science Review* 81 (4):1121-1137.
Rogowski, Ronald. 1989. *Commerce and Coalitions : How Trade Affects Domestic Political Alignments*. Princeton, N.J.: Princeton University Press.
Rosenbloom, Joshua. 1989. "Is Wage Dispersion a Good Index of Labor Market Integration? A Comment on Rothenberg." *Journal of Economic History* 49 (1):166-69.
Rothenberg, Winifred B. 1988. "The Emergence of Farm Labor Markets and the Transformation of the Rural Economy: Massachusetts, 1750-1855." *Journal of Economic History* 48 (3):537-66.
Rueda, David. 2005. "Insider–Outsider Politics in Industrialized Democracies: The Challenge to Social Democratic Parties." *American Political Science Review* 99 (1):61-74.
Samuelson, Paul A. 1971. Ohlin Was Right. *Swedish Journal of Economics* 73 (4):365-84.
SAP. 2007. "The Swedish Social Democratic Party - An introduction." Stockholm: Socialdemokraterna.
Schattschneider, E. E. 1935. *Politics, Pressures, and the Tariff.* New York: Prentice-Hall.
Scheve, Kenneth F., and Matthew J. Slaughter. 2001. "What Determines Individual Trade Policy Preferences?" *Journal of International Economics* 54 (2):267-292.

Schmitt, John, and Ben Zipperer. 2006. "Is the U.S. a Good Model for Reducing Social Exclusion in Europe?" In *CEPR*. Washington, D.C.: Center for Economic and Policy Research.

Shapiro, Carl, and Joseph E. Stiglitz. 1984. "Equilibrium Unemployment as a Worker Discipline Device." *The American Economic Review* 74 (3):433-44.

Stolper, Wolfgang F., and Paul A. Samuelson. 1941. "Protection and Real Wages." *The Review of Economic Studies* 9 (1):58-73.

Tinbergen, J. 1946. "Some Measures of Elasticities of Substitution." *The Review of Economic Statistics* 28 (3):109-16.

Tsebelis, George. 2002. *Veto Players: How Political Institutions Work*. Princeton, N.J.: Princeton University Press.

UNIDO. 2005. "UNIDO INDSTAT3 2005, Industrial Statistics Database at the 3-digit level of ISIC (Rev. 2)." United Nations Industrial Development Organization.

USDOS. 2008. "Background Note: Sweden." United States Department of State.

Verdier, Daniel. 1995. "The Politics of Public Aid to Private Industry- The Role of Policy Networks." *Comparative Political Studies* 28 (1):3-42.

Wacziarg, Romain, and Jessica Seddon Wallack. 2004. "Trade liberalization and intersectoral labor movements." *Journal of International Economics* 64:411-39.

Walde, Klaus, and Pia Weiss. 2006. "Relative Price Changes, Wages and Unemployment in a Specific Factors Model with Search Frictions." *Review of Development Economics* 10 (3):400-10.

Wallerstein, Michael. 1990. "Centralized Bargaining and Wage Restraint." *American Journal of Political Science* 34 (4):982-1004.

Wallerstein, Michael. 1999. "Wage-Setting Institutions and Pay Inequality in Advanced Industrial Societies." *American Journal of Political Science* 43 (3):649-80.

Wittman, Donald. 1977. "Candidates with Policy Preferences: A Dynamic Model." *Journal of Economic Theory* 14:180-89.
Wittman, Donald. 1983. "Candidate Motivation: A Synthesis of Alternative Theories." *American Political Science Review* 77 (1):142-57.
Wood, Adrian. 1995. "How Trade Hurt Unskilled Workers." *Journal of Economic Perspectives* 9 (3):57-80.
Wood, Stewart. 2001. "Labour Market Regimes under Threat? Sources of Continuity in Germany, Britain, and Sweden." In *The New Politics of the Welfare State*, ed. P. Pierson. New York: Oxford University Press.
Zuckman, Jill. 2007. McCain in Michigan: Retraining for idled workers. In *The Swamp*.

Sociologie et questions de société
aux éditions L'Harmattan

Dernières parutions

EN AVANT LA RETRAITE !
Mieux gérer la transition
Helson Juliette, Lévy Daniel
Aujourd'hui, un retraité naît toutes les 37 secondes ! Peut-on exister socialement quand on est à la retraite ? Y a-t-il des «risques sociaux» chez les retraités ? Quels sont les choix qui s'offrent à eux pour donner du sens à leur vie ? Ce livre, ponctué de récits, de témoignages éclairants, d'exercices personnels, vous accompagne durant la transition entre le monde du travail et le début d'une vie où vous serez l'acteur libre et responsable de vos décisions.
(22.50 euros, 226 p.)
ISBN : 978-2-343-07483-2, ISBN EBOOK : 978-2-336-39718-4

LA LAÏCITÉ, DÉFI DU XXIe SIÈCLE
Delfau Gérard
Cet ouvrage renouvelle la réflexion sur la laïcité en explorant son histoire depuis 1789. Elle ne se limite pas à la neutralité de l'État, ni à la nécessaire fermeté face à l'islamisme. C'est un processus de longue durée, multiforme, et par nature inachevé, comme le montrent les débats sur l'IVG, le «mariage pour tous», ou la Fin de vie. L'enjeu principal, c'est l'égalité des droits pour les femmes et les minorités sexuelles, que contestent tous les intégrismes. Et l'horizon, c'est la liberté absolue de conscience.
(Coll. Débats Laïques, 20.00 euros, 238 p.)
ISBN : 978-2-343-07828-1, ISBN EBOOK : 978-2-336-39562-3

DU NÉANT SARKOZYEN AU VIDE HOLLANDIEN
Généalogie de l'art de gouverner sous la Ve République
Fonseca David
Nicolas Sarkozy et François Hollande ont tous deux voulu refonder le pouvoir sous la Ve République. Sans contester cette prétention, cet essai essaye d'en dérouler la logique interne pour en faire surgir les singularités et contradictions. L'auteur expose ces présidences à leur propres discours et détaille les tensions qui les entourent. De la politique du néant à la politique du vide, ces tentatives de refonder le pouvoir sont toujours rattrapées par ce à quoi elles tenteraient d'échapper.
(29.00 euros, 276 p.)
ISBN : 978-2-343-07405-4, ISBN EBOOK : 978-2-336-39419-0

JE SUIS CHARLIE
Ainsi suit-il...
Collectif
L'un des traits majeurs de la situation nouée en France au lendemain des attentats de janvier 2015 fut le rassemblement presque unanime du peuple sous la houlette du gouvernement. Ce livre collectif s'attache, avec le recul nécessaire, à analyser la face cachée de ce moment inédit de notre histoire politique et critique le trait intolérant de cet attroupement : pendant quelques semaines, il n'a pas fait bon de ne pas être Charlie.
(Coll. Quelle drôle d'époque !, 22.00 euros, 212 p.)
ISBN : 978-2-343-07563-1, ISBN EBOOK : 978-2-336-39456-5

IDÉALITÉ ET RÉALITÉ DES RELATIONS ENTRE LES NATIONS
Kouassi Kanga Bertin
Les relations entre les nations telles que nous les rêvons dans nos théories pures et dans nos discours sont loin de refléter la réalité. De quoi tenons-nous l'existence d'une communauté internationale ? Pourquoi certains États se cramponnent-ils tant à des sanctions économiques aux effets mitigés qu'ils assimilent à la sanction du droit ? Pourquoi la guerre demeure-t-elle toujours la solution du règlement des conflits internationaux ? Comment perpétue-t-on les inégalités entre les États par l'idée d'une justice pénale internationale ? Voici des analyses juridiques, politiques et économiques qui aident à développer le fonctionnement du monde actuel.
(40.00 euros, 504 p.)
ISBN : 978-2-343-06998-2, ISBN EBOOK : 978-2-336-39480-0

ET LE VÉLO DANS TOUT ÇA ?
Le territoire et la mobilité vus de ma selle – Chroniques cyclo-logiques 2
Pressicaud Nicolas
L'auteur a réuni ici une trentaine d'articles traitant de différents domaines où le vélo devrait trouver sa place. Comptes rendus commentés de colloques, de lectures et d'expériences, ils en pointent le plus souvent un manque de considération. Ce faisant, par ces textes, l'auteur témoigne d'une certaine vision «cyclo-logique» de l'aménagement et de la mobilité, combinant préoccupation environnementale, sens de l'économie et souci d'équité sociale.
(27.50 euros, 268 p.)
ISBN : 978-2-343-06520-5, ISBN EBOOK : 978-2-336-39422-0

TOUCHE PAS À MON SEXE !
Cette féminité qu'on assassine
Zwang Gérard
Faisant autorité dans la description anatomique et physiologique des organes génitaux externes féminins, Gérard Zwang entonne ici un vibrant plaidoyer en faveur du respect absolu de ce legs imprescriptible. Il incite chaque femme vivant sous nos climats à révérer dévotieusement le trésor que lui a offert Dame Nature : au seuil de l'asile vaginal, siège de l'étreinte, cette bonne mère l'a dotée d'un luxueux portique, aussi singulier que son visage.
(21.00 euros, 206 p.)
ISBN : 978-2-343-07594-5, ISBN EBOOK : 978-2-336-39604-0

LA FACE CACHÉE DE LA PARENTALITÉ
Une approche sociologique de l'accompagnement de la fonction parentale
Sas-Barondeau Martine
Cet ouvrage traite de la parentalité à travers l'analyse des dispositifs d'accompagnement de la fonction parentale, financés par les caisses d'allocations familiales (CAF). Des experts ont préconisé des axes de politique familiale visant à contrecarrer les effets de l'instabilité conjugale sur l'éducation des enfants et la délinquance juvénile. De quelle teneur est cette politique et de quelle vision de la société contemporaine est-elle porteuse ? Comment les professionnels du secteur social s'emparent-ils de cette modalité d'action sociale qu'est l'accompagnement de la fonction parentale ? En quoi celui-ci est-il une réponse pertinente et adaptée aux attentes et besoins des parents ?
(Coll. Logiques sociales, 25.50 euros, 242 p.)
ISBN : 978-2-343-07398-9, ISBN EBOOK : 978-2-336-39484-8

ETHNICITÉS ET CONSTRUCTION IDENTITAIRE DANS L'AIRE ANGLOPHONE
Sous la direction de Michel Prum
Comment la construction identitaire s'opère-t-elle dans le cadre des communautés ethniques ? Comment s'élaborent dans un jeu de miroirs et de perceptions croisées, ces nombreuses identités qui font la diversité de nos sociétés actuelles ? Cet ouvrage se concentre sur l'aire anglophone, la Grande-Bretagne d'abord mais aussi les pays du Commonwealth, et se termine par un hommage vibrant à l'anthropologue Franz Boas qui a fondé l'antiracisme américain et a posé l'ethnicité comme simple construction identitaire.
(Coll. Racisme et eugénisme, 20.00 euros, 188 p.)
ISBN : 978-2-343-07505-1, ISBN EBOOK : 978-2-336-39531-9

QU'EST-CE QUE TRANSMETTRE ?
Sociologie d'une pratique
Giraud Claude
Si nos sociétés sont en crise d'autorité, elles le sont *a fortiori* à propos de la transmission qui a lieu de façon constante. Est-ce que ce sont les objets transmis qui font problème ? Est-ce que ce sont les processus de transmission, ou encore ceux qui s'approprient et qui transforment qui font problème ? Cet ouvrage prétend ainsi apporter des pistes de réponses et fait suite aux travaux de l'auteur sur les liens négatifs, les dynamiques organisationnelles et sur ce qui fait société.
(Coll. Logiques sociales, 15.00 euros, 132 p.)
ISBN : 978-2-343-07379-8, ISBN EBOOK : 978-2-336-39642-2

SOCIOLOGIE ET PSYCHANALYSE n°21
Quelle praxis, quelle clinique ?
Sous la direction de Gilles Arnaud et Pascal Fugier
Le présent volume met en dialogue les différents courants qui sont à la fois le produit et la réécriture de l'histoire collective liant sociologie et psychanalyse : du dialogue interdisciplinaire socio-analytique à la psychologie sociale et sociologie cliniques, en passant par l'anthropologie d'inspiration psychanalytique ou encore la sociopsychanalyse. L'objectif est ici de donner à voir cette diversité d'approches

dans un même ouvrage, en les considérant comme autant de modalités originales de mise en acte de ce qui fait « copule » entre les deux disciplines.
(Coll. Clinique et changement social, 20.50 euros, 184 p.)
ISBN : 978-2-343-07854-0, ISBN EBOOK : 978-2-336-39695-8

LES COMBATTANTS EUROPÉENS EN SYRIE
Sous la direction d'Ann Jacobs et Daniel Flore
Le présent ouvrage rassemble les actes de la quatrième journée franco-belge de droit pénal, consacrée aux combattants européens en Syrie. Après une introduction décrivant le contexte du terrorisme islamiste, la problématique est d'abord abordée sous l'angle des analyses et actions de l'Union européenne et ensuite sous l'angle du droit des conflits armés. Il est enfin passé au crible du droit français et de ses dernières modifications ainsi que du droit belge, tant pénal que procédural.
(Coll. Comité international des pénalistes francophones, 25.00 euros, 250 p.)
ISBN : 978-2-343-07389-7, ISBN EBOOK : 978-2-336-39356-8

REGARDS PLURIELS SUR L'INCERTAIN POLITIQUE
Entre dérives identitaires, urbanisation, globalisation économique, réseaux numériques et féminisation du social
Sous la direction de Hervé Marchal et de Christophe Baticle
Cet ouvrage identifie les formes actuelles du politique, du Mali au Québec en passant par la Turquie, l'Espagne, Madagascar, la France ou encore l'Italie. Que se passe-t-il concrètement en matière de redéfinition du politique ? Quelles formes prennent les mouvements protestataires à travers le monde ? Les notions d'espace public, d'autochtonie, d'identité, de nation, de citoyenneté sont, entre autres, analysées. L'incertain politique est pensé à travers des pratiques, mouvements et luttes qui restent à identifier pour comprendre notre monde contemporain.
(Coll. Recherche et transformation sociale, 24.50 euros, 234 p.)
ISBN : 978-2-343-07373-6, ISBN EBOOK : 978-2-336-39226-4

ÉNERGIE, CHIMÈRES ET SUPERCHERIES
Sibresse Marie-Abel
Cet ouvrage a pour but de montrer quelle est la problématique de l'énergie sous les angles, historiques, scientifiques, techniques, technologiques et économiques. Tout choix politique concernant l'énergie ne devrait être opéré qu'après une approche globale de la question. Pourtant, dans la plupart des cas, ce n'est pas fait. Un exemple : le diesel est accusé de polluer plus que les autres moteurs thermiques, ce qui est globalement faux et thermodynamiquement le diesel est bien meilleur que ses concurrents.
(28.00 euros, 270 p.)
ISBN : 978-2-343-07183-1, ISBN EBOOK : 978-2-336-39269-1

L'HARMATTAN ITALIA
Via Degli Artisti 15; 10124 Torino
harmattan.italia@gmail.com

L'HARMATTAN HONGRIE
Könyvesbolt ; Kossuth L. u. 14-16
1053 Budapest

L'HARMATTAN KINSHASA
185, avenue Nyangwe
Commune de Lingwala
Kinshasa, R.D. Congo
(00243) 998697603 ou (00243) 999229662

L'HARMATTAN CONGO
67, av. E. P. Lumumba
Bât. – Congo Pharmacie (Bib. Nat.)
BP2874 Brazzaville
harmattan.congo@yahoo.fr

L'HARMATTAN GUINÉE
Almamya Rue KA 028, en face
du restaurant Le Cèdre
OKB agency BP 3470 Conakry
(00224) 657 20 85 08 / 664 28 91 96
harmattanguinee@yahoo.fr

L'HARMATTAN MALI
Rue 73, Porte 536, Niamakoro,
Cité Unicef, Bamako
Tél. 00 (223) 20205724 / +(223) 76378082
poudiougopaul@yahoo.fr
pp.harmattan@gmail.com

L'HARMATTAN CAMEROUN
BP 11486
Face à la SNI, immeuble Don Bosco
Yaoundé
(00237) 99 76 61 66
harmattancam@yahoo.fr

L'HARMATTAN CÔTE D'IVOIRE
Résidence Karl / cité des arts
Abidjan-Cocody 03 BP 1588 Abidjan 03
(00225) 05 77 87 31
etien_nda@yahoo.fr

L'HARMATTAN BURKINA
Penou Achille Some
Ouagadougou
(+226) 70 26 88 27

L'HARMATTAN SÉNÉGAL
10 VDN en face Mermoz, après le pont de Fann
BP 45034 Dakar Fann
33 825 98 58 / 33 860 9858
senharmattan@gmail.com / senlibraire@gmail.com
www.harmattansenegal.com

L'HARMATTAN BÉNIN
ISOR-BENIN
01 BP 359 COTONOU-RP
Quartier Gbèdjromèdé,
Rue Agbélenco, Lot 1247 I
Tél : 00 229 21 32 53 79
christian_dablaka123@yahoo.fr

Achevé d'imprimer par Corlet Numérique - 14110 Condé-sur-Noireau
N° d'Imprimeur : 128197 - Dépôt légal : avril 2016 - *Imprimé en France*

www.ingramcontent.com/pod-product-compliance
Lightning Source LLC
LaVergne TN
LVHW011012061026
849535LV00006B/1835